Lecture Notes in Computer Science 8129

Commenced Publication in 1973
Founding and Former Series Editors:
Gerhard Goos, Juris Hartmanis, and Jan van Leeuwen

T0254866

André Rauber Du Bois   Phil Trinder (Eds.)

Programming Languages

17th Brazilian Symposium, SBLP 2013
Brasília, Brazil, October 3-4, 2013
Proceedings

Volume Editors

André Rauber Du Bois
Universidade Federal de Pelotas
Programa de Pós-Graduação em Computação
Rua Gomes Carneiro 1
96010-610 Pelotas, RS, Brazil
E-mail: dubois@inf.ufpel.edu.br

Phil Trinder
Glasgow University
School of Computing Science
Lilybank Gardens
Glasgow G12 8QQ, UK
E-mail: phil.trinder@glasgow.ac.uk

ISSN 0302-9743   e-ISSN 1611-3349
ISBN 978-3-642-40921-9   e-ISBN 978-3-642-40922-6
DOI 10.1007/978-3-642-40922-6
Springer Heidelberg New York Dordrecht London

Library of Congress Control Number: 2013948121

CR Subject Classification (1998): D.3.1-2, D.3.4, D.2.5-6, D.2.9, D.1.1, D.1.5, D.2.11

LNCS Sublibrary: SL 2 – Programming and Software Engineering

Typesetting: Camera-ready by author, data conversion by Scientific Publishing Services, Chennai, India

Printed on acid-free paper

Springer is part of Springer Science+Business Media (www.springer.com)

Preface

The Brazilian Symposium on Programming Languages (SBLP) is a series of annual conferences promoted by the Brazilian Computer Society (SBC) since 1996. In the last four years, it has been organized in the context of CBSoft (Brazilian Conference on Software: Theory and Practice), co-located with a number of other events on computer science and software engineering.

SBLP 2013 was the 17th edition of the symposium, and was held in Brasília, Brazil, organized by the Department of Computer Science of the University of Brasília (UnB). It was collocated with the 2013 editions of SBMF (Brazilian Symposium on Formal Methods), SBES (Brazilian Symposium on Software Engineering), and SBCARS (Brazilian Symposium on Software Components, Architecture and Reuse), under CBSoft 2013. The previous editions in SBLP were held in Natal (2012), São Paulo (2011), Salvador (2010), Gramado (2009), Fortaleza (2008), Natal (2007), Itatiaia (2006), Recife (2005), Niterói (2004), Ouro Preto (2003), Rio de Janeiro (2002), Curitiba (2001), Recife (2000), Porto Alegre (1999), Campinas (1997), and Belo Horizonte (1996).

The Program Committee (PC) of SBLP 2013 comprised 36 members, from 8 countries. SBLP 2013 received 31 submissions, including 4 short papers, with authors from Argentina, Brazil, Mexico, The Netherlands, Portugal, USA, and Uruguay. Each paper was reviewed by at least four reviewers, including 14 reviewers outside the PC. The referee reports were discussed by the reviewers, generally leading to a consensus. The final selection was made by the PC co-chairs, based on the reviews and PC discussion. As in previous editions, the authors of the 10 full papers selected will be invited to submit extended versions of their works to be considered for publication in a special issue of a reputed journal in computer science. The technical program of SBLP 2013 also included keynote talks from Tim Harris (Oracle Labs, UK), and Ryan R. Newton (Indiana University).

We would like to thank the referees for their reviews, the members of the PC for their reviews and contributions to the discussion and decision-making, and the invited speakers for accepting our invitation and enriching the technical program with interesting talks. We also thank the authors, the sponsors, and the Organizing Committee of CBSoft 2013 for contributing to the success of SBLP 2013.

October 2013
André Rauber Du Bois
Phil Trinder

Organization

SBLP 2013 was organized by the Department of Computer Science, University of Brasilia, and sponsored by the Brazilian Computer Society (SBC), in the context of CBSoft 2013 (Fourth Brazilian Conference on Software: Theory and Practice).

Organizing Committee

Genaina Nunes Rodrigues	UnB, Brazil
Rodrigo Bonifácio	UnB, Brazil
Diego Aranha	UnB, Brazil

Steering Committee

Francisco Heron de Carvalho Junior	UFC, Brazil
Christiano Braga	UFF, Brazil
Ricardo Massa Ferreira Lima	UFPE, Brazil
André Rauber Du Bois	UFPel, Brazil

Program Committee Chairs

André Rauber Du Bois	UFPel, Brazil
Phil Trinder	Glasgow University, UK

Program Committee

Alberto Pardo	Universidad de La República, Uruguay
Alex Garcia	IME, Brazil
Álvaro Freitas Moreira	UFRGS, Brazil
André Santos	UFPE, Brazil
Carlos Camarão	UFMG, Brazil
Christiano Braga	UFF, Brazil
Edwin Brady	University of St. Andrews, UK
Fernando Castor Filho	UFPE, Brazil
Fernando Quintão Pereira	UFMG, Brazil
Francisco H. de Carvalho Junior	UFC, Brazil
Hans-Wofgang Loidl	Heriot-Watt University, UK
Jeremy Singer	Glasgow University, UK
João Saraiva	Universidade do Minho, Portugal

João F. Ferreira	Teesside University, UK
Lucilia Figueiredo	UFOP, Brazil
Luis Soares Barbosa	Universidade do Minho, Portugal
Manuel António Martins	Universidade de Aveiro, Portugal
Marcelo A. Maia	UFU, Brazil
Marcello Bonsangue	Leiden University/CWI, The Netherlands
Marcelo d'Amorim	UFPE, Brazil
Marco Tulio Valente	UFMG, Brazil
Mariza A. S. Bigonha	UFMG, Brazil
Martin A. Musicante	UFRN, Brazil
Noemi Rodriguez	PUC-Rio, Brazil
Peter Mosses	Swansea University, UK
Zongyan Qiu	Pekin University, China
Rafael Dueire Lins	UFPE, Brazil
Ricardo Massa	UFPE, Brazil
Roberto S. Bigonha	UFMG, Brazil
Roberto Ierusalimschy	PUC-Rio, Brazil
Sandro Rigo	UNICAMP, Brazil
Sergio Soares	UFPE, Brazil
Simon Thompson	University of Kent, UK
Varmo Vene	University of Tartu, Estonia

Additional Referees

A. Annamaa	M. Garcia	A. Rademaker
J. Cunha	F. Medeiros Neto	P. Torrini
C. de Faveri	H. Nestra	M. Viera
J. P. Fernandes	R. Neves	V. Vojdani
R. Ferreira	E. Piveta	

Sponsoring Institutions

CNPq - Conselho Nacional de Desenvolvimento Científico e Tecnológico
http://www.cnpq.br
CAPES - Coordenação de Aperfeiçoamento de Pessoal de Nível Superior
http://www.capes.gov.br
Ministério da Educação, Brazilian Government
http://www.mec.gov.br
Instituto Nacional de Ciência e Tecnologia para Engenharia de Software
http://www.ines.org.br
Google
http://www.google.com

Abstracts of Invited Papers

Big-Tent Deterministic Parallelism

Ryan R. Newton

Indiana University, USA
rrnewton@cs.indiana.edu

Abstract. Nondeterminism is essential for achieving flexible parallelism: it allows tasks to be scheduled onto cores dynamically, in response to the vagaries of an execution. But if schedule nondeterminism is *observable* within a program, it becomes much more difficult for programmers to discover and correct bugs by testing, let alone to reason about their programs in the first place. While much work has focused on identifying methods of deterministic parallel programming, *guaranteed* determinism in real parallel programs remains a lofty and rarely achieved goal. It places stringent constraints on the programming model: concurrent tasks must communicate in restricted ways that prevent them from observing the effects of scheduling, a restriction that must be enforced at the language or runtime level.

This talk will overview the known forms of deterministic-by-construction parallel languages, including: Kahn process networks, pure data-parallelism, single assignment languages, functional programming, and type-effect systems that enforce limited access to state by threads. However, I will argue that existing approaches remain fragmented and under-exploited, and that an effort is called for both to extend the scope of deterministic approaches and to better integrate known approaches. The ultimate target is a full-featured programming environment that enables a practical form of guaranteed-deterministic parallelism not possible today.

I will present our recent work in this area. We have extended Haskell's `Par` monad with arbitrary monotonic data structures called LVars. These go beyond single-assignment and include any shared data structures to which information is added but never removed. Specifically, each LVar is associated with a *lattice* from which its states are drawn; writes become *join* operations; and reads block on a monotonic threshold functions, preventing observation of the order in which information is added. I will describe a prototype implementation of this model called LVish, and will describe both its facilities for task-parallelism with monotonic shared data, and its ability to support other idioms: for example, parallel in-place update of array locations via a monad-transformer we call `VecParT`. Haskell provides an attractive environment for implementing such approaches, because deterministic parallelism constructs can be presented as *dischargable effects*, and used within ordinary (non-`IO`) purely functional code. The result is that parallel programming mechanisms can be arbitrarily composed. For example, LVish programs can internally execute GPU code with Accelerate, or use threaded array parallelism with

REPA, or do in-place parallel array computations with a `VecParT` transformer, all while modifying and reading monotonic data structures, and all while retaining a full guarantee of determinism.

Language Design, in Theory and Practice

Tim Harris

Oracle Labs, Cambridge, UK
timothy.l.harris@oracle.com

Abstract. The end of the "free lunch" of rising CPU clock rates has led to a resurgence of interest in techniques for parallel programming. Some techniques are well established, coming from fields such as databases and high-performance computing. Other techniques are more recent, such as programming models that target GPUs, or that build on the emerging transactional memory systems. To be effective, many emerging techniques require changes at multiple layers of the stack: a hardware component, support in the operating system, and changes to the language runtime system in addition to the evolution of the language itself.

A common theme is that the role of hardware is becoming more significant. This setting creates new challenges for the programming languages community: how do we reconcile the need for portable programs and well-defined languages with the ability to use specialized hardware where it is available.

I will talk about my experience trying to tackle instances of these problems, and I will try to identify some lessons learned. I will focus on three examples. First, transactional memory, and the tensions that exist between specifying simple language constructs, enabling "transactionalization" of existing code, and enabling efficient implementations in hardware and software. Second, the message passing abstractions exposed by the Barrelfish research OS, and the tension between providing well-defined semantics, while being able to build over diverse forms of communication stack. Finally, I will talk about my current work on supporting multiple parallel applications together on the same machine, and how previous work has influenced the design choices there.

Table of Contents

Exception Handling for Error Reporting in Parsing Expression Grammars

André Murbach Maidl[1], Fabio Mascarenhas[2], and Roberto Ierusalimschy[1]

[1] Department of Computer Science, PUC-Rio, Rio de Janeiro, Brazil
{amaidl,roberto}@inf.puc-rio.br
[2] Department of Computer Science, UFRJ, Rio de Janeiro, Brazil
fabiom@dcc.ufrj.br

Abstract. Parsing Expression Grammars (PEGs) are a new formalism to describe a top-down parser of a language. However, error handling techniques that are often applied to top-down parsers are not directly applicable to PEGs. This problem is usually solved in PEGs using a heuristic that helps to simulate the error reporting technique from top-down parsers, but the error messages are generic. We propose the introduction of labeled failures to PEGs for error reporting, as labels help to produce more meaningful error messages. The labeled failures approach is close to that of generating and handling exceptions often used in programming languages, being useful to annotate and label grammar pieces that should not fail. Moreover, our approach is an extension to the PEGs formalism that is expressive enough to implement some previous work on parser combinators. Finally, labeled failures are also useful to compose grammars preserving the error messages of each separate grammar.

Keywords: parsing, error reporting, parsing expression grammars, packrat parsing, parser combinators.

1 Introduction

When a parser receives an erroneous input, it should indicate the existence of syntax errors. However, a generic error message (e.g. `syntax error`) does not help the programmer to find and fix the errors that the input may have. Therefore, the least that is expected from a parser is that it should produce an error message indicating the position of an error in the input and some information about the context of this error. The LL and LR methods detect syntax errors very efficiently because they have the *viable prefix* property, that is, these methods detect a syntax error as soon as a token is read and cannot be used to form a viable prefix of the language [1].

Usually, there are two ways to handle errors: error reporting and error recovery. In error reporting, the parser aborts with an informative message when the first error is found. In error recovery, the parser is adapted to not abort on the first error, but to try processing the rest of the input, informing all errors that it found. Such error handling techniques are described in more detail in [1] and

A. Rauber Du Bois and P. Trinder (Eds.): SBLP 2013, LNCS 8129, pp. 1–15, 2013.
© Springer-Verlag Berlin Heidelberg 2013

[5]. In this paper we focus on error reporting because error recovery can produce cascading errors.

Parsing Expression Grammars (PEGs) [4] are a new formalism for describing the syntax of programming languages. We can view a PEG as a formal description of a top-down parser for the language it describes. The syntax of PEGs has similarities to Extended Backus-Naur Form (EBNF), but, unlike EBNF, PEGs avoid ambiguities in the definition of the grammar's language due to the use of an ordered choice operator. More specifically, a parser implemented by a PEG is a recursive descent parser with restricted backtracking. This means that the alternatives of a non-terminal are tried in order; when the first alternative recognizes an input prefix, no other alternative of this non-terminal is tried, but when an alternative fails to recognize an input prefix, the parser backtracks on the input to try the next alternative.

On the one hand, PEGs are an expressive formalism for describing top-down parsers [4]; on the other hand, PEGs cannot use error handling techniques that are often applied to top-down parsers, because these techniques assume the parser reads the input without backtracking [2]. In top-down parsers without backtracking, it is possible to signal a syntax error when there is no alternative to continue reading. In PEGs, it is more complicated to identify the cause of an error and the position where it happened because failures during parsing are not necessarily errors, but just an indication that the parser should backtrack and try a different alternative.

Ford [2] provided a heuristic to the problem of error handling in PEGs. His heuristic simulates the error reporting technique that is implemented in top-down parsers without backtracking. However, the error messages produced by both regular top-down parsers and parsers that use this heuristic are still generic. The best the parsers can do is to tell the user the position where the error happened, what was found in the input and what they were expecting.

In this paper we present a new approach for error reporting in PEGs, based on the concept of *labeled failures*. In our approach, each label may be tied to a specific error message and resembles the concept of exceptions from programming languages. Our approach is not tied to a specific implementation of PEGs, being an extension to the PEGs formalism itself. We show how to use labeled failures to implement error reporting. We also show that our extension is expressive enough to implement alternative error reporting techniques from top-down parsers with backtracking.

The rest of this paper is organized as follows: in Section 2 we contextualize the problem of error handling in PEGs and we also explain in detail the heuristic that Ford used to implement error reporting. In Section 3 we discuss alternative work on error reporting for top-down parsers with backtracking. In Section 4 we introduce the concept of labeled failures, show how to use it for error reporting, and show how labeled failures can encode some of the techniques of Section 3. Finally, we draw our conclusions in Section 5.

2   Error Reporting in PEGs

In this section we use examples to present in more detail how a PEG behaves badly on the presence of syntax errors. After that, we present a heuristic proposed by Ford [2] to implement error reporting in PEGs. Rather than using the original definition of PEGs by Ford [4], our examples use the equivalent and more concise definition proposed by Medeiros et al. [12,13]. We will extend this definition in Section 4 to present a semantics for PEGs with labeled failures.

A PEG G is a tuple (V, T, P, p_S) where V is a finite set of non-terminals, T is a finite set of terminals, P is a total function from non-terminals to *parsing expressions* and p_S is the initial parsing expression. We describe the function P as a set of rules of the form $A \leftarrow p$, where $A \in V$ and p is a parsing expression. A parsing expression, when applied to an input string, either fails or consumes a prefix of the input resulting in the remaining suffix. The abstract syntax of parsing expressions is given as follows:

$$p = \varepsilon \mid a \mid A \mid p_1 p_2 \mid p_1/p_2 \mid p* \mid !p$$

Intuitively, ε successfully matches the empty string, not changing the input; a matches and consumes itself or fails otherwise; A tries to match the expression $P(A)$; $p_1 p_2$ tries to match p_1 followed by p_2; p_1/p_2 tries to match p_1; if p_1 fails, then it tries to match p_2; $p*$ repeatedly matches p until p fails, that is, it consumes as much as it can from the input; the matching of $!p$ succeeds if the input does not match p and fails when the the input matches p, not consuming any input in both cases; we call it the negative predicate or the lookahead predicate.

Hereafter, we present the fragment of a PEG for the Tiny language [11] to show how error reporting differs between top-down parsers without backtracking and PEGs. Tiny is a simple programming language with a syntax that resembles Pascal's.

$$
\begin{aligned}
Tiny &\leftarrow CmdSeq \\
CmdSeq &\leftarrow (Cmd\ \text{SEMICOLON})\ (Cmd\ \text{SEMICOLON})* \\
Cmd &\leftarrow IfCmd\ /\ RepeatCmd\ /\ AssignCmd\ /\ ReadCmd\ /\ WriteCmd \\
IfCmd &\leftarrow \text{IF}\ Exp\ \text{THEN}\ CmdSeq\ (\text{ELSE}\ CmdSeq\ /\ \varepsilon)\ \text{END} \\
RepeatCmd &\leftarrow \text{REPEAT}\ CmdSeq\ \text{UNTIL}\ Exp \\
AssignCmd &\leftarrow Name\ \text{ASSIGNMENT}\ Exp \\
ReadCmd &\leftarrow \text{READ}\ Name \\
WriteCmd &\leftarrow \text{WRITE}\ Exp
\end{aligned}
$$

PEGs usually express the language syntax down to the character level, without the need of a separate lexer. For instance, we can write the lexical rule IF as follows:

$$IF \leftarrow if\ !IDRest\ Skip$$

That is, the rule matches the keyword *if* provided that it is not a prefix of an identifier and then the rule skips surrounding white spaces and comments.

The non-terminal *IDRest* recognizes any character that may be present on a
proper suffix of an identifier while the non-terminal *Skip* recognizes white spaces
and comments. In the presented fragment, we omitted the lexical rules and the
definitions of *Exp* and *Name* for brevity.

Now, we present an example of erroneous Tiny code to compare approaches
for error reporting. The program has a missing semicolon (;) in the assignment
in line 5:

```
1 n := 5;
2 f := 1;
3 repeat
4   f := f * n;
5   n := n - 1
6 until (n < 1);
7 write f;
```

A hand-written top-down parser without backtracking that aborts on the first
error presents an error message like this:

```
factorial.tiny:6:1: syntax error, unexpected 'until', expecting ';'
```

The error is reported in line 6 because the parser cannot complete a valid
prefix of the language, since it unexpectedly finds the token `until` when it was
expecting a command terminator (;).

In PEGs, we can try to report errors using the remaining suffix, but this
approach usually does not help the PEG to produce an error message like the
one shown above. In general, when a PEG finishes parsing the input, a remaining
suffix that is not the empty string means that parsing did not reach the end of file
due to a syntax error. However, this remaining suffix usually does not indicate
the position where the longest parse ends. This problem happens because the
failure of a parsing expression does not necessarily mean an error. Actually, the
failure usually means that the PEG should backtrack the input to try a different
alternative. For this reason, the remaining suffix probably indicates a position
far away from the real position where the first error happened when parsing
finishes without consuming all the input.

In our example, the problem happens when the PEG tries to recognize the
sequence of commands inside the `repeat` command. Even though the program
has a missing semicolon (;) in the assignment in line 5, making the PEG fail to
recognize the sequence of commands inside the `repeat` command, this failure is
not treated as an error. Instead, this failure makes the recognition of the `repeat`
command also fail. For this reason, the PEG backtracks the input to line 3 to try
other command alternatives that exist in the language. Since it is not possible to
recognize a command other than `repeat` in line 3, the parsing finishes without
consuming all the input. Hence, if the PEG uses the remaining suffix to produce
an error message, the PEG shows a wrong position where the error happened.

We can also make the PEG fail whenever it does not consume all the input,
instead of checking whether the remaining suffix is the empty string. To do that,

we change the starting symbol to fail when it does not reach the end of file. Even though the failure of the PEG indicates the presence of syntax errors, it does not indicate a possible position where the first error happened.

According to Ford [2], although there is no perfect method to identify which information is the most relevant to report an error, using the information of the farthest position that the PEG reached in the input is a heuristic that provides good results. PEGs implement top-down parsers and try to recognize the input from left to right, so the position farthest to the right in the input that a PEG reaches during parsing usually is close to the real error [2].

Ford used this heuristic to add error reporting to his packrat parsers [2]. A packrat parser generated by Pappy [3], Ford's PEG parser generator, tracks the farthest position and uses this position to report an error when parsing fails because it finished without consuming all the input. In other words, this heuristic helps packrat parsers to simulate the error reporting technique that is implemented in top-down parsers without backtracking.

During our research, we realized that we can use the farthest position heuristic to add error reporting to any implementation of PEGs that provides semantic actions. The idea is to annotate the grammar with semantic actions that track the farthest failure position. For instance, in Leg [16], a PEG parser generator with Yacc-style semantic actions, we can annotate the rule *CmdSeq* as follows:

```
CmdSeq = Cmd (";" Skip | &{ updateffp() })
         (Cmd (";" Skip | &{ updateffp() }))*
```

The parser calls the function `updateffp` when the matching of a semicolon fails. The function `updateffp` is a semantic action that updates the farthest failure position in a global variable if the current parsing position is greater than the position that is stored in this global. After the update, the semantic action forces another failure to not interrupt backtracking.

Since this semantic action propagates failures and runs only when a parsing expression fails, we could annotate all terminals and non-terminals in the grammar without changing the behavior of the PEG. In practice, we just need to annotate terminals to implement error reporting.

However, storing just the farthest failure position does not give the parser all the information it needs to produce an informative error message. That is, the parser has the information about the position where the error happened, but it lacks the information about what terminals failed at that position. Thus, we should include the name of the terminals in the annotations so the parser can also track these names to compute the set of expected terminals at a certain position.

Basically, we give an extra argument to each semantic action. This extra argument is a hard-coded name for the terminal that we want to keep track along with the farthest failure position. For instance, now we annotate the *CmdSeq* rule in Leg as follows:

```
CmdSeq = Cmd (";" Skip | &{ updateffp(";") })
         (Cmd (";" Skip | &{ updateffp(";") }))*
```

We then extend the implementation of `updateffp` to also update the set of expected terminals; the update of the farthest failure position continues the same. If the current position is greater than the farthest failure, the set contains only the given name. If the current position equals the farthest failure, the given name is added to the set.

Parsers generated by Pappy also track the set of expected terminals, but with limitations. The error messages include only symbols and keywords that were defined in the grammar as literal strings. That is, the error messages do not include terminals that were defined through character classes.

The approach of naming terminals in the semantic actions avoids the kind of limitation found in Pappy, though it increases the annotation burden because who is implementing the PEG is also responsible for adding one semantic action for each terminal and its respective name.

The annotation burden can be lessened in implementations of PEGs that treat parsing expressions as first-class objects, as we are able to define functions to annotate the lexical parts of the grammar to track errors, record information about the expected terminals to produce good error messages, and enforce lexical conventions such as the presence of surrounding white spaces. For instance, in LPeg [7,8], a PEG library for Lua that defines patterns as first-class objects, we can annotate the rule *CmdSeq* as follows:

```
CmdSeq = V"Cmd" * symb(";") * (V"Cmd" * symb(";"))^0;
```

The function `symb` works like a parser combinator [6]. It receives a string as its only argument and returns a pattern that is equivalent to the parsing expression that we used in the Leg example. That is, `symb(";")` is equivalent to `";" Skip | &{ updateffp(";") }`. Notice that the patterns `V"A"`, `p1 * p2`, and `p^0` are equivalent to the following parsing expressions: A, $p_1 p_2$, and $p*$.

We implemented error tracking and reporting using semantic actions as a set of parsing combinators on top of LPeg and used these combinators to implement the PEG for Tiny. It produces the following error message for the example we have been using in this section:

```
factorial.tiny:6:1: syntax error, unexpected 'until',
                    expecting ';', '=', '<', '-', '+', '/', '*'
```

We tested the PEG for Tiny with other erroneous inputs and in all cases the PEG identified an error in the same place as a top-down parser without backtracking. In addition, the PEG for Tiny produced error messages that are similar to the error messages produced by packrat parsers generated by Pappy. We annotated other grammars too and successfully obtained similar results. However, the error messages are still generic.

3   Error Reporting in Top-Down Parsers with Backtracking

In this section we discuss alternative approaches for error reporting in top-down parsers with backtracking other than the heuristic explained in Section 2.

Mizushima et al. [14] proposed a cut operator ($\uparrow$) to reduce the space consumption of packrat parsers; the authors claimed that the cut operator can also be used to implement error reporting in packrat parsers, but the authors did not give any details on how the cut operator could be used for this purpose. The cut operator is borrowed from Prolog to annotate pieces of a PEG where backtracking should be avoided. PEGs' ordered choice works in a similar way to Prolog's green cuts, that is, they limit backtracking to discard unnecessary solutions. The cut proposed to PEGs is a way to implement Prolog's white cuts, that is, they prevent backtracking to rules that will certainly fail.

The semantics of cut is similar to the semantics of an `if-then-else` control structure and can be simulated through predicates. For instance, the PEG (with cut) $A \leftarrow B \uparrow C/D$ is functionally equivalent to the PEG (without cut) $A \leftarrow BC/!BD$ that is also functionally equivalent to the rule $A \leftarrow B[C, D]$ on Generalized Top-Down Parsing Language (GTDPL), one of the parsing techniques that influenced the creation of PEGs [2,3,4]. On the three cases, the expression D is tried only if the expression B fails. Nevertheless, this translated PEG still backtracks the input whenever B successfully matches and C fails. Thus, it is not trivial to use this translation to implement error reporting in PEGs.

Even though error handling is an important task for parsers, we did not find any other research about error handling in PEGs, beyond the heuristic proposed by Ford and the cut operator proposed by Mizushima et al. However, parser combinators [6] present some similarities with PEGs so we will briefly discuss them for the rest of this section.

In functional programming it is common to implement recursive descent parsers using parser combinators [6]. A parser is a function that we use to model symbols of the grammar. A parser combinator is a higher-order function that we use to implement grammar constructions such as sequencing and choice. Usually, we use parser combinators to implement parsers that return a list of results. That is, we use non-deterministic parser combinators that return a list of results to implement recursive descent parsers with full backtracking. We get parser combinators that have the same semantics as PEGs by changing the return type from list of results to `Maybe`. That is, we use deterministic parser combinators that return `Maybe` to implement recursive descent parsers with limited backtracking. In this paper we are referring to deterministic parser combinators.

Like PEGs, parser combinators also use ordered choice and try to accept input prefixes. More precisely, parsers implemented using parser combinators also backtrack the input in case of failure. For this reason, when the input string contains syntax errors, the longest parse usually indicates a position far away from the position where the error really happened.

Hutton [6] introduced the `nofail` combinator to implement error reporting in a quite simple way: we just need to distinguish between failure and error during parsing. More specifically, we can use the `nofail` combinator to annotate the grammar's terminals and non-terminals that should not fail; when they fail, the failure should be transformed into an error that aborts parsing. This technique

Table 1. Behavior of sequence and choice in the four-values technique

p_1	p_2	$p_1 p_2$	$p_1 \mid p_2$
Error	Error	Error	Error
Error	Fail	Error	Error
Error	Epsn	Error	Error
Error	OK (x)	Error	Error
Fail	Error	Fail	Error
Fail	Fail	Fail	Fail
Fail	Epsn	Fail	Epsn
Fail	OK (x)	Fail	OK (x)
Epsn	Error	Error	Error
Epsn	Fail	Fail	Epsn
Epsn	Epsn	Epsn	Epsn
Epsn	OK (x)	OK (x)	OK (x)
OK (x)	Error	Error	OK (x)
OK (x)	Fail	Error	OK (x)
OK (x)	Epsn	OK (x)	OK (x)
OK (x)	OK (y)	OK (y)	OK (x)

is also called the *three-values* technique because the parser finishes with one of the following values: OK, Fail or Error.

Röjemo [17] presented a cut combinator that we can also use to annotate the grammar pieces where parsing should be aborted on failure, on behalf of efficiency and error reporting. The cut combinator is different from the cut operator (↑) for PEGs because the combinator is abortive and unary while the operator is not abortive and nullary. The cut combinator introduced by Röjemo has the same semantics as the nofail combinator introduced by Hutton. However, the cut implementation uses an approach based on continuations while the nofail implementation uses an approach based on constructs.

Partridge and Wright [15] showed that error detection can be automated in parser combinators when we assume that the grammar is LL(1). Their main idea is: if one alternative successfully consumes at least one symbol, no other alternative can successfully consume any symbols. Their technique is also known as the *four-values* technique because the parser finishes with one of the following values: Epsn, when the parser finishes with success without consuming any input; OK, when the parser finishes with success consuming some input; Fail, when the parser fails without consuming any input; and Error, when the parser fails consuming some input. Three values were inspired by Hutton's work [6], but with new meanings.

In the four-values technique, we do not need to annotate the grammar because the authors changed the semantics of the sequence and choice combinators to automatically generate the Error value according to the table 1. In summary, the sequence combinator propagates an error when the second parse fails after consuming some input while the choice combinator does not try further alternatives if the current one consumed at least one symbol from the input. In case of error, the four-values technique detects the first symbol following the longest parse of the input and uses this symbol to report an error.

The four-values technique assumes that the input is composed by tokens which are provided by a separate lexer. However, being restricted to LL(1) grammars can be a limitation because parser combinators, like PEGs, usually operate on strings of characters to implement both lexer and parser together. For instance, a parser for Tiny that is implemented with Parsec [10] does not parse the following program: `read x;`. That is, the matching of `read` against `repeat` generates an error. Such behavior is confirmed in table 1 by the third line from the bottom.

Parsec is a parser combinator library for Haskell that employs a technique equivalent to the four-values technique for implementing LL(1) predictive parsers that automatically report errors [10], so in this paper we refer to Parsec using the four-values technique. A predictive parser is a recursive descent parser without backtracking. Parsec inspired Ford on his heuristic that tracks the longest parse of the input to implement error reporting in packrat parsers and on the creation of a parser combinator library for Haskell to implement packrat parsers.

The authors of Parsec introduced the `try` combinator to avoid the LL(1) limitation found in the four-values technique. More precisely, we use `try` to annotate parts of the grammar where arbitrary lookahead is needed, though Parsec is a library for implementing LL(1) predictive parsers. Dual to the `nofail` combinator, the `try` combinator transforms an error into a failure. That is, the `try` combinator pretends that a parser p did not consume any input when p fails. For this reason, it should be used carefully because it breaks Parsec's automatic error detection system when it is overused.

Parsec's restriction to LL(1) grammars made it possible to implement in the library an error reporting technique similar to the one applied to top-down parsers. Parsec produces error messages that include the error position, the character at this position and the FIRST set of the productions that were expected at this position. Parsec also implements the error injection combinator (`<?>`) for naming productions. This combinator gets two arguments: a parser p and a string `exp`. The string `exp` replaces the FIRST set of a parser p when all the alternatives of p failed. This combinator is useful to name terminals and non-terminals to get better information about the context of a syntax error.

Swierstra and Duponcheel [18] showed an implementation of parser combinators for error recovery, although most libraries and parser generators that are based on parser combinators implement only error reporting. Their work shows an implementation of parser combinators that repair the input in case of error, produce an appropriated message, and continue parsing the rest of the input.

4 Labeled Failures for Error Reporting

Exceptions are a common mechanism for signaling and handling errors in programming languages. Exceptions let programmers classify the different errors their programs may signal by using distinct types for distinct errors, and decouple error handling from regular program logic.

In this section we add *labeled failures* to PEGs, a mechanism akin to exceptions and exception handling, with the goal of improving error reporting preserving PEGs composability. We also discuss how to use PEGs with labels to implement some of the techniques that we have discussed in the previous section: the `nofail` combinator [6], the `cut` combinator [17], the four-values technique [15] and the `try` combinator [10].

A labeled PEG G is a tuple $(V, T, P, L, \texttt{fail}, p_S)$ where L is a finite set of labels and $\texttt{fail} \in L$. The other parts use the same definitions from Section 2. The abstract syntax of labeled parsing expressions adds the *throw* operator $\Uparrow^l$, which generates a failure with label l, and adds an extra argument S to the ordered choice operator, which is the set of labels that the ordered choice should catch. S must be a subset of L.

$$p = \varepsilon \mid a \mid A \mid p_1 p_2 \mid p_1 /^S p_2 \mid p* \mid !p \mid \Uparrow^l$$

The semantics of PEGs with labels is defined by the relation $\overset{\text{PEG}}{\rightsquigarrow}$ among a parsing expression, an input string and a result. The result is either a string or a label. The notation $G[p] \; xy \overset{\text{PEG}}{\rightsquigarrow} y$ means that the expression p matches the input xy, consumes the prefix x and leaves the suffix y as the output. The notation $G[p] \; xy \overset{\text{PEG}}{\rightsquigarrow} l$ indicates that the matching of p fails with label l on the input xy.

Figure 1 presents the semantics of PEGs with labels using natural semantics [19]. Intuitively, ε successfully matches the empty string, not changing the input; a matches and consumes itself and fails with label $\texttt{fail}$ otherwise; A tries to match the expression $P(A)$; $p_1 p_2$ tries to match p_1, if p_1 matches an input prefix, then it tries to match p_2 with the suffix left by p_1, the label l is propagated otherwise; $p_1 /^S p_2$ tries to match p_1 in the input and tries to match p_2 in the same input only if p_1 fails with a label $l \in S$, the label l is propagated otherwise; $p*$ repeatedly matches p until the matching of p silently fails with label $\texttt{fail}$, and propagates a label l when p fails with this label; $!p$ successfully matches if the input does not match p with the label $\texttt{fail}$, fails producing the label $\texttt{fail}$ when the input matches p, and propagates a label l when p fails with this label, not consuming the input in all cases; $\Uparrow^l$ produces the label l.

We faced some design decisions in our formulation that are worth discussing.

We use $\texttt{fail}$ as a label to maintain compatibility with the original semantics of PEGs. For the same reason, we define the expression p_1/p_2 as syntactic sugar for $p_1 /^{\{\texttt{fail}\}} p_2$.

We use a set of labels in the ordered choice as a convenience. We could have each ordered choice handling a single label, and it would just lead to duplication: an expression $p_1 /^{\{l_1, l_2, \ldots, l_n\}} p_2$ would become $(\ldots ((p_1 /^{l_1} p_2) /^{l_2} p_2) \ldots /^{l_n} p_2)$.

The repetition stops silently only on the $\texttt{fail}$ label to maintain the following identity: the expression $p*$ is equivalent to a fresh non-terminal A plus the rule $A \leftarrow p\,A \mid \varepsilon$.

The negative predicate succeeds only on the $\texttt{fail}$ label to allow the implementation of the positive predicate: the expression $\&p$ that implements the positive predicate in the original semantics of PEGs [2,3,4] is equivalent to the expression $!!p$. Both expressions successfully match if the input matches p, fail producing the label $\texttt{fail}$ when the input does not match p, and propagate a label l when p fails with this label, not consuming the input in all cases.

Empty
$$\frac{}{G[\varepsilon]\; x \overset{\text{PEG}}{\rightsquigarrow} x}\;(\textbf{empty.1})$$

Terminal
$$\frac{}{G[a]\; ax \overset{\text{PEG}}{\rightsquigarrow} x}\;(\textbf{char.1}) \qquad \frac{}{G[b]\; ax \overset{\text{PEG}}{\rightsquigarrow} \text{fail}}, b \neq a\;(\textbf{char.2}) \qquad \frac{}{G[a]\; \varepsilon \overset{\text{PEG}}{\rightsquigarrow} \text{fail}}\;(\textbf{char.3})$$

Non-terminal
$$\frac{G[P(A)]\; x \overset{\text{PEG}}{\rightsquigarrow} X}{G[A]\; x \overset{\text{PEG}}{\rightsquigarrow} X}\;(\textbf{var.1})$$

Concatenation
$$\frac{G[p_1]\; xy \overset{\text{PEG}}{\rightsquigarrow} y \quad G[p_2]\; y \overset{\text{PEG}}{\rightsquigarrow} X}{G[p_1\; p_2]\; xy \overset{\text{PEG}}{\rightsquigarrow} X}\;(\textbf{con.1}) \qquad \frac{G[p_1]\; x \overset{\text{PEG}}{\rightsquigarrow} l}{G[p_1\; p_2]\; x \overset{\text{PEG}}{\rightsquigarrow} l}\;(\textbf{con.2})$$

Ordered Choice
$$\frac{G[p_1]\; xy \overset{\text{PEG}}{\rightsquigarrow} y}{G[p_1\; /^S p_2]\; xy \overset{\text{PEG}}{\rightsquigarrow} y}\;(\textbf{ord.1}) \qquad \frac{G[p_1]\; x \overset{\text{PEG}}{\rightsquigarrow} l}{G[p_1\; /^S p_2]\; x \overset{\text{PEG}}{\rightsquigarrow} l}, l \notin S\;(\textbf{ord.2})$$

$$\frac{G[p_1]\; x \overset{\text{PEG}}{\rightsquigarrow} l \quad G[p_2]\; x \overset{\text{PEG}}{\rightsquigarrow} X}{G[p_1\; /^S p_2]\; x \overset{\text{PEG}}{\rightsquigarrow} X}, l \in S\;(\textbf{ord.3})$$

Repetition
$$\frac{G[p]\; x \overset{\text{PEG}}{\rightsquigarrow} \text{fail}}{G[p*]\; x \overset{\text{PEG}}{\rightsquigarrow} x}\;(\textbf{rep.1}) \qquad \frac{G[p]\; xyz \overset{\text{PEG}}{\rightsquigarrow} yz \quad G[p*]\; yz \overset{\text{PEG}}{\rightsquigarrow} z}{G[p*]\; xyz \overset{\text{PEG}}{\rightsquigarrow} z}\;(\textbf{rep.2})$$

$$\frac{G[p]\; x \overset{\text{PEG}}{\rightsquigarrow} l}{G[p*]\; x \overset{\text{PEG}}{\rightsquigarrow} l}, l \neq \text{fail}\;(\textbf{rep.3})$$

Negative Predicate
$$\frac{G[p]\; x \overset{\text{PEG}}{\rightsquigarrow} \text{fail}}{G[!p]\; x \overset{\text{PEG}}{\rightsquigarrow} x}\;(\textbf{not.1}) \qquad \frac{G[p]\; xy \overset{\text{PEG}}{\rightsquigarrow} y}{G[!p]\; xy \overset{\text{PEG}}{\rightsquigarrow} \text{fail}}\;(\textbf{not.2})$$

$$\frac{G[p]\; x \overset{\text{PEG}}{\rightsquigarrow} l}{G[!p]\; x \overset{\text{PEG}}{\rightsquigarrow} l}, l \neq \text{fail}\;(\textbf{not.3})$$

Throw
$$\frac{}{G[\Uparrow^l] \overset{\text{PEG}}{\rightsquigarrow} l}\;(\textbf{throw.1})$$

Fig. 1. Natural Semantics of PEGs with labels

Now, we use labeled failures to implement error reporting in the fragment of the Tiny grammar that we presented in Section 2. In the following example, the expression $[p]^l$ is syntactic sugar for $(p\; /\; \Uparrow^l)$. We use the expression $[p]^l$ to annotate the pieces of the PEG that should not fail and that should generate a label l to name the error and interrupt backtracking when they fail, saving the error position. That is, we use the fail label only for backtracking and other labels for tagging errors.

$Tiny \leftarrow CmdSeq$

$CmdSeq \leftarrow (Cmd~[\text{SEMICOLON}]^{\text{sc}})~(Cmd~[\text{SEMICOLON}]^{\text{sc}})*$

$Cmd \leftarrow IfCmd~/~RepeatCmd~/~AssignCmd~/~ReadCmd~/~WriteCmd$

$IfCmd \leftarrow \text{IF}~[Exp]^{\text{eif}}~[\text{THEN}]^{\text{then}}~[CmdSeq]^{\text{cs1}}(\text{ELSE}~[CmdSeq]^{\text{cs2}}/\varepsilon)~[\text{END}]^{\text{end}}$

$RepeatCmd \leftarrow \text{REPEAT}~[CmdSeq]^{\text{csr}}~[\text{UNTIL}]^{\text{until}}~[Exp]^{\text{erep}}$

$AssignCmd \leftarrow Name~[\text{ASSIGNMENT}]^{\text{bind}}~[Exp]^{\text{ebind}}$

$ReadCmd \leftarrow \text{READ}~[Name]^{\text{read}}$

$WriteCmd \leftarrow \text{WRITE}~[Exp]^{\text{write}}$

We use labeled failures to mark only the pieces of the PEG that should not fail. The PEG detects an error situation when parsing finishes with a certain label that was not caught, so it can identify the error information that is tied to that certain label to report a more meaningful error message. For instance, if we use this PEG for Tiny to parse the example from Section 2, parsing finishes with the sc label and the PEG can use it to produce an error message like below:

```
factorial.tiny:6:1: syntax error, there is a missing ';'
```

Note how the semantics of the repetition works with the rule *CmdSeq*. Inside the repetition, the `fail` label means that there are no more commands to be matched and the repetition should stop while the sc label means that a semicolon (;) failed to match. It would not be possible to write the rule *CmdSeq* using repetition if we had chosen to stop the repetition with any label, instead of stopping only with the `fail` label, because the repetition would accept the sc label as the end of the repetition when it should propagate this label.

Like PEGs, parsers written using parser combinators also finish with success or failure and usually backtrack in case of failure, making it difficult to implement error reporting. In Section 3 we have briefly discussed some related work [6,17,15,10] that solve this problem. Now, we will discuss how these techniques can be expressed using PEGs with labels.

In Hutton's deterministic parser combinators, the `nofail` combinator is used to distinguish between failure and error. We can express the `nofail` combinators using PEGs with labels as follows:

$$\text{nofail}~p \equiv p~/~\Uparrow^{\text{error}}$$

That is, `nofail` is an expression that transforms the failure of p into an error to abort backtracking. Note that the `error` label should not be caught by any ordered choice. Instead, the ordered choice propagates this label and catches solely the `fail` label. The idea is that parsing should finish with one of the following values: success, `fail` or `error`.

The annotation of the Tiny grammar to use `nofail` is similar to the annotation we have done using labeled failures. Basically, we just need to change the grammar to use `nofail` instead of $[p]^l$. For instance, we can write the rule *CmdSeq* as follows:

$CmdSeq \leftarrow (Cmd~(\text{nofail SEMICOLON}))~(Cmd~(\text{nofail SEMICOLON}))*$

If we are writing a grammar from scratch, there is no advantage to use `nofail` instead of more specific labels, as the annotation burden is the same and with `nofail` we lose more specific error messages.

The `cut` combinator was introduced to reduce the space inefficiency of `nofail`, which is space inefficient when implemented in a lazy language due to the error propagation. The semantics of PEGs abstracts the implementation details that differentiate `cut` and `nofail`, thus, in PEGs they are expressed in the same way.

The four-values technique changed the semantics of parser combinators to implement predictive parsers for LL(1) grammars that automatically identify the longest input prefix in case of error, without needing annotations in the grammar. We can express this technique using labeled failures by transforming the original PEG with the following rules:

$$[\![\varepsilon]\!] \equiv \Uparrow^{\texttt{epsn}} \tag{1}$$

$$[\![a]\!] \equiv a \tag{2}$$

$$[\![A]\!] \equiv A \tag{3}$$

$$[\![p_1 p_2]\!] \equiv [\![p_1]\!] \, ([\![p_2]\!] \, / \, \Uparrow^{\texttt{error}} \, /^{\{\texttt{epsn}\}} \, \varepsilon) \, /^{\{\texttt{epsn}\}} \, [\![p_2]\!] \tag{4}$$

$$[\![p_1 / p_2]\!] \equiv [\![p_1]\!] \, /^{\{\texttt{epsn}\}} \, ([\![p_2]\!] \, / \, \Uparrow^{\texttt{epsn}}) \, / \, [\![p_2]\!] \tag{5}$$

This translation is based on three labels, `epsn` means that the expression successfully finished without consuming any input, `fail` means that the expression failed without consuming any input, and `error` means that the expression failed after consuming some input. In our translation we do not have an `ok` label because resulting suffix means that the expression successfully finished after consuming some input. It is straightforward to check that the translated expressions behave according to the table 1 from Section 3.

Parsec introduced the `try` combinator to annotate parts of the grammar where arbitrary lookahead is needed. We need arbitrary lookahead because PEGs and parser combinators usually operate on the character level. The authors of Parsec also showed a correspondence between the semantics of Parsec as implemented in their library and Partridge and Wright's four-valued combinators, so we can emulate the behavior of Parsec using labeled failures by building on the five rules above and adding the following rule for `try`:

$$[\![\texttt{try } p]\!] \equiv [\![p]\!] \, /^{\{\texttt{error}\}} \, \Uparrow^{\texttt{fail}} \tag{6}$$

If we take the Tiny grammar from Section 2, insert `try` in the necessary places, and pass this new grammar through the transformation $[\![\,]\!]$, then we get a PEG that automatically identifies errors in the input with the `error` label. For instance, we can write the rule *RepeatCmd* as follows:

$$RepeatCmd \leftarrow (\texttt{try REPEAT}) \; CmdSeq \; \texttt{UNTIL} \; Exp$$

5 Conclusions

In this paper we discussed error reporting in PEGs. Unfortunately, PEGs behave badly on the presence of syntax errors because backtracking usually makes the

PEG report a position far away from the position where the error happened. Ford [2] showed how he changed his implementation of PEGs to add his farthest position heuristic to have error reporting in packrat parsers. We showed that we can use this heuristic without changing the implementation of PEGs, when it provides mechanisms to produce semantic actions. Although the farthest position heuristic helps PEGs to produce error messages that are close to the ones produced by predictive top-down parsers, these error messages are still generic.

The main contribution of this paper is the introduction of labeled failures to PEGs. The new approach closely resembles the technique of generating and handling exceptions. In this approach, the *throw* operator $\Uparrow^l$ throws labeled failures and the ordered choice catches these failures.

We introduced labeled failures to PEGs as a way to annotate error points in the grammar and tie them to more meaningful error messages. We showed that PEGs with labels report an error when parsing finishes with a label that was not caught. In practice, if we use labeled failures along with the heuristic proposed by Ford, PEGs give specific error messages that report the right place of the error. Furthermore, these error messages can be customized according to the labels that are being used. We also showed that our approach can express several techniques for error reporting on parser combinators as presented in related work [6,17,15,10].

The grammar annotation demands care: if we mistakenly annotate expressions that should be able to fail, this actually modifies the behavior of the parser beyond error reporting. In any case, labeled PEGs introduce an annotation burden that is lesser than the annotation burden introduced by error productions in LR parsers, because error productions usually introduce *reduce-reduce* conflicts to the parser [9].

We implemented the semantics of PEGs with labels using Haskell as a prototype to help us testing our approach. We tested the annotation of Tiny and Lua grammars using this prototype. The tests succeeded in our goal of reporting errors in the correct places and with specific error messages. We also tested in our prototype the translations that we have presented in the previous section, and successfully obtained the expected results.

Finally, labeled failures also help to compose PEGs preserving specific error messages of each separate PEG. For instance, we can compose an annotated PEG that parses HTML with an annotated PEG that parses JavaScript, having specific error messages for each PEG. Composing two different PEGs is an interesting case study to be implemented. It would be also interesting to investigate other cases where exception handling may be useful in PEGs beyond error reporting.

References

1. Aho, A.V., Lam, M.S., Sethi, R., Ullman, J.D.: Compilers: Principles, Techniques, and Tools, 2nd edn. Addison-Wesley Longman Publishing Co., Inc., Boston (2006)

2. Ford, B.: Packrat parsing: a practical linear-time algorithm with backtracking. Master's thesis, Massachusetts Institute of Technology (September 2002)
3. Ford, B.: Packrat Parsing: Simple, Powerful, Lazy, Linear Time. In: ICFP 2002: Proceedings of the 7th ACM SIGPLAN International Conference on Functional Programming, pp. 36–47. ACM, New York (2002)
4. Ford, B.: Parsing Expression Grammars: A Recognition-Based Syntactic Foundation. In: POPL 2004: Proceedings of the 31st ACM SIGACT-SIGPLAN Symposium on Principles of Programming Languages, pp. 111–122. ACM, New York (2004)
5. Grune, D., Jacobs, C.J.: Parsing Techniques: A Practical Guide, 2nd edn. Springer Publishing Company, Incorporated (2010)
6. Hutton, G.: Higher-Order Functions for Parsing. Journal of Functional Programming 2(3), 323–343 (1992)
7. Ierusalimschy, R.: LPeg - Parsing Expression Grammars for Lua (2008), http://www.inf.puc-rio.br/~roberto/lpeg/lpeg.html (visited on March 2013)
8. Ierusalimschy, R.: A Text Pattern-Matching Tool based on Parsing Expression Grammars. Software - Practice & Experience 39(3), 221–258 (2009)
9. Jeffery, C.L.: Generating LR Syntax Error Messages from Examples. ACM Transactions on Programming Languages and Systems 25(5), 631–640 (2003)
10. Leijen, D., Meijer, E.: Parsec: Direct Style Monadic Parser Combinators For The Real World. Technical Report UU-CS-2001-35, Department of Computer Science, Utrecht University (2001)
11. Louden, K.C.: Compiler Construction: Principles and Practice. PWS Publishing Co., Boston (1997)
12. Medeiros, S., Mascarenhas, F., Ierusalimschy, R.: From Regular Expressions to Parsing Expression Grammars. In: Brazilian Symposium on Programming Languages (2011)
13. Medeiros, S., Mascarenhas, F., Ierusalimschy, R.: Left Recursion in Parsing Expression Grammars. In: de Carvalho Junior, F.H., Barbosa, L.S. (eds.) SBLP 2012. LNCS, vol. 7554, pp. 27–41. Springer, Heidelberg (2012)
14. Mizushima, K., Maeda, A., Yamaguchi, Y.: Packrat Parsers Can Handle Practical Grammars in Mostly Constant Space. In: PASTE 2010: Proceedings of the 9th ACM SIGPLAN-SIGSOFT Workshop on Program Analysis for Software Tools and Engineering, pp. 29–36. ACM, New York (2010)
15. Partridge, A., Wright, D.: Predictive parser combinators need four values to report errors. Journal of Functional Programming 6(2), 355–364 (1996)
16. Piumarta, I.: Peg/leg — recursive-descent parser generators for C (2007), http://piumarta.com/software/peg/ (visited on March 2013)
17. Röjemo, N.: Efficient Parsing Combinators. Technical report, Department of Computer Science, Chalmers University of Technology (1995)
18. Swierstra, S.D., Duponcheel, L.: Deterministic, Error-Correcting Combinator Parsers. In: Launchbury, J., Sheard, T., Meijer, E. (eds.) AFP 1996. LNCS, vol. 1129, pp. 184–207. Springer, Heidelberg (1996)
19. Winskel, G.: The Formal Semantics of Programming Languages: An Introduction. MIT Press, Cambridge (1993)

LuaRocks - A Declarative and Extensible Package Management System for Lua

Hisham Muhammad[1], Fabio Mascarenhas[2], and Roberto Ierusalimschy[1]

[1] Department of Computer Science, PUC-Rio, Rio de Janeiro, Brazil
{hisham,roberto}@inf.puc-rio.br
[2] Department of Computer Science, UFRJ, Rio de Janeiro, Brazil
fabiom@dcc.ufrj.br

Abstract. While sometimes dismissed as an operating systems issue, or even a matter of systems administration, module management is deeply linked to programming language design. The main issues are how to instruct the build and runtime environments to find modules and handle their dependencies; how to package modules into redistributable units; how to manage interaction of code written in different languages; and how to map modules to files. These issues are either handled by the language itself or delegated to external tools. Language-specific package managers have risen as a solution to these problems, as they can perform module management portably and in a manner suited to the overall design of the language. This paper presents LuaRocks, a package manager for Lua modules. LuaRocks adopts a declarative approach for specifications using Lua itself as a description language and features an extensible build system that copes with the heterogeneity of the Lua ecosystem.

Keywords: programming language environments, scripting languages, modules and libraries, package management.

1 Introduction

While it is sometimes dismissed as an operating systems issue, or even a matter of systems administration, module management (and by extension package management) is deeply linked to programming language design. The questions of how modules are built, packaged, deployed, detected, and used are mostly dependent on decisions in the design and implementation of the languages in which they are written.

In languages that feature a separate compilation step, there's the issue of how to specify dependencies between modules, and how to instruct the compiler to find them. Some languages take care of this matter internally, such as the management of units in Pascal or classes in Java. Others, like C, relegate it to external tools — in the case of C, the preprocessor is used to forward-declare prototypes and tools like Make are used to handle dependencies between objects during build. In contrast, the Java compiler extracts the classes and interfaces a source file references, finds the files where they are defined, and compiles them

A. Rauber Du Bois and P. Trinder (Eds.): SBLP 2013, LNCS 8129, pp. 16–30, 2013.

on demand. Still, building complex projects usually involves more than sources (including, for instance, generation and conversion of icons, interface description files and other assets, as well as inter-language dependencies), leading to the creation of external tools such as Apache Ant [13].

Packaging modules into redistributable units is another design issue. Some languages define packaging formats as part of their specification. Java has policies for the namespace hierarchy and defines the JAR format, with rules for the file format and its metadata. It also includes a library for reading and writing such archives in its standard library (`java.util.jar`). The .NET Common Language Infrastructure also defines package formats for module bundles, called assemblies, which contain compiled classes and metadata, as well as versioning information [16]. In the other extreme, languages such as C leave the definition of library formats entirely to the operating system and language implementors: support for modularization through dynamic libraries is implemented through OS-specific linkers and runtime support libraries. In all cases, the handling of modules requires some interaction with the operating system due to portability concerns, including varying installation directories and lookup paths.

Languages also employ different approaches when adding support for modules written in different languages. Extensible languages like Perl, Python, Ruby and Lua provide C APIs that allow dynamic libraries to interact with the runtime state of the language's virtual machine [21], as well as facilities to load those libraries into the runtime and register them as modules. Some languages also feature foreign-function interfaces, through which the mapping between functions of external libraries and the language environment are written in the host language itself; an example is the Racket FFI [5]. Those interfaces may be bundled into the language's standard libraries [14], or may be external modules themselves [22]. Loading those external libraries and modules again requires interaction with the operating system, and the extent to which this is performed internally or done by external tools is up to the language's design to define. In the case of modules written in different languages, this means one has two sets of design and implementation aspects to deal with (or even three, when C APIs are used as a bridge between two other languages, as is the case, for example, of LuaJava [18]).

Finally, there is the issue of deployment. While languages such as C and Pascal traditionally left the mapping between modules and files, the physical locations of those files, and the installation processes of the modules to be specified as implementation details, the desire for portability and increased code reuse has led the communities of many languages to attempt to standardize these definitions. From those efforts, a number of language-specific deployment tools have emerged: CPAN for Perl [8], RubyGems for Ruby [7], PIP for Python [29], Cabal for Haskell [17], and so on. While originally developed as external tools, many of these have in fact been integrated into the standard distribution of those languages, and are now considered to be part of their standard libraries, showing that deployment has grown from an OS issue into a core language concern.

These tools are essentially portable, language-specific package managers. Package management, however, is a task of the operating system in platforms such as Linux, and this overlap between OS and language concerns may put the necessity of these language-specific tools into question. This feeling is understandable, but comparing the numbers of packages provided by distributions versus the number of modules available in mature module repositories from scripting languages, it becomes clear that the approach of converting everything into native packages is untenable: for example, while the repository for the Ubuntu Linux distribution features 37,000 packages in total, Perl's CPAN alone contains over 23,000 packages, with the advantage that the language's repository is portable to various platforms. Besides, some platforms simply lack universal package management (Microsoft Windows being a notable case). The portability aspect and the great number of packages make a good case for having package managers for programming languages.

This paper presents one such language-specific package manager: LuaRocks, for the Lua programming language. Lua was originally designed as an embeddable language, to be loaded as a library into other programs. As such, it features extensive facilities for inter-language interaction, through a complete and reentrant C API and a first-class type for boxed C pointers. However, features oriented towards the use of Lua as the host program language are more recent: Lua only gained a module system two major revisions ago, in version 5.0, ten years after the first release of the language [15]. With the module system, many of the concerns enumerated above naturally emerged: namespace issues, build methods, packaging formats, deployment and redistribution of modules. The focus of the language in being a portable language with a small footprint meant that Lua would not take the approach of dealing with these issues internally. Instead, it provides the minimal core of an extensible module system, concerning the integration with the language runtime (package loaders, namespace management), and all other tasks are left for external tools to perform. LuaRocks is an integrated solution for these tasks related to module management, providing a portable build system for both C and Lua code, package format specifications and a package management tool for remote deployment of modules.

2   Related Work

This section provides background on package managers, tracing their origins as operating system tools and the history of language-specific package management. As systems grow in complexity, library dependencies become harder to track. Package management is the most common solution for this problem [33]; on environments without system-wide package management, these conflicts have to be tracked on a file-by-file basis [23], which is a more fragile approach [34].

2.1   Operating System Package Managers

The idea of having a unified system for building and installing packages can be traced back to open source operating systems in the 1990s. The growth of both the free software movement and the commercial internet meant that a large number of independently developed projects were available in source form. However, much of this software could not be built unmodified in a variety of platforms, often requiring OS-specific patches to adapt them to the peculiarities of each system. In 1993, the Debian project introduced dpkg [19], a program for installing, removing and keeping track of installed *packages*, which are archives containing all files that compose a given compiled program. In 1994, FreeBSD introduced the Ports collection, a system of Makefiles that provided a unified interface for building software from third-party (*upstream*) developers while automatically applying compatibility patches [20]. Having a Makefile in the Ports collection means that a program can be easily installed into FreeBSD by using standardized commands.

Linux distributions soon adopted this concept. Red Hat Linux was the first distribution to gain popularity on the merits of its package management system, called RPM [3]. RPM combined both the facilities for creating binary packages found in dpkg with the unified method for building sources from Ports. Later, Debian introduced APT, a front-end tool to dpkg which included dependency resolution, recursively scanning for package dependencies, fetching necessary packages over the network and installing them in topologically-sorted order [19]. Over time, many other package management tools emerged, and these features have grown to become the essential expected feature set: fetching packages remotely; resolving dependency graphs; and installing, removing and listing packages. Current versions of FreeBSD Ports also allow the installation of precompiled packages, and RPM performs dependency management. Some of these features have also evolved in sophistication, for instance, with the distinction between *build dependencies* (packages that need to be installed in the system where the package is being compiled, such as a parser generator or a set of C header files) and *runtime dependencies* (packages that need to be installed in the system where the package will run, such as a shared library).

In recent years, deployment tools for centralized package management have been adopted in platforms for distribution and sale of binary packages as well: these are usually named "application stores". Some examples are the Apple App Store, Google Play and the Amazon Appstore.

2.2 Language-Specific Package Managers

The history of language-specific package managers can be traced to online repositories of software. CPAN [8], the Comprehensive Perl Archive Network, was mainly influenced by CTAN, a repository for TeX class files. Created in 1995, CPAN is the oldest repository for language modules and over the years evolved into a fully-featured package manager. Figure 1 lists 15 of the most popular language specific package managers, along with their start years and number of available packages. Over the last 15 years, many languages, especially those associated with the notion of scripting [24], have gained package managers of their own. Some languages define a official package format as part of their specification, such as JAR for Java, and some include the package management tool along

Language	package manager / repository	packages	included in lang. distr.	official pkg. format	repository start year	direct publishing
Java	Maven/Central	56697	no	yes	2005	no*
Ruby	RubyGems	55035	yes	yes	2003	yes
Python	pip/PyPI	32180	no	yes	2003	yes
JavaScript	npm (node.js)	27688	yes	yes*	2009	yes
Perl	CPAN	24092	yes	yes	1995	no
C#/.NET	NuGet	11823	no	no	2011	yes
PHP	Composer/Packagist	9757	no	no	2011	yes
Clojure	Leiningen/Clojars	6004	no	yes	2009	yes
Haskell	Cabal/Hackage	5062	no**	yes	2007	yes
R	CRAN	4450	yes	yes	1997	no
Objective-C	CocoaPods	1391	no	no	2011	no
Common Lisp	Quicklisp	850	no	no	2010	no
Go	go	744	yes	no	2009	no***
Racket	PLaneT	510	yes	yes	2004	yes
Lua	LuaRocks	266	no	no	2007	no

* The Maven Central is a two-tier repository: it aggregates a number of approved repositories, some of which may provide direct publishing functionality.
** Cabal is not included with Haskell implementations such as GHC and Hugs, but it is part of the Haskell Platform "batteries" package from haskell.org.
*** The Go repository is in fact just a wiki of links to projects which can be imported directly with the Go import statement; editing the list requires contributor access.

Fig. 1. Language-specific package managers, as of April 16, 2013

with the sources of the language reference implementation. These are identified in Figure 1 as well.

Following the steps of CPAN, CRAN [1] was started in 1997 as a repository and later package manager for R, a niche language in the field of statistics. In 2003, RubyGems was created for the Ruby language. Unlike its predecessors, RubyGems [7] allows any developer to publish modules directly in the public repository, without any curating process. By lowering the barrier of entry early on, RubyGems gained enormous popularity and became the largest module repository among scripting languages. In fact, the aspect that seems to affect most directly the number of available packages in a repository is whether the repository allows developers to publish packages directly or if it requires some kind of approval step. From the 15 languages listed in Figure 1, 8 allow direct publishing of modules; 7 of them are in the top 9 positions when ranked by number of available packages. The two exceptions in the top positions are Maven's Central, which is an aggregator of repositories, and CPAN, which has a large total of packages due to being much older than the other repositories. Maven [2] is a build and deployment tool for Java, which eventually evolved into a full-fledged package manager. Maven Central is currently the largest language-specific package repository in existence, with over 56000 packages [32].

Package management systems for Python have had an eventful evolution [35]. The package management tool has been added and then removed from the main Python distribution, and the original tool, `easy_install`, was eventually replaced by `pip`. Still, the package repository, PyPI (Python Package Index) has seen continuous growth [29]. PHP originally had two official package repositories, PEAR and PECL, respectively for PHP extensions and library bindings. These are not open for direct publishing of modules. Eventually, a new package manager, Composer, was created alongside a new open repository, called Packagist. Composer and Packagist quickly eclipsed the original repositories: while PEAR/PECL have less than 900 packages, Packagist features over 9700 [26].

The JavaScript world did not have a package manager until 2009, when `npm` was created. This tool has the peculiarity among package managers of being not only language-specific, but in fact framework-specific, being a tool created to be used with Node.js, an event-driven platform for server-side development [28].

Objective-C, like C and C++, does not define its own package format, but it has an unofficial package management system for class libraries. The CocoaPods project [9] was started in 2011 and hosts modules for iOS and Mac OS X platforms. It has the distinction of being the only one of the language-specific package management systems studied that is not implemented in the target language itself: instead, CocoaPods is written in Ruby, and it is in fact distributed as a Ruby gem. In the .NET platform, there is also no official package manager, but NuGet [25] is a popular tool, which integrates with the Visual Studio IDE.

The Go language adopts a very unusual approach towards module management. Go bundles the compiler, build and deployment tools, and instead of using a centralized repository, adds support for decentralized cross-reference of modules in the language itself: its `import` statement can refer to full URLs which point to source code repositories [4].

Cabal [17] is the package manager for Haskell. Due to the language's sophisticated type system, Haskell modules are known for their intricate dependency relations, as minor interface changes cause incompatibilities and there is no way for incompatible packages to coexist in an installed environment [31]. Other package managers worth mentioning are: PLaneT [27], for Racket; Quicklisp [6], for Common Lisp (which aims to be compatible with several implementations of the language standard); and Leiningen [12], for Clojure (a language that targets the Java Virtual Machine and therefore also uses the JAR format for packages).

Architecturally, all these tools are very similar to their OS-level counterparts, as they perform the same basic tasks: fetching modules; resolving dependencies; and building, installing, and removing modules. A common issue is avoiding conflicts with packages installed by the OS package manager, and how to inform the language runtime about newly installed modules. Old versions of Ruby, for example, required the user to write `require "rubygems"` to enable gem-installed modules, but more recently this support has been integrated by default. Modules that feature dependencies on external libraries, such as bindings to C libraries, are another point of concern. Each package manager specifies its own syntax for locating these libraries, and they often make OS-specific assumptions such as filenames and paths. Integration between OS-level and language-level package managers is a problem that cannot be solved in the general case. For example, a module providing bindings to a JPEG library may be aware that the library is provided by an OS package called `jpeg-dev` in one platform, `libjpeg6-dev` in another, or even by a file called `JPEG.DLL` available somewhere in the library path, when the OS does not feature a standard package manager.

3   The Design of LuaRocks

LuaRocks is written as a pure Lua application and does not assume the availability of any other Lua modules in the system. To perform operations not provided by stock Lua, such as manipulating directories or downloading remote files, it can either launch external programs (e.g. `wget`) or use additional modules such as LuaSocket, depending on what is available. On Windows, a set of helper binaries is included in the distribution that aids the bootstrapping process.

On the surface, LuaRocks behaves like any other package manager. It provides two command-line tools: `luarocks`, the main interface; and `luarocks-admin`, for managing remote repositories. These tools support typical commands, such as `luarocks install` ⟨*package_name*⟩ and `luarocks remove` ⟨*package_name*⟩, respectively for installing and removing packages, while performing recursive dependency matching as expected. While all package managers perform essentially the same tasks, the specifics of each environment impose some design restrictions while opening up some possibilities. In this section, we discuss the novel aspects in the design of LuaRocks. They explore the potential of Lua as a data description language, its sandboxing facilities, and the extensible solutions LuaRocks uses to deal with the heterogeneity of operating systems and build tools that developers use. We also discuss the approach we take to versioning, which makes it easier to deal with package conflicts.

3.1   Declarative Specifications

Package management tools usually define a file format through which packages are specified. Those files can be as simple as a Makefile, as is the case with FreeBSD Ports [20], or may contain various metadata and embedded build scripts, such as .spec files for the RPM package manager. For specifying LuaRocks packages, which we call "rocks", we devised a file format called "rockspec", which is actually a Lua file containing a series of assignments to predefined variable names such as `dependencies` and `description`, defining metadata and build rules for the package.

Rockspecs are loaded by LuaRocks as Lua scripts inside a sandbox that allows the use of Lua syntactical constructs, but no access to its standard libraries or external libraries. This ensures that the loading of the package specification is safe: loading a rockspec file (for example, for syntax verification with the `luarocks lint` command) can at most lock the command-line tool through an endless loop, but it is not able to access any system resources. Even the

```
%define luaver 5.1
%define lualib %{_libdir}/lua/%{luaver}
%define luapkg %{_datadir}/lua/%{luaver}
Name: luasocket
Version: 2.0.2
Release: 8%{?dist}
Summary: Network socket extension for Lua
# ...
Source0: http://.../luasocket-2.0.2.tar.gz
Patch0: lua-socket-unix-sockets.patch
# ...
%prep
%setup -q -n luasocket-%{version}
%patch0 -p1 -b .unix
%build
make %{?_smp_mflags} CFLAGS="%{optflags}
↪ -fPIC"
%install
rm -rf $RPM_BUILD_ROOT
make install
↪ INSTALL_TOP_LIB=$RPM_BUILD_ROOT%{lualib}
↪ INSTALL_TOP_SHARE=$RPM_BUILD_ROOT%{luapkg}
%clean
rm -rf $RPM_BUILD_ROOT
# ...
```

(a) RPM .spec file

```
package = "LuaSocket"
version = "2.0.2-5"
source = {
  url = "http://.../luasocket-2.0.2.tar.gz",
}
description = {
  summary = "Network support for the Lua
language",
  -- ...
}
build = {
  type = "make",
  build_variables = {
    CFLAGS = "$(CFLAGS) -I$(LUA_INCDIR)",
    LDFLAGS = "$(LIBFLAG) -O -fpic",
    LD = "$(CC)"
  },
  install_variables = {
    INSTALL_TOP_SHARE = "$(LUADIR)",
    INSTALL_TOP_LIB = "$(LIBDIR)"
  },
  -- ...
}
```

(b) LuaRocks rockspec

Fig. 2. Excerpts from specification files for LuaSocket 2.0.2 using RPM (from Fedora 18) and LuaRocks, including basic package identification, download URL and build instructions

possibility of an endless loop can be removed using hooks in the Lua virtual machine, making the loading of rockspecs completely safe for use by servers that accept arbitrary rockspecs.

While the loading of a rockspec is imperative, it is not a "build script", but a declarative specification of the package and its build process. Imperative build scripts impose a strict order on operations. A rockspec does not list the sequence of build operations in order as a makefile or an RPM .spec would (Figure 2a), but rather contains definitions which describe the build method declaratively (Figure 2b). The use of declarative descriptions gives us more liberty as tool implementors to make changes to the way the build process is implemented from one version of LuaRocks to another.

Rockspecs allow developers to make higher-level descriptions of their build processes, as we will see in more detail in Section 3.2, and let the tool handle low-level details such as portability adaptations. As a simple example, the invocation of the make command is explicit in Figure 2a and implicit in Figure 2b, which allows LuaRocks to adjust the command name to gmake in some BSD environments. LuaRocks also provides a general method for conditionally replacing entries in a rockspec in a per-platform basis. For example, a field named source.platforms.win32.url will overwrite the source.url field on Windows platforms and will be ignored on other operating systems. Through platforms subtables, a developer can conditionally specify platform-specific build flags, module dependencies and external library requirements.

After LuaRocks compiles and installs a rockspec, the rockspec maintainer can package it as a .rock file, which is a .zip archive containing all modules, the rockspec and a manifest file. Manifest files are essentially plain-text databases for package management, implemented as Lua tables which are loaded in the same sandbox used for rockspecs and saved using a simple serialization procedure.

While each rock has its own manifest in a `rock_manifest` file (containing also the MD5 checksum for each deployed file), LuaRocks also caches a global manifest for all packages in a system `manifest` file for quicker initialization. This global manifest has indexes for efficiently finding dependencies between packages, which package owns a module, and which modules a package owns. This same style of global manifest is used in remote repositories as a directory of available packages. In short, LuaRocks stores all of its metadata as Lua source files, making heavy use of Lua facilities for sandboxes and data description.

3.2   Extensible Build System

One aspect in which the design of LuaRocks resembles OS-level package managers more than typical language-specific package managers is in its handling of build tools. Often, language-specific repositories are built around one specific tool: for example, `easy_install` and later `pip` for Python, Rake for Ruby, ExtUtils::MakeMaker and later Module::Build for Perl. The package manager then delegates the build process to the build tool and focuses on tracking installed files and dependencies. Lua, however, does not have a standard build system. By the time LuaRocks was created, a number of Lua-based build tools had been proposed, but none have gained traction in the developer community. Most Lua modules were distributed by upstream authors along with Unix Makefiles only, or with no build scripts at all, and the user is expected to build and deploy the modules by hand. Some developers also use other tools, such as CMake.

To support these uses, LuaRocks supports several build tools, like OS-level package managers normally do. OS-level package managers typically let developers call their preferred build tools explicitly in imperative specification scripts, as seen in the call to `make` in the .spec file from Figure 2a. This is an open-ended approach that allows the use of any build tool, at the cost of having hard-coded references and a low abstraction level, akin to a shell script or a batch file.

LuaRocks, however, does this in a more controlled manner, with a system of plugins for the different build tools. Each plugin is implemented as a Lua module, and selected through the `build.type` field in the rockspec. For example, using `build.type="make"` (as in Figure 2b) causes LuaRocks to load the module `luarocks.build.make`, which is then responsible for providing the necessary plumbing that connects LuaRocks with the build tool.

The `build` field has additional entries specific for the *build type*, which are passed to the plugin. These entries, and a set of context variables describing the system where LuaRocks is installed, can be used to parameterize the build. For example, in Figure 2b, the plugin responsible for the "`make`" build type interprets the `build.build_variables` and `build.install_variables` entries, passing the appropriate variables to the build tool. Other customizations are possible: for

```
package = "midialsa"; version = "1.17-1"
source = {
    url = "http://www.pjb.com.au/comp/lua/midialsa-1.17.tar.gz",
    md5 = "0482df57c2262ff75f09cec5568352a7"
}
description = {
    summary = "Provides access to the ALSA sequencer", detailed = [[ ... ]],
    homepage = "http://www.pjb.com.au/comp/lua/midialsa.html", license = "MIT/X11"
}
dependencies = { "lua >= 5.1" }
external_dependencies = { ALSA = { header = "alsa/asoundlib.h", library = "asound" }
}
build = {
    type = "builtin",
    modules = {
        ['C-midialsa'] = {
            incdirs = { "$(ALSA_INCDIR)" }, libdirs = { "$(ALSA_LIBDIR)" },
            libraries = { "asound" }, sources = { "C-midialsa.c" }
        },
        midialsa = "midialsa.lua"
    },
    copy_directories = { "doc", "test" }
}
```

Fig. 3. Rockspec for a module using the `builtin` build type

instance, the default `make` target for installation is "`install`", but one can override that using `build.install_target`. Any of these fields can be specified in a platform-specific manner. For example, a rockspec may specify build variables specific to the Windows platform in a `build.platforms.win32.install_target` field.

The first release of LuaRocks shipped with support for three build types: `make`, `cmake` and `command`. The `command` type is a catch-all backend for unsupported build tools: it allows writing a pair of operating system commands in the rockspec (`build.build_command` and `build.install_command`) which LuaRocks then calls. Early on in its history, however, a fourth standard type was added, called `builtin`. The `builtin` type, as the name suggests, is a lightweight built-in build tool integrated with LuaRocks. It was designed to cover the common cases when a module is either written in pure Lua, or contains C code that can be compiled without sophisticated pre-configuration.

Figure 3 depicts a complete rockspec that uses the `builtin` build type. This is the rockspec for midialsa, Lua bindings for the MIDI features of the Advanced Linux Sound Architecture (ALSA). This package installs a module written in Lua, `midialsa`, which provides a high-level Lua API, and a module written in C, `C-midialsa`, which links to the ALSA library and provides core functions for the Lua module. This is a fairly typical setup for library bindings.

The `builtin` build type expects a `modules` map. In the simpler cases, such as pure Lua modules, it associates the name of each module to the source file that implements it. For modules written in C, one can specify more metadata. These are typically paths where to find headers and libraries needed to build the module, names of libraries the module depends on, and the source files for the module. In Figure 3, `C-midialsa` specifies that it needs to be linked to the `asound` library and has its implementation in the `C-midialsa.c` file.

The example also references two context variables that LuaRocks provides, `ALSA_LIBDIR` and `ALSA_INCDIR`. LuaRocks defines these variables after detecting the location of the `alsa/asoundlib.h` and `asound` library the rockspec specifies in the `external_dependencies` section of the rockspec.

To deal with variations between operating systems, external dependencies to libraries are given as abstractly as possible: based on `libraries = "asound"`, LuaRocks will look for files matching one of various possibilities: `libasound.so`, `libasound.so.*`, `libasound.dylib`, `ASOUND.DLL`, `ASOUND.LIB` and so on, depending on the running platform. LuaRocks searches for these files in a series of OS-specific directories. This flexible approach for dependency verification has proven to be a good compromise solution that limits the amount of OS-specific information in the specification file and keeps platform-specific metadata to a minimum. The locations of system header and library directories can, if necessary, be adjusted permanently by the user in a configuration file, or on a case-by-case basis with command-line arguments.

The `builtin` plugin launches the C compiler and linker, passing proper flags for the system it is running on. It has internal support for the GCC and Visual Studio toolchains by default, but it is also largely configurable. All programs and flags used can be overridden using familiar variables such as `CC`, `LD` and `CFLAGS` in the LuaRocks configuration file, in particular making it easy to use alternative compiler toolchains, including cross-compilers.

The `builtin` build type provides LuaRocks with a build tool that is declarative, like the rest of the rockspec format. Platform-specific details are abstracted as much as possible, and can be added only when needed. This gives an easy way for developers who often shipped Unix-only makefiles to support Windows builds with little effort. Still, developers wishing to continue using other tools such as make, CMake, and GNU Autotools can easily do so. LuaRocks integrates well with these tools, as all configuration variables it provides are available for all build plugins, including those by detected external dependencies such as `ALSA_LIBDIR` in the above example, and others such as `PREFIX` and `CFLAGS`.

For all build types, LuaRocks executes the build stage targeting a temporary sandbox directory in its `PREFIX` variable, later moving the generated files to their final locations. This forces relocatability: there is no way for a module compiled through LuaRocks to hard-code its install location. In other words, any module built with LuaRocks can be packed into a .rock file with `luarocks pack` ⟨*rock*⟩ and then installed in a different directory. This is important when deploying binaries, particularly on Windows environments.

3.3   Versioning

Another feature that sets LuaRocks apart from other package managers is the fact that it supports multiple simultaneous versions of the same package in a single installed tree, so that one can, for example, install two modules A and B, where A depends on C version < 2 and B depends on C version ≥ 2. LuaRocks allows all four modules to remain installed in the same directory simultaneously, and provides runtime support so that the correct version of C is used for either A or B.

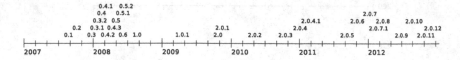

Fig. 4. Timeline of LuaRocks releases

When LuaRocks installs a new version of a module, it renames the old version so they can coexist in the same directory (adding the rock name and version as a prefix). The idea is that Lua will always find the latest installed version of each module, as that file will have a standard pathname such as /usr/local/lib/lua/5.1/socket.so.

Users who need support for loading versions other than the latest one can use a custom module loader that LuaRocks provides. Module loaders are the extensibility mechanism for the Lua module system. Whenever a module is requested, Lua tries to load it using a series of loader functions registered in a list. The LuaRocks module loader keeps in memory a "context", which is the list of previously loaded modules, the rocks they belong to, and their dependencies, so that when Lua needs to load a new module, the LuaRocks module loader can choose a version based on dependencies from the current context.

This approach to versioning alleviates the so called "dependency hell" experienced in many other package managers. If the user wants to write a script using a module that happens to depend on a version of another module that is different than what is already installed on their system, they are free to install that additional dependency without worrying that other modules that depend on the previously installed version will break. When using package managers that lack this feature, the workaround is to create separate local module trees in different directories and configure the runtime environment accordingly whenever each script is run. Some languages even feature tools that encapsulate this usage pattern, creating replicated environments to avoid conflicting dependencies: RVM [30] for Ruby and Virtualenv [11] for Python are two examples.

4 Development History

The initial release of LuaRocks was published in August 2007. After thirteen 0.x releases, LuaRocks 1.0 was released in September 2008 (See Figure 4), and the rockspec format specification has been frozen ever since. LuaRocks 2.0 was released in October 2009, introducing the custom module loader.

Given that Lua has a history as a language for embedding into applications and games, where the only additional modules are those specific to the underlying program, the developer community for reusable modules is small compared to languages with a focus on areas such as, for example, web development. Still, the LuaRocks repository has shown a steady growth. Figure 5, generated from archive snapshots of the repository index, shows the growth of the collection, from October 2009 when LuaRocks 2.0 was released and the repository contained

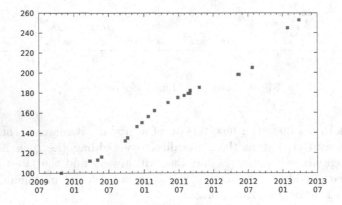

Fig. 5. Number of packages in the LuaRocks repository during the 2.0 series, from October 2009 to March 2013

exactly 100 packages, up to March 2013, when we just surpassed 250 packages. During this time, the 2.0 series had a number of point releases. Save for bugfixes, these releases are essentially compatible. They were mainly driven by feedback and contributions from users, and were focused on improving portability, adding new commands to the `luarocks` and `luarocks-admin` command-line tools, and improving user experience with better platform detection.

The `builtin` build plugin proved to be quite popular. As of this writing, of the 258 projects in the LuaRocks repositories, 195 of them use the `builtin` build type, and only 26 use `make`[1]. In particular, from those 195 rocks, 29 of them originally used the `make` build type and later switched to `builtin`, suggesting that it was a good strategy to allow developers to warm up to the idea of using LuaRocks by letting them start to use it along with their existing build systems. The `make` build type often exposed shortcomings in the developers' makefiles, such as poor support for specifying custom install paths and linker flags. This was often noticed when Mac users attempted to install rocks written by Linux developers and vice versa, and also as developers transitioned from x86 to x86-64. The `builtin` type handles those issues transparently.

5   Conclusion

In recent years, language-specific package managers have become an essential part of programming language ecosystems, as the internet allows large communities of developers to build upon each other's work by reusing modules. The exact role and scope of language-specific package managers vary from language to language, as the definitions of what is handled by the language and what is

---

[1] From the 37 remaining projects, 10 use `command`, mostly for invoking GNU Autotools, and 27 use `none`, which is a blank build type for merely copying .lua files (a predecessor of `builtin`).

delegated to the package manager are language design decision themselves. Still, these developments have been underrepresented in academic literature so far.

This paper presented LuaRocks, a package manager for the Lua programming language. LuaRocks brings some novel concepts to language-specific package manager design, such as a completely declarative integrated build system, thorough use of the language itself as its data description language (which allows the tool to bootstrap itself without any external dependencies) and support for coexisting versions of modules in local repositories, with runtime support for dependency resolution based on the extensibility mechanisms of the Lua language.

LuaRocks is used in production systems around the world and is included in repositories of several Linux distributions. As of this writing, the rocks repository features 750 rockspecs for 258 different projects. LuaRocks users have reported success using it in a number of platforms, such as Windows (either natively, with Cygwin, or with Mingw32), Linux, Mac OS X, FreeBSD, OpenBSD, NetBSD and Solaris. The directions of development nowadays are essentially dictated by the needs of the community, while trying to balance concerns of compatibility, portability and ease of use. For many developers, especially those familiar with other languages that already have similar ecosystems in place, LuaRocks is their introduction to writing and sharing Lua modules.

The declarative rockspec format proved to be a success among developers, and its specification remains largely frozen since LuaRocks 1.0. Still, we have identified some possibilities for improvement of the format over the years, and the next major release may include a revision of the specification, while keeping backward compatibility. LuaRocks is prepared to recognize incompatibilities through the `rockspec_format` field, so the transition shouldn't be traumatic.

Another frequent request is implementing support for LuaRocks to upgrade itself. The tool already has experimental support for that, but it is not enabled by default, since the interaction with installations made through OS-level package managers still has to be assessed. Another plan is to eventually allow direct publishing of modules by developers. This requires development of server-side infrastructure, but the LuaRocks community has already started efforts in this direction, with an alternative repository called MoonRocks which allows direct publishing [10].

References

1. Adler, J.: R in a Nutshell, pp. 37–47. O'Reilly Media (October 2012) ISBN 144931208X
2. Apache Software Foundation. Apache Maven Project,
   https://maven.apache.org/
3. Bailey, E.: Maximum RPM, p. 450. Sams (August 1997) ISBN 0672311054
4. Balbaert, I.: The Way To Go: A Thorough Introduction to the Go Programming Language, pp. 203–223. iUniverse (March 2012) ISBN 1469769166
5. Barzilay, E., Orlovsky, D.: Foreign Interface for PLT Scheme. In: Fifth Workshop on Scheme and Functional Programming, Snowbird Utah, USA (September 22, 2004)

6. Beane, Z.: Quicklisp, http://www.quicklisp.org/
7. Berube, D.: Practical Ruby Gems. Apress (April 2007) ISBN 1590598113
8. Christiansen, T., Foy, B.D., Wall, L., Orwant, J.: Programming Perl, 4th edn., pp. 629–644. O'Reilly Media, ISBN 0596004923
9. CocoaPods, http://www.cocoapods.org
10. Corcoran, L.: MoonRocks, http://rocks.moonscript.org/
11. Gift, N., Jones, J.: Python for Unix and Linux System Administration, pp. 279–283. O'Reilly Media (August 2008) ISBN 0596515820
12. Hagelberg, P., et al.: Leiningen, http://leiningen.org/
13. Hatcher, E., Loughran, S.: Java Development with Ant, p. 672. Manning Publications (August 2002) ISBN 1930110588
14. Heller, T., et al.: Python CTypes, http://docs.python.org/3/library/ctypes.html
15. Ierusalimschy, R., Figueiredo, L.H., Celes, W.: The evolution of Lua. In: History of Programming Languages III, San Diego, USA (June 2007)
16. ISO/IEC 23271:2012. Information Technology — Common Language Infrastructure (CLI)
17. Jones, I., Peyton Jones, S., Marlow, S., Wallace, M., Patterson, R.: The Haskell Cabal: A Common Architecture for Building Applications and Tools. In: Haskell Workshop (2005)
18. Kepler Project. LuaJava — A script tool for Java, http://keplerproject.org/luajava/
19. Krafft, M.: The Debian System: Concepts and Techniques, p. 608. No Starch Press (September 2005) ISBN 1593270690
20. Lehey, G.: The Complete FreeBSD: Documentation from the Source, 4th edn., pp. 167–180. O'Reilly Media (April 2003) ISBN 0596005164
21. Muhammad, H., Ierusalimschy, R.: C APIs in extension and extensible languages. Journal of Universal Computer Science 13(6)
22. Mascarenhas, F.: Alien — Pure Lua extensions, http://mascarenhas.github.com/alien/
23. Microsoft, MSDN Library, Side-by-side Assemblies (Windows) (August 2010), http://msdn.microsoft.com/en-us/library/aa376307.aspx
24. Osterhout, J.: Scripting: Higher Level Programming for the 21st Century. IEEE Computer 31(3), 23–30 (1998)
25. Outercurve Foundation. NuGet Gallery, https://nuget.org/
26. Packagist, http://www.packagist.org
27. PLaneT Package Repository, http://planet.racket-lang.org/
28. Powers, S.: Learning Node, pp. 63–79. O'Reilly Media (October 2012) ISBN 1449323073
29. Python Package Index, https://pypi.python.org/pypi
30. Ruby Version Manager, https://rvm.io/
31. Snoyman, M.: Solving Cabal Hell, http://www.yesodweb.com/blog/2012/11/solving-cabal-hell
32. Sonatype Inc. The Central Repository, https://search.maven.org
33. Spinellis, D.: Package Management Systems. IEEE Software 29(2), 84–86 (2012), doi:10.1109/MS.2012.38
34. Worthmuller, S.: No End to DLL Hell! Dr. Dobb's Journal (September 2010), http://www.drdobbs.com/windows/no-end-to-dll-hell/227300037
35. Ziadć, T.: Chronology of Packaging, http://ziade.org/2012/11/17/chronology-of-packaging/

On the Performance of Multidimensional Array Representations in Programming Languages Based on Virtual Execution Machines

Francisco Heron de Carvalho Junior, Cenez Araújo Rezende,
Jefferson de Carvalho Silva, Francisco José Lins Magalhães,
and Renato Caminha Juaçaba-Neto

Mestrado e Doutorado em Ciência da Computação,
Universidade Federal do Ceará, Brazil
heron@lia.ufc.br

Abstract. This paper evaluates the performance of virtual execution machines (VM) of the CLI and JVM standards for the common approaches to represent multidimensional arrays in high performance computing applications. In particular, it shows which representation is the best for each virtual machine implementation, showing that the choices may be surprisingly contradictory, even with respect to previous results of other works on performance evaluation of VMs.

1 Introduction

Object-oriented programming languages based on virtual execution environments (VEE), such as Java and C#, are consolidated in software industry, motivated by the security, safety and interoperability they provide to software products and the productivity they provide to software development and maintenance. These languages have caught the attention of Fortran and C users from computational sciences and engineering, interested in modern techniques and tools for large-scale software development [28]. However, most of them still consider that the performance of VEEs does not attend the needs of HPC (High Performance Computing) applications.

In the 1990s, the performance bottlenecks of JVM (Java Virtual Machine) for HPC have been extensively investigated. New techniques have been proposed to circumvent them, also incorporated in CLI (Common Language Infrastructure) virtual execution machines [15], such as .NET and Mono. In the 2000s, most of these efforts moved to the design of new high-level programming languages aimed at the HPC needs [21]. However, the performance of virtual machines have been significantly improved with *just-in-time* (JIT) compilation during this period. Also, the new CLI standard have introduced new features for addressing HPC requirements, such as rectangular arrays, direct interface to native code, language interoperability and unsafe pointers.

After a decade of developments in the design and implementation of virtual execution machines, there is still a lack of rigorous studies about their serial

A. Rauber Du Bois and P. Trinder (Eds.): SBLP 2013, LNCS 8129, pp. 31–45, 2013.

performance in the context of HPC applications [17]. Recent works have evaluated current JVM machines by taking parallel processing into consideration (i.e. including communication/synchronization costs) [31,9], both in shared-memory and distributed-memory platforms, using a subset of NPB-JAV [16], a Java implementation of the NPB (NAS Parallel Benchmarks) suite [11]. Also, for our knowledge, it is only devoted to W. Vogels the publication of a comprehensive performance comparison between JVM and CLI machines [35]. Finally, the existing works barely take into consideration the analysis of different approaches to implement multidimensional arrays, which is relevant in the HPC context.

This paper reports the results of a performance evaulation with the following goals in mind: to compare the current performance of virtual execution engines that follow the CLI and JVM standards for different approaches to implementing multidimensional arrays, using real-world numerical simulation programs; to obtain a more realist measure of the performance gap between virtual and native execution; and to identify bottlenecks in the current implementation of virtual machines, regarding the support to multidimensional arrays.

As far we know, this paper is the first one to report a comprehensive study about the performance of distinct approaches to implementing multidimensional arrays in programming languages based on virtual execution, which are: index mapping to unidimensional arrays; jagged arrays; and rectangular arrays. It points out at invalid generalizations of results reported in previous works, contradicting some common sense ideas of programmers that do not apply depending on the virtual machine implementations, and quantifying the cost of array-bounds-checking [1].

The results of this paper complement the results of previous works on the performance evaluation of JVM and CLI for scientific/engineering code [31,8,35,16], finding that they present some contradictory results due to the lack of analysis of different forms of implementing multidimensional arrays, as well as providing recommendations on how to optimize the performance of array intensive code according to the features of the virtual machine.

Section 2 introduces virtual execution technology and presents the motivations of the experimental work whose results are presented in this paper, based on an analysis of related works. Section 3 presents the methodology adopted in the experiments, whose results are presented and discussed in Section 4. Section 5 summarizes the results and contributions of this paper and suggests further works on improving the performance of virtual machines.

2   Context and Related Works

Programming languages based on virtual execution environments (VEE) abstract away from the hardware and operating systems of computing systems, reaching high portability. In heterogeneous environments, the benefits of virtual execution, such as security and cross-platform portability, are clear, in particular for applications that are distributed across a network, such as the internet.

---

[1] The results of this paper is available at http://npb-for-hpe.googlecode.com

Java was launched by Sun Microsystem in the 1990s. The Java Virtual Machine (JVM) has an available implementation for virtually any platform. Its intermediate representation, the so-called *bytecode*, is dynamically compiled, on demand, through just-in-time (JIT) compilation. The JIT compiler implementation dictates the performance of virtual execution machines such as JVM. The most important industrial-strength implementations of JVM are now supported by Oracle [7] and IBM [2]. OpenJDK [6], also popular, is an open-source project directly related to the Oracle's JVM.

The CLI standard [15] has been introduced in the beginning of 2000s, specifying virtual execution machines with distinguishing features, such as: support for multiple programming languages and their interoperability [19]; a strongly typed and polymorphic intermediate representation, called IL (Intermediate Language); version control; ahead-of-time compilation; true multidimensional arrays; unsafe execution using pointers, like in C; and so on.

.NET [5] and Mono [1] are interoperable implementations of CLI. The .NET framework has been developed by Microsoft for the Windows Platform, whereas Mono is an open source project started by Novell, with implementations for a wide range of platforms, including Windows. Mono and its related products are now property of Xamarin. Also, IKVM.NET [3] is an implementation of the Java Platform for Mono and .NET, including an implementation of JVM, standard Java class libraries, and tools for Java and Mono/.NET interoperability.

2.1 Virtual Execution Environments in HPC

In the end of 1990s, Java started to attract the attention of programmers from scientific and engineering community, due to its productivity and interoperability features. However, the poor performance of the first JVM implementations, the difficulties to introduce usual loop optimizations in JIT compilers, and the absence of true multidimensional arrays were considered prohibitive for HPC applications, motivating researchers in quantifying the performance bottlenecks of JVM and proposing solutions to circumvent them [27,24], including language extensions [33], support for multidimensional arrays [23,18], specific-purpose scientific computing libraries [4,32,34], interfaces for interoperability with native scientific computing libraries [12], and compiler support [13], including loop optimizations [10] and array-bounds-checking (ABC) elimination [20,29,25,36]. However, it was JIT compilation that made VEEs attractive for HPC software.

.NET attempted to narrow the performance gap between native and virtual execution, by introducing true multidimensional arrays and JIT optimizations. W. Vogels [35] was the first to compare CLI and JVM implementations, showing that .NET performance is competitive with the performance of the best JVM implementations, but not providing significative gains. Surprisingly, jagged arrays outperformed rectangular arrays in .NET, justified by further JIT optimizations.

In 2003, Frumkin *et al.* [16] proposed NPB-JAV, a multi-threaded Java implementation of the NAS Paralell Benchmarks (NPB) [11], reporting that performance of Java was still lagging far behind Fortran and C. Also in 2003, Nikishkov *et al.* [26] compared the performance of Java (object-oriented design) and C using a three-dimensional finite element code, reporting similar performance conditioned to code tuning and the choice of the virtual machine implementation.

In a special issue of a journal devoted to the 2001 Java Grande-ISCOPE (JGI'2001) conference, published in 2003, two papers deserves special attention. The paper of Riley et al. [30] reported slowdown factors between 1.5 and 2.0 for carefully object-oriented designed Java implementations of real-world applications from computational fluid dynamics (CFD), running in Sun and IBM JVMs. In turn, the paper of Bull et al. [14] compared directly the performance of Java Grande Benchmarks [22] re-written in C and Fortran with their performance in Java, accross a number of JVM implementations and computing platforms, showing small performance gaps, notably for Intel Pentium.

The most recent works on the performance evaluation of virtual machines are due to Taboada et al. [31] and Amedro et. al. [9], with focus on parallel programming. Contrariwise to the previous works, they presented results where the performance of virtual execution is near to the performance of native execution. However, their evaluation is only based on Oracle JVM implementation. The results of Section 4 will show that some conclusions of these works cannot be generalized to other implementations. Also, we consider important to evaluate pure sequential execution, not affected by communications and synchronization costs of parallel execution, since an efficient parallel program cannot be obtained from inefficient sequential code.

2.2 Multidimensional Arrays

In computational intensive programs from scientific and engineering domains, arrays of multiple dimensions are the most used data structures. For this reason, HPC programmers use techniques for efficient access to multidimensional arrays, based on their layout in memory, attempting to promote spacial locality for optimizing cache performance [17]. For that, Fortran supports *rectangular arrays*, whose elements may be accessed as in standard mathematical notation, and stored consecutively in memory. In C and C++, rectangular arrays are static.

Java was conceived without rectangular arrays, which has been viewed as an annoying limitation for using Java in HPC, together with bytecode interpretation. Java supports *jagged arrays* (*arrays-of-arrays*), where a $N_1 \times N_2 \times \cdots \times N_k$ array (k dimensions, with N_i elements in the i-th dimension), where $k > 2$, must be represented as an unidimensional array whose elements are pointers to $N_2 \times \cdots \times N_k$ multidimensional arrays. By consequence, only the N_k elements in the last dimension of the array may be consecutive in memory. The memory requirements of jagged arrays and rectangular ones are different. Jagged arrays require much more memory due to the additional pointers for redirecting the elements of the first $k - 1$ indexes, in a k dimensional array.

In turn, CLI designers decided to introduce rectangular arrays, as well as other features considered relevant in HPC, such as cross-language interoperability, integration to unmanaged code and ahead-of-time (AOT) compilation. Due to the lack of support for rectangular arrays, Java programmers in the HPC domain usually implement multidimensional arrays by using the common C/C++ technique for implementing dynamic rectangular arrays, by explicitly mapping their indexes to the indexes of unidimensional (unboxed) arrays, ensuring that all elements are consecutive in memory. For instance, let a be a $N_1 \times N_2 \times \cdots \times N_k$ array and let A be a unidimensional array that will represent a in a Java program. In the case of row-major memory layout, the element $a_{i_1, i_2, \ldots, i_k}$ must be mapped to the element $index\,(i_1, i_2, \ldots, i_k)$, where

$$index\,(x_1, x_2, \ldots, x_k) = \sum_{i=1}^{k} \left(x_i * \prod_{j=i+1}^{k} N_j \right).$$

In HPC practice, the $index$ function is "inlined" for avoiding function calls.

These techniques, originated from the experience of HPC programmers with native languages, are followed by NPB-JAV. However, this paper shows that they may cause overheads in virtual machine-based languages, depending on the choice of virtual machine implementation.

3 Methodology

For achieving the experimental goals announced in Section 1, it is required the use of near-optimal code from realistic HPC applications. For this reason, we have adopted NPB (NAS Parallel Benchmarks), a benchmark suite derived from CFD (Computational Fluid Dynamics) applications by the Advanced Supercomputing Division of NASA for evaluating the performance of parallel computing platforms [11]. It has reference implementations written by expert HPC programmers in Fortran, C and Java [16]. NPB has been widely used along the years for evaluating the performance of programming language abstractions, compilers, and execution environments.

The NAS Parallel Benchmarks (NPB) comprises eight programs, from which one *benchmark* and three *simulated applications* have been selected for the purposes of the experiment reported in this paper. They are: **FT** (Fast Fourier Transform), **SP** (Scalar Pentadiagonal Linear System Solver), **BT** (Block-Triagonal Linear System Solver), and **LU** (LU Factorization).

NPB specifies a set of *problem classes*, which define standard workloads to be applied to the programs, based on realistic problem instances. They are referenced by letters: S and W, originally for testing purposes; A, B, C, and so on, defining realistic workload levels.

3.1 Experimental Factors

For the purposes of this performance evaluation, the following experimental factors and levels have been selected:

- **Program**: **SP, BT, LU** and **FT**;
- **Problem class**: **S, W, A** and **B**;

- **Virtual machine**: IBM JVM 1.7 (**JVM$_1$**), Oracle JVM 1.7 (**JVM$_2$**), Mono 2.11.3 (**CLI$_1$**), .NET 4.0.3 (**CLI$_2$**) and IKVM 0.46.0.1 (**JVM$_3$**);
- **Multidimensional array representation**: unidimensional arrays with in-line index arithmetic (**AU**) and with index arithmetic encapsulated in methods (**AU***), row-major ordered jagged arrays (**AJR**), column-major ordered jagged arrays (**AJC**), row-major ordered rectangular arrays (**ARR**) and column-major ordered rectangular arrays (**ARC**).

3.2 Derivation of Program Versions

We have derived Java sequential versions of SP, BT, LU and FT from NPB-JAV [16], officially supported by NPB 3.0, corresponding to the **AU** version. For supporting the other kinds of multidimensional arrays, versions of each program have been derived for **AU***, **AJR**, and **AJC**. Then, C# versions were derived from the Java versions, except for **AU***. Finally, the **ARR** and **ARC** versions have been written only in C#, which supports rectangular arrays.

3.3 Performance Measures

The performance measures have been collected in a Dell Studio XPS 810, equipped with an Intel Core i5 processor (Cores: 4, RAM: 8GB, Clock: 2.66MHz). The operating system is Ubuntu 12.04.1 LTS (GNU/Linux 3.2.0-30-generic x86_64).

For each combination of levels of the experimental factors, we have collected a sample of execution times from 10 runs, defining the set of *observations*.

The sample size has been derived from a preliminary experiment with 100 observations for the problem classes S and W, with outliers elimination, where we calculated that the sample size does not need to be greater than 10 to achieve acceptable confidence in the use of the average as the central tendency measure, by assuming normal distribution.

4   Results and Discussion

The experimental data is summarized in the graphs of figures 1-3. Each graph shows the average execution times (y axis) of the levels of **array kind** for each **problem class** (x axis), for one combination of **program** and **virtual machine**. The graphs also includes the execution times of the native versions. Logarithmic scale is used for better interpretation and visualization, since the workloads of the NPB problem classes increases in one level of magnitude.

Using logarithm scale, if the difference between the execution times of two program versions is nearly the same from one problem class to another one that represents a bigger workload, there is a strong evidence that the computation workload do not affect the two versions in different ways. For instance, by comparing the differences between the execution times of row-major (**AJR**, **ARR**) and column-major versions (**AJC**, **ARC**) across the problem classes, the overhead of column-major traversing tends to increase slightly with the workload, as expected. So, we focus our attention in comparing **AJR**, **ARR** and **AU**.

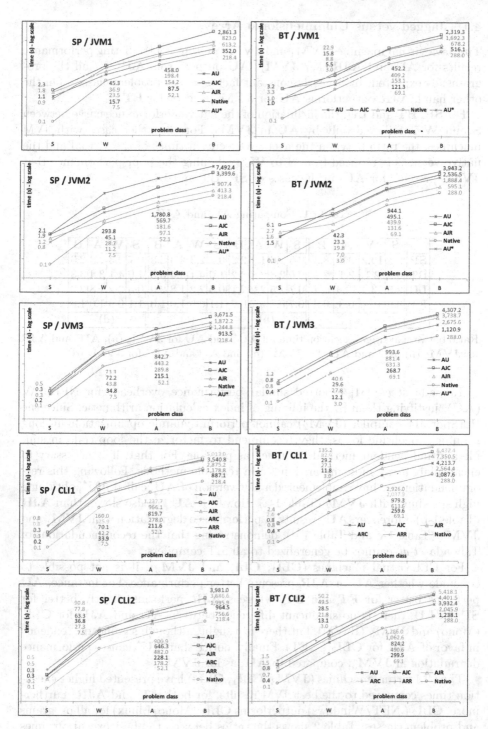

Fig. 1. SP and BT - Performance Figures

4.1 Jagged versus Unidimensional Arrays

The Java virtual machines JVM_1 and JVM_2 present contradicting performance results for **AU** and **AJR**. For JVM_1, **AU** outperforms **AJR** for all the programs, as expected, by a nearly constant factor across problem classes. On the other hand, **AJR** outperforms **AU** for JVM_2, except for **FT**.

For **SP**, **BT** and **LU**, the inclination of the native performance curve between **S** and **W** is followed only by **AU** in JVM_2. For the other cases with JVM machines, the ratio between the average execution times of the virtual and the native versions is reduced from **S** to **W**, explaining the poor performance that JVM_2 presents for **AU**, in the cases of **SP**, **BT** and **LU**.

Table 1. Comparing **AU** and **AU***

	S	W	A	B	S	W	A	B	S	W	A	B	S	W	A	B
SP	2.8	10.2	9.8	8.3	0.6	2.6	1.9	2.2	0.7	2.3	2.3	2.3	0.7	2.3	2.3	2.3
BT	0.9	2.1	2.1	2.1	0.6	2.8	3.3	3.2	1.0	4.1	3.4	3.3	1.0	4.1	3.4	3.3
LU	2.5	13.4	13.4	12.0	0.7	2.5	2.2	2.1	0.5	2.2	1.8	2.0	0.5	2.2	1.8	2.0
FT	0.9	0.9	0.8	0.9	0.7	0.7	0.7	0.9	1.1	0.9	1.0	1.0	1.1	0.9	1.0	1.0
	(a)				(b)				(c)				(d)			

Ratio between average execution times of **AU*** and **AU** for JVM_2 (a), **AU*** and **AJR** for JVM_2 (b), **AU** and **AU*** for JVM_1 (c), and **AU** and **AU*** for JVM_3 (d).

Taboada *et al.* [31] reported similar performance overheads for NPB-JAV (**AU**), justifying them by the inlining of index calculation arithmetic. Since the HotSpot JIT compiler (JVM_2) cannot perform dynamic optimizations in long running monolithic loops, they recommend to factorize the loop code in simple and independent methods as much as possible. For that, it is necessary to encapsulate array indexing arithmetic in reusable methods. Following this recommendation, we have implemented a new version of **AU**, called **AU***, obtaining high speedups with JVM_2 (Table 1-a). However, **AU*** is also slower than **AJR** (Table 1-b). Moreover, **AU*** results in performance degradation with JVM_1 and JVM_3 (Table 1-c and Table 1-d), demonstrating that the recommendations of Taboada *et al.* cannot be generalized to all JIT compilers.

For CLI virtual machines (CLI_1, CLI_2 and JVM_3), it is not possible to conclude whether **AU** or **AJR** presents better performance. For instance, **AU** performs better for **FT** and **BT**, whereas **AJR** performs slightly better for **SP**. In **LU**, there is no significant difference between **AU** and **AJR** for CLI_1 (Mono) and JVM_3 (IKVM), but there is a slight, although significant, tendency in favor of **AJR** for CLI_2 (.NET). Finally, notice that **AU*** causes performance degradation in JVM_3, compared to **AU**, as for JVM_1.

The CLI virtual machines (JVM_3, CLI_1, CLI_2) have presented higher execution times compared to the best JVM results, for both **AU** and **AJR**. Furthermore, CLI_2 (.NET/Windows) outperforms CLI_1 (Mono/Linux) for all programs and problem classes. Table 2 shows the ratios between the best execution times obtained using a CLI virtual machine and using a JVM one, for **AU** and **AJR**.

Table 2. CLI *versus* JVM in **AU** and **AJR**

	S	W	A	B	S	W	A	B
SP	0.3	2.2	2.4	2.5	0.1	2.4	1.8	2.9
BT	0.4	2.1	2.1	2.1	0.2	3.1	3.7	4.3
LU	0.3	2.1	2.5	2.3	0.2	1.8	1.7	2.9
FT	2.0	1.9	1.9	2.0	1.5	1.4	1.4	–
	(a)				(b)			

Ratio between the best execution time of CLI_1 and CLI_2 and the best execution time of JVM_1 and JVM_2 for **AU** (a) and **AJR** (b).

u[k][j][i][m]	u[m+i*isize2 + j*jsize2 + k*ksize2]

`ldfld float64[][][][] <CLASS>::u`
`ldloc.2`
`ldelem.ref`
`ldloc.1`
`ldelem.ref`
`ldloc.0`
`ldelem.ref`
`ldloc.3`
`ldelema [mscorlib]System.Double`
 	
`<CLASS> ≡ NPB3_0_JAV.SPThreads.SPBase`
	`ldfld float64[] <CLASS>::u`
	`ldloc.3`
	`ldloc.0`
	`ldarg.0`
	`ldfld int32 <CLASS>::isize1`
	`mul`
	`add`
	`ldloc.1`
	`ldarg.0`
	`ldfld int32 <CLASS>::jsize1`
	`mul`
	`add`
	`ldloc.2`
	`ldarg.0`
	`ldfld int32 <CLASS>::ksize1`
	`mul`
	`add`
	`ldelema [mscorlib]System.Double`

Fig. 2. CIL Codes for Accessing a Multidimensional Array (Comparing **AU** and **AJR**)

Figure 2 compares the CIL code generated by the C# compiler for accessing the array u in **SP** and **BT**, using jagged array (a) and unidimensional array (b). An access to a jagged array is dominated by a sequence of *indirection operations* (`ldloc/ldref.i`), for each index i, followed by a *fetch operation* (`ldelema`). The JIT compiler emits the array bounds checking code to protect `ldref` instructions. In turn, the unidimensional version performs arithmetic to calculate the array index, followed by a *fetch operation*. Indirection operations perform very fast if data is in cache, justifying the better performance compared to index calculation arithmetic. Moreover, this may be the reason why **AU** performs better than **AJR** only for **FT**. **FT** stores complex numbers, distinguishing the real and imaginary parts in the last dimension of the arrays (size 2), which is not large enough to take advantage of data locality for better cache performance.

Table 3. Virtual *versus* Native Execution

	S	W	A	B		S	W	A	B		S	W	A	B		S	W	A	B
SP	15.2	1.5	1.7	1.6	**BT**	10.6	1.9	1.8	1.8	**LU**	18.8	1.8	1.6	1.7	**FT**	2.5	2.7	2.6	2.9

The best results across all the experimental cases have been obtained by JVM_1 using **AU**, followed by JVM_2 using **AJR**. As expected, their performance are still worse compared to native execution, in Fortran, by the factors

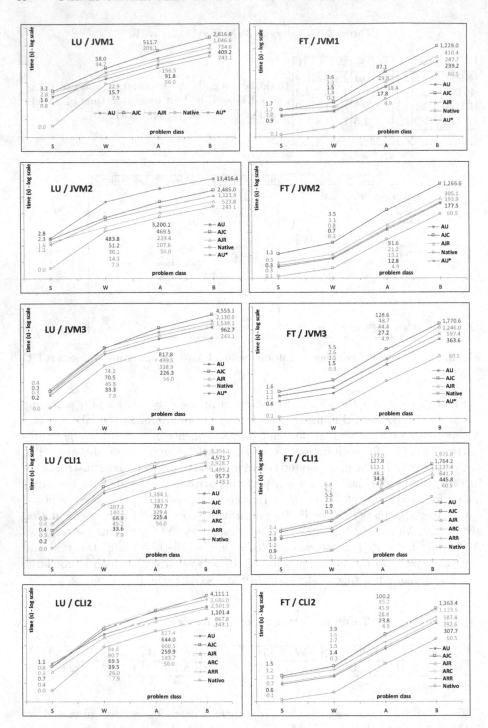

Fig. 3. LU and FT - Performance Figures

presented in Table 3, confirming, for large workloads, the results found by Riley *et al.* [30]. However, we think that the advantages of using object-oriented languages, regarding modularity and abstraction, make them competitive for bigger problem instances, where virtual execution presents better results.

For HPC programmers, it is a surprise that **AJR** may be competitive to **AU** in Java, since they avoid jagged arrays due to three beliefs that come from their familiarity with C and Fortran. Firstly, the elements of a jagged arrays are not consecutive in memory, making difficult to take advantage of spatial locality of array accesses for better performance of the memory hierarchy system. Secondly, the cost of array bounds checking is proportional to the number of dimensions. Thirdly, the time of jagged array accesses is also proportional to the number of dimensions. Thus, this is a useful result for helping HPC programmers to improve the quality of their code, since jagged arrays is the best way to implement multidimensional arrays in Java, in terms of safety and code readability.

Together, the above beliefs and the results of Taboada *et al.*[31] suggest that Java HPC programmers must use unidimensional arrays encapsulated in classes, with methods for accessing the elements through multiple dimensions, avoiding the scattering of the index calculation arithmetic in the source code. However, this paper shows that the performance of this approach depends on the underlying virtual machine implementation. For JVM_1 (IBM), it is better to use jagged arrays or, even better, to inline array accesses, whereas for JVM_2 (Oracle), it is better to use jagged arrays and inlining is prohibitive. This kind of poor performance portability is a coherent argument against the use of Java HPC applications, since it requires that programmers write code that will run efficiently only in a specific JVM implementation.

Table 4. Performance of Rectangular Arrays

	S	W	A	B	S	W	A	B
SP	1.4	1.4	1.4	1.4	3.1	7.0	5.5	5.7
BT	1.7	1.6	1.7	1.7	4.1	9.0	8.8	8.5
LU	1.1	1.5	1.5	1.6	3.9	6.4	6.5	6.1
FT	1.9	1.9	1.9	1.9	3.9	3.9	3.6	3.3
	(a)				(b)			

(a) Ratio between execution times of CLI_1 and CLI_2 for **ARR**

(b) Ratio between execution times of CLI_2 and the best execution times across all the other virtual machines.

4.2   Rectangular versus Jagged Arrays

As discussed before, CLI compliant virtual execution machines have introduced the support for rectangular arrays, also referred as true multidimensional arrays, for the needs of scientific computing code, where it is important to traverse array elements by supposing they are stored consecutively in memory for taking advantage of spatial data locality. Also, array elements may be accessed in constant time, whereas in jagged arrays the access time depends on the number of array dimensions. However, the results for rectangular versions of **SP**, **BT**, **LU** and **FT** (**ARR** and **ARC**) are disappointing, both for CLI_1 and CLI_2.

Compared to **AU** and **AJR**, **ARR** performs worse. In some cases of CLI_1 (Mono), **ARR** performs worse even than **AJC**. CLI_2 (.NET) outperforms Mono for rectangular arrays. For quantifying the differences, Table 4 shows the ratio of execution times between CLI_1 and CLI_2 for **ARR** (a) and between **ARR** of CLI_2 and the best execution time across all the evaulated virtual machines (b).

Table 5. Optimizations and ABC in Mono

		Optimizations			ABC Off		
		S	W	A	S	W	A
AU	SP	1.03	1.03	1.03	1.08	1.07	1.07
	BT	1.01	1.01	1.01	1.15	1.12	1.11
	LU	0.95	1.00	1.00	1.11	1.11	1.11
	FT	0.97	0.97	0.97	1.04	1.04	1.04
AJR	SP	1.04	1.04	1.05	1.28	1.30	1.28
	BT	0.98	0.98	0.99	1.26	1.27	1.27
	LU	0.88	1.03	1.03	1.33	1.34	1.32
	FT	0.96	0.96	0.95	1.11	1.12	1.12
ARR	SP	1.10	1.10	1.10	1.13	1.14	1.13
	BT	1.16	1.15	1.16	1.31	1.29	1.29
	LU	1.12	1.12	1.13	1.21	1.19	1.20
	FT	1.13	1.14	1.12	1.02	1.02	1.02

4.3   Particular Features of Mono

Mono provides some additional features for improving the performance of program execution. In the following sections, we discuss the most important ones.

JIT Optimizations. Mini, the Mono JIT compiler, supports a set of compiler optimizations that is applied to the CIL code. The users may enable each optimization separately through the flag `--optimize`. In the experiments described above, all optimization flag has been enabled, under the assumption that HPC users will try the most aggressive alternatives to reduce execution time. In Table Table 5, the optimized execution times are compared with the execution times by ignoring the optimization flag. In **AU** and **AJR**, no gains in performance have being observed. In **ARR**, there are modest gains, between 10% and 16%.

ABC Disabling. The overhead of array bounds checking (ABC) motivates many HPC programmers to avoid using safe programming languages, such as Java and C#, despite the sophisticated static analysis techniques applied for ABC elimination [36]. Table 5 presents the speedup obtained by turning off ABC in **AU**, **AJR** and **ARR**, in Mono. For **AU** and **AJR**, ABC may be turned off by setting the unsafe optimization flag (`-O=unsafe`). However, this approach does not apply to **ARR**, forcing us to disable emission of ABC code in the source code of Mono, requiring its recompilation. The ABC overhead of **AJR** and **ARR** is greater than **AU**, since it has more dimensions bounds checking. Also, the speedups are nearly independent of the problem class (array size).

5   Conclusions and Further Works

This paper evaluated the serial performance of current implementations of CLI and JVM virtual execution machines for different implementations of multidimensional arrays, for HPC programs from sciences and engineering, showing a relevant dependency of their performance with respect to the kind of multidimensional array and the virtual machine implementation. So, it provides useful guidelines for decisions of programmers that want to take advantage of the features of high-level programming languages in HPC applications.

JVM implementations still outperform CLI ones for bigger workloads (**W**, **A** and **B**), despite the CLI support for rectangular arrays. However, the better performance of CLI for the smallest workload (**S**) evidences that this is caused by dynamic JIT optimizations of JVM implementations. One could investigate how to port JIT optimizations of JVM implementations to CLI ones.

The most efficient combinations of virtual machine implementation and kind of multidimensional arrays are the IBM JVM (**JVM$_1$**) with **AU** and the Oracle/Open JVM (**JVM$_2$**) with **AJR**. This second approach, using jagged arrays, is a more natural solution in Java, resulting in a more readable code.

In the results reported in this paper, virtual was still slower than native execution by factors between 1.9 and 2.8 for realistic workloads (**A** and **B**), which could be yet reduced by applying certain coding recommendations for enabling further optimizations of the JIT compiler [9]. However, they are not portable, as demonstrated in this paper for the refactoring strategy proposed by Taboada *et al.* [31], causing high speedups in Oracle JVM and prohibitive overheads in the IBM JVM and CLI implementations.

The overhead of array-bounds-checking (ABC) is still relevant in virtual execution, despite ABC elimination techniques. This paper reported overheads around 30% for Mono, but it makes possible to bypass ABC through unsafe code blocks, where memory addresses may be accessed directly. However, this approach makes array-intensive programs very hard to understand and debug.

Finally, the findings of this paper suggest directions for investigations about the bottlenecks of JVM and CLI virtual machines with multidimensional arrays, by taking advantage that the source code of some industrial-strength virtual machines are open, such as OpenJDK, Jikes RVM, SSCLI and Mono.

References

1. The Mono Project (2006), http://www.mono-project.com
2. IBM Java Development Kit (May 2012)
3. IKVM.NET Home Page (May 2012)
4. JSci - A science API for Java (May 2012)

5. Microsoft .NET Framework (2012), `http://www.microsoft.com/net`
6. OpenJDK (May 2012)
7. Oracle Java Development Kit (May 2012)
8. Amedro, B., Baude, F., Caromel, D., Delbe, C., Filali, I., Huet, F., Mathias, E., Smirnov, O.: An Efficient Framework for Running Applications on Clusters, Grids and Clouds, ch. 10, pp. 163–178. Springer (2010)
9. Amedro, B., Caromel, D., Huet, F., Bodnartchouk, V., Delbé, C., Taboada, G.: HPC in Java: Experiences in Implementing the NAS Parallel Benchmarks. In: Proceedings of the 10th WSEAS International Conference on Applied Informatics and Communications (AIC 2010) (August 2010)
10. Artigas, P.V., Gupta, M., Midkiff, S.P., Moreira, J.E.: Automatic Loop Transformations and Parallelization for Java. In: Proceedings of the 14th International Conference on Supercomputing (ICS 2000), pp. 1–10. ACM Press, New York (2000)
11. Bailey, D.H., et al.: The NAS Parallel Benchmarks. International Journal of Supercomputing Applications 5(3), 63–73 (1991)
12. Baitsch, M., Li, N., Hartmann, D.: A Toolkit for Efficient Numerical Applications in Java. Advances in Engineering Software 41(1), 75–83 (2010)
13. Budimlic, Z., Kennedy, K.: JaMake: A Java Compiler Environment. In: Margenov, S., Waśniewski, J., Yalamov, P. (eds.) LSSC 2001. LNCS, vol. 2179, pp. 201–209. Springer, Heidelberg (2001)
14. Bull, J.M., Smith, L.A., Ball, C., Pottage, L., Freeman, R.: Benchmarking Java against C and Fortran for scientific applications. Concurrency and Computation: Practice and Experience 15(35), 417–430 (2003)
15. ECMA International. Common Language Infrastructure (CLI), Partitions I to VI. Technical Report 335, ECMA International (June 2006)
16. Frumkin, M.A., Schultz, M., Jin, H., Yan, J.: Performance and Scalability of the NAS Parallel Benchmarks in Java. In: 17th International Symposium on Parallel and Distributed Processing (IPDPS 2003), p. 139 (April 2003)
17. Grama, A., Gupta, A., Karypis, J., Kumar, V.: Introduction to Parallel Computing. Addison-Wesley (1976)
18. Gundersen, G., Steihaug, T.: Data structures in Java for matrix computations. Concurrency and Computation: Practice and Experience 16(8), 799–815 (2004)
19. Hamilton, J.: Language Integration in the Common Language Runtime. SIGPLAN Notices 38(2), 19–28 (2003)
20. Luján, M., Gurd, J.R., Freeman, T.L., Miguel, J.: Elimination of Java Array Bounds Checks in the Presence of Indirection. In: Proceedings of the 2002 Joint ACM-ISCOPE Conference on Java Grande (JGI 2002), pp. 76–85. ACM Press, New York (2002)
21. Lusk, E., Yelick, K.: Languages for High-Productivity Computing - The DARPA HPCS Language Support. Parallel Processing Letters (1), 89–102 (2007)
22. Mathew, J.A., Coddington, P.D., Hawick, K.A.: Analysis and development of Java Grande benchmarks. In: Proceedings of the ACM 1999 Conference on Java Grande (JAVA 1999), pp. 72–80. ACM Press, New York (1999)
23. Moreira, J.E., Midkiff, S.P., Gupta, M.: Supporting Multidimensional Arrays in Java. Concurrency and Computation: Practice and Experience 15(35), 317–340 (2003)
24. Moreira, J.E., Midkiff, S.P., Gupta, M., Artigas, P.V., Wu, P., Almasi, G.: The NINJA project. Communications of the ACM 44(10), 102–109 (2001)
25. Nguyen, T.V.N., Irigoin, F.: Efficient and Effective Array Bound Checking. ACM Trans. on Programming Languages and Systems 27(3), 527–570 (2005)

26. Nikishkov, G.P., Nikishkov, Y.G., Savchenko, V.V.: Comparison of C and Java Performance in Finite Element Computations. Computers & Structures 81(24-25), 2401–2408 (2003)
27. Philippsen, M., Boisvert, R.F., Getov, V., Pozo, R., Moreira, J.E., Gannon, D., Fox, G.: JavaGrande - High Performance Computing with Java. In: Sørevik, T., Manne, F., Moe, R., Gebremedhin, A.H. (eds.) PARA 2000. LNCS, vol. 1947, pp. 20–36. Springer, Heidelberg (2001)
28. Post, D.E., Votta, L.G.: Computational Science Demands a New Paradigm. Physics Today 58(1), 35–41 (2005)
29. Qian, F., Hendren, L., Verbrugge, C.: A Comprehensive Approach to Array Bounds Check Elimination for Java. In: Nigel Horspool, R. (ed.) CC 2002. LNCS, vol. 2304, pp. 325–342. Springer, Heidelberg (2002)
30. Riley, C.J., Chatterjee, S., Biswas, R.: High-Performance Java Codes for Computational Fluid Dynamics. Concurrency and Computation: Practice and Experience 15(35), 395–415 (2003)
31. Taboada, G.L., Ramos, S., Expósito, R.R., Tourino, J., Doallo, R.: Java in the High Performance Computing arena: Research, practice and experience. Science of Computer Programming 78(5), 425–444 (2013)
32. Todorov, V.: Java and Computing for Robust Statistics. In: Developments in Robust Statistics, pp. 404–416. Physica-Verlag GmbH & Co. (2002)
33. van Reeuwijk, C., Kuijlman, F., Sips, H.J.: Spar: A Set of Extensions to Java for Scientific Computation. Concurrency and Computation: Practice and Experience 15(35), 277–297 (2003)
34. VanderHeyden, W.B., Dendy, E.D., Padial Collins, N.T.: CartaBlanca A Pure-Java, Component-Based Systems Simulation Tool for Coupled Nonlinear Physics on Unstructured Grids. Concurrency and Computation: Practice and Experience 15(35), 431–458 (2003)
35. Vogels, W.: Benchmarking the CLI for high performance computing. Software IEE Proceedings 150(5), 266–274 (2003)
36. Würthinger, T., Wimmer, C., Mössenböck, H.: Array bounds check elimination for the Java HotSpot client compiler. In: Proceedings of the 5th International Symposium on Principles and Practice of Programming in Java (PPPJ 2007), p. 125. ACM Press, New York (2007)

Modular Bialgebraic Semantics
and Algebraic Laws

Ken Madlener[1], Sjaak Smetsers[1], and Marko van Eekelen[1,2]

[1] Institute for Computing and Information Sciences
Radboud University Nijmegen
[2] School of Computer Science
Open University of the Netherlands
{K.Madlener,S.Smetsers,M.vanEekelen}@cs.ru.nl

Abstract. The ability to independently describe operational rules is indispensable for a modular description of programming languages. This paper introduces a format for open-ended rules and proves that conservatively adding new rules results in well-behaved translations between the models of the operational semantics. Silent transitions in our operational model are truly unobservable, which enables one to prove the validity of algebraic laws between programs. We also show that algebraic laws are preserved by extensions of the language and that they are substitutive. The work presented in this paper is developed within the framework of bialgebraic semantics.

1   Introduction

In order to scale to the complexity of real-world programming languages, a modular way of describing semantics is highly desirable. When dealing with incrementally constructed languages, one should anticipate on future extensions or changes to the language. Moreover, a concrete program seldom uses all the constructs provided by the language. When reasoning about a program it is convenient to narrow the semantics down to the part of the language which is actually used. True modularity offers the possibility to build an ad hoc semantics, easing the construction of correctness proofs.

Mosses [14] advocates to define higher-level language constructs out of so-called "funcons", language-independent fundamental programming constructs. It is highly desirable that algebraic rules between programs are preserved under the addition of new funcons, since this avoids the repetition of proofs.

The present paper provides a fundamental perspective on this issue, built on the framework of Turi and Plotkin's bialgebraic semantics [18]. One of the advantages of this work is that it can be implemented in a functional language such as HASKELL as well as in a theorem prover like COQ. In fact, part of this work has already been formalized within COQ, based on [11].

Each operation corresponding to a funcon has a number of defining operational rules, which may manipulate the state, or invoke an external operation. For example, the rule for a condition-less loop would be $\mathsf{loop}\ x \Longrightarrow \mathsf{seq}\ x\ (\mathsf{loop}\ x)$.

A. Rauber Du Bois and P. Trinder (Eds.): SBLP 2013, LNCS 8129, pp. 46–60, 2013.
© Springer-Verlag Berlin Heidelberg 2013

The double arrow indicates that the transition is deemed silent, it does not generate an observable side-effect. To handle two subsequential commands, loop invokes the external operation seq. This mechanism is comparable to interfaces in object-oriented languages. Thus, we consider the operational rules corresponding to some construct as open-ended, empowering true modularity in language descriptions. By commencing with an empty language and then incrementally extending this with new constructs, a full language is obtained.

Silent transitions are indispensable in providing independent descriptions of the operations. An alternative version of the previous rule, which avoids the use of a silent transition, can be defined by performing a "look-ahead", i.e. $x \xrightarrow{a} x' \vdash \mathsf{loop}\ x \xrightarrow{a} \mathsf{seq}\ x'\ (\mathsf{loop}\ x)$. The problem with this version is that the resulting rule is no longer modular. It makes implementation assumptions on seq, namely that seq always makes a step on its first statement. Such assumptions clearly violate the independency principle. On the other hand, representing silent transitions as distinguished labels does not make them truly unobservable, as loop x is no longer (behaviorally) equivalent to seq x (loop x), unless one resorts to the more complex notion of weak bisimulations. Moreover, rules for silent transitions are often not purely structural. For example, the rule seq skip $x \Longrightarrow x$ inspects the first argument of the head operation before it can be applied.

In this paper we treat structural operational rules and rules for silent transitions as separate classes. A generalization of the categorical interpretation by Turi and Plotkin [18] of the GSOS rule format accommodates the structural rules. For the silent transitions we apply an altered construction of Klin [7].

The standard notion of bisimulation between computations expresses that both computations exhibit the same observational behavior. Unfortunately, standard bisimulation is not preserved by language extensions [15]. De Simone [4] introduced Formal-Hypothesis bisimulations, which take into account that variables in terms being evaluated may exhibit arbitrary behavior. A pair of FH-bisimilar (open) terms is called an algebraic law. We prove that our notion of language extension preserves algebraic laws. Moreover, we show that algebraic laws are substitutive, in the sense of [16]. This property eases reasoning about programs, since it allows program fragments to be replaced by other simpler fragments, provided these are FH-bisimilar.

In summary, the contributions of this paper are threefold:

- We introduce a rule format, called "open GSOS", which enables the modular description of operational semantics. Moreover, we provide a definition for conservative extensions of open GSOS rules, and show that there exists a well-behaved translation between the operational semantics described by open GSOS rules and the operational semantics described by conservative extensions of these rules.
- We add support for rules with silent transitions to open GSOS, in such a manner that silent transitions are truly unobservable while well-behavedness of the translation between the base and extended operational semantics remains intact.

– We formalize the notion of algebraic laws within the bialgebraic framework, prove that these laws are preserved through conservative language extensions, and prove that they are substitutive. This transfers results from [15] and [16] to the setting of bialgebraic semantics.

The reader is expected to have some familiarity with category theory and bialgebraic semantics. Proofs that were omitted for space reasons can be found in the accompanying technical report [12].

2 Preliminaries

This section recalls some basic definitions. A good introduction to the field of bialgebraic semantics is provided in [8], further background can be found in [5].

The (open) terms TX, generated by an endofunctor F, where X acts as the variables, are the least solution to the equation $Y \cong X + FY$. This means that there is an isomorphism $\kappa_X : TX \to X + FTX$, and we call the left and right components of the inverse morphism $\eta_X : X \to TX$ and $\psi_X : FTX \to TX$ respectively. One can show that the functor T is a monad, i.e. it has a unit, $\eta : Id \to T$, and a join operation $\mu : TT \to T$, subject to the following conditions:

$$\mu \circ T\mu = \mu \circ \mu_T, \qquad \mu \circ \eta_T = \mu \circ T\eta = id.$$

Algebras such as ψ_X play a crucial role in the syntax, and dually coalgebras play a crucial role for the behavior. A B-coalgebra consists of a state-space, i.e. a set X of states, together with a morphism $c : X \to BX$. Sometimes we will also call c itself a coalgebra. One calls the pair $\langle D, \pi \rangle$ a copointed endofunctor if there is a natural transformation $\pi : D \to Id$. The leading example will be $DX := X \times BX$ (we assume that the underlying category has products).

A relation $R \subseteq X \times X$ is a bisimulation relation between the coalgebras c, d if there exists a morphism γ such that the following diagram commutes:

$$
\begin{array}{ccccc}
X & \xleftarrow{\;\pi_1\;} & R & \xrightarrow{\;\pi_2\;} & X \\
{\scriptstyle c}\downarrow & & \downarrow{\scriptstyle \exists\gamma} & & \downarrow{\scriptstyle d} \\
BX & \xleftarrow{\;B\pi_1\;} & BR & \xrightarrow{\;B\pi_2\;} & BX
\end{array}
$$

Here, R is considered to be an object of the underlying category. When B is a polynomial functor, it is equivalent to say that any pair $\langle x, y \rangle \in R$ implies that $\langle cx, dy \rangle \in Rel(B)(R)$, where $Rel(B)(R) \subseteq BX \times BX$ is the lifting of R to B, see Chapter 3 in [5].

In Section 4 we will need to make the additional assumption that the underlying category is **CPPO**-enriched. This holds true when the homsets, V say, are cppo's (i.e. (small) posets with a least element and closed under LUBs and omega chains), and that composition is continuous in both arguments. Tarski's theorem asserts that for every continuous $\Psi : V \to V$, if $\Psi f \geq f$, then the least fixpoint of Ψ exists, and it is equivalent to $\Psi^* f := \bigsqcup_{n \in \mathbb{N}} \Psi^n f$.

$$\text{if true } x\ y \Longrightarrow x \qquad\qquad \text{seq skip } x \Longrightarrow x$$
$$\text{if false } x\ y \Longrightarrow y \qquad x \xrightarrow{a} x' \vdash \text{seq } x\ y \xrightarrow{a} \text{seq } x'\ y$$
$$x \xrightarrow{a} x' \vdash \text{if } x\ y\ z \xrightarrow{a} \text{if } x'\ y\ z \qquad \text{loop } x \Longrightarrow \text{seq } x\ (\text{loop } x)$$

$$\text{catch skip} \Longrightarrow \text{skip}$$
$$x \xrightarrow{\{\text{ex}'=\text{false},\dots\}} x' \vdash \text{catch } x \xrightarrow{\{\text{ex}'=\text{false},\dots\}} \text{catch } x'$$
$$x \xrightarrow{\{\text{ex}'=\text{true},\dots\}} x' \vdash \text{catch } x \xrightarrow{\{\text{ex}'=\text{false},\dots\}} \text{skip}$$
$$\text{break} \xrightarrow{\{\text{ex}'=\text{true},-\}} \text{stuck}$$

Fig. 1. Example operational rules

3 Rule Format

In [18] it was shown that the operational rules in the GSOS format can be understood as a natural transformation $FD \to BT$. In this section we introduce a more general rule format, which we call "open GSOS", tailored to the independent description of operational rules.

3.1 Open GSOS

As an example, consider the constructs in Figure 1. We can define the higher-level construct while by combining these:

$$\text{while } c\ b := \text{catch (loop (if } c\ b\ \text{break)}).$$

In this section we will strictly consider rules for non-silent transitions. For the behavior functor, set $BX := S \to B_0 X$, where $B_0 X := 1 + S \times X$, and S represents the states. In this case, the type for the GSOS format is isomorphic to $FD \times S \to 1 + S \times T$. The option "1" is for operations which do not have any defining operational rules, i.e. skip, stuck, true, false. Such operations are called *values*, as they are only to be inspected by the rules [3]. We can send values to 1, to ensure that the rules are completely defined, e.g. skip $\mapsto 1$.

The rule for seq can be defined as follows:

$$\langle \text{seq } \langle x, x_B \rangle \ \langle y, y_B \rangle, s \rangle \longmapsto B_0 \left(\lambda x', \text{seq } x'\ y \right) (x_B\ s),$$

where the argument pairs stand for the variable and the behavior of that variable, respectively, thus $x, y : X$ and $x_B, y_B : BX$. The signature functor is $FX := \text{seq } (x\ y : X)$.

The rules for catch, which catches loop breaks, have been provided in MSOS notation [13]. The curly brackets indicate the pattern the label is matched on. Primed component names (e.g. ex') indicate an update of the state. We can interpret the catch rules as follows:

$$\langle \text{catch } \langle x, x_B \rangle, s \rangle \longmapsto \begin{cases} B_0 \left(\lambda x', \text{catch } x' \right) (x_B\ s) & \text{if is\_ex } (x_B\ s) = \text{false} \\ B_0 \left(\lambda x', \text{skip} \right) (\text{reset\_ex } (x_B\ s)) & \text{if is\_ex } (x_B\ s) = \text{true} \end{cases}$$

This rule requires that states come with a component $s.\text{ex} \in \{\text{true}, \text{false}\}$. To query if an exception has been thrown, we use is_ex : $BX \to \{\text{true}, \text{false}\}$ (which reads $s.\text{ex}$ from the input), and resetting the exception component is done through reset_ex : $B_0 X \to B_0 X$.

We have defined a rule for the signature $FX := \text{catch } (x : X)$, however, the result points to skip, which is not included in F. We introduce a generalization of the GSOS rule format that permits such a discrepancy between the set of defined operations, the *ingoing* signature functor F, and the resulting terms T', which are generated by the *outgoing* signature functor F'.

Definition 1 (Open GSOS). *Suppose that we have functors F, F', B, and that T' is the free monad generated by F'. A rule in open GSOS format is a natural transformation $\rho : FD \to BT'$.*

We will assume the existence of a natural transformation $\iota_{F,F'} : F \to F'$ between signature functors. The intuition is that $\iota_{F,F'}$ corresponds to the set inclusion of the operations (function symbols) corresponding to each of the signatures, and henceforth we shall call this morphism an *inclusion*, but formally all we require is that $\iota_{F,F'}$ is natural. It is straightforward to extend $\iota_{F,F'}$ to the terms by induction, yielding a monad morphism $\iota_{T,T'} : T \to T'$. Likewise we have an inclusion for the behavior functors and the obvious extension to the copointed behavior functors. When the types are obvious, we will omit the subscripts.

3.2 Operational Model

The following is a generalization of [18]. In this section, the monads T and T' are the free monads over F and F', respectively.

Definition 2. *Suppose that there exists a natural transformation $\iota : T \to T'$ between monads T and T'. An* open distributive law *of T, T' over the copointed functor D is a natural transformation $\Lambda : TD \to DT'$, subject to the following three coherence conditions:*

$$
\begin{array}{ccc}
D \xrightarrow{\eta_D} TD & TTD \xrightarrow{T\Lambda} TDT' \xrightarrow{\Lambda_{T'}} DT'T' & TD \xrightarrow{\Lambda} DT' \\
\searrow_{D\eta'} \quad \downarrow_{\Lambda} & \mu_D \downarrow \qquad\qquad\qquad\qquad \downarrow_{D\mu'} & T\pi_1 \downarrow \qquad \downarrow_{(\pi_1)_{T'}} \\
DT' & TD \xrightarrow{\qquad\qquad \Lambda \qquad\qquad} DT' & T \xrightarrow{\iota} T'
\end{array}
$$

From left to right, the first condition says that the law should behave trivially on variables, the second condition characterizes the compositionality of the semantics, and the third condition says that the first component of the result is essentially the input, included into T'.

Proposition 1. *There exists a map $\rho \mapsto \Lambda^\rho$, which is a one-to-one correspondence between natural transformations $\rho : FD \to BT'$ and open distributive laws $\Lambda^\rho : TD \to DT'$.*

In the proof, Λ^ρ is obtained from ρ by induction over the terms.

Any open distributive law Λ, whether obtained from an open GSOS rule or not, induces an *operational model*:

$$op_\Lambda \frac{X \xrightarrow{h} BX}{TX \xrightarrow{T\langle id,h\rangle} TDX \xrightarrow{\Lambda_X} DT'X \xrightarrow{(\pi_2)_{T'X}} BT'X}.$$

The operational model takes an environment h (hypotheses about the behavior of variables) and maps it over the terms, and then applies the distributive law. The projection π_2 leaves us with the resulting behavior. Throughout the rest of this paper we will use the notation $h_+ := (\iota_{B,B_+})_X \circ h$, to denote the inclusion of the environment h into the extended behavior.

3.3 Operational Conservative Extensions

A language extension relates two open GSOS rules, the *base language* and the *extended language*. We call an extension *conservative* when the base language, as included in the extended language, retains its original behavior, see also [1]. In the rest of this paper we will omit the word "conservative", as everything we do is in this spirit.

As a convention, we will write F_+, F'_+ (T_+, T'_+) for the in- and outgoing signatures (terms) of the extended language, respectively, and B_+ (D_+) for the (copointed) behavior functor.

Definition 3. *Let $\rho : FD \to BT'$ and $\rho_+ : F_+D_+ \to B_+T'_+$ be open GSOS rules. Then ρ_+ is a rule extension of ρ if the diagram below holds.*

$$\begin{array}{ccccc}
FD & \xrightarrow{\iota_D} & F_+D & \xrightarrow{F_+\iota} & F_+D_+ \\
{\scriptstyle \rho}\downarrow & & & & \downarrow{\scriptstyle \rho_+} \\
BT' & \xrightarrow{B\iota} & BT'_+ & \xrightarrow{\iota_{T'_+}} & B_+T'_+
\end{array}$$

Let $\Lambda : TD \to DT'$ and $\Lambda_+ : T_+D \to D_+T_+$ be natural transformations. Then Λ_+ is a law extension of Λ if the diagram below holds.

$$\begin{array}{ccccc}
TD & \xrightarrow{\iota_D} & T_+D & \xrightarrow{T_+\iota} & T_+D_+ \\
{\scriptstyle \Lambda}\downarrow & & & & \downarrow{\scriptstyle \Lambda_+} \\
DT' & \xrightarrow{D\iota} & DT'_+ & \xrightarrow{\iota_{T'_+}} & D_+T'_+
\end{array}$$

We view the full language as a closed set of rules that is obtained by gradually extending a base language with new rules. If we take the liberty to assume a category of partial functions as the underlying category, we can also view the rule extension as the inequality $\rho_X \le (\rho_+)_X$ between the two families of morphisms $\{\rho_X\}_{X \in C}$ and $\{(\rho_+)_X\}_{X \in C}$, and the full language would be the join of all sublanguages. However, this is not general enough for Section 4.

Proposition 2. *Suppose that the signature inclusions satisfy:*

$$\iota_{F',F'_+} \circ \iota_{F,F'} = \iota_{F_+,F'_+} \circ \iota_{F,F_+}.$$

Then, if ρ_+ is an extension of ρ, then Λ^{ρ_+} is an extension of Λ^ρ.

Proposition 3. *Suppose that Λ_+ is an extension of Λ. Let $h : X \to BX$ be arbitrary. Then it holds that op_{Λ_+} is an extension of op_Λ, i.e.*

$$
\begin{array}{ccc}
TX & \xrightarrow{\;\;\iota_X\;\;} & T_+X \\
{\scriptstyle op_\Lambda h}\big\downarrow & & \big\downarrow{\scriptstyle op_{\Lambda_+} h_+} \\
BT'X \xrightarrow{\;\;B\iota_X\;\;} BT'_+X & \xrightarrow{\;\;\iota_{T'_+X}\;\;} & B_+T'_+X
\end{array}
$$

4   Silent Transitions

It is trivial to represent silent transitions by adjusting the behavior functor to $X + BX$. However, the problem with this approach is that for example the terms seq skip x and x have different semantics, since in this case the silent transitions are not truly unobservable, therefore and bisimilarity does not hold.

In this section, we introduce a merging of silent transition rules with an existing open distributive law, resulting in an operational model where silent transitions are truly unobservable. We will need to assume that the underlying category is **CPPO**-enriched, to ensure the existence of a least fixpoint construction. Specifically, the examples are aimed at a category of partial maps.

4.1   Unfolding Rules and Their Conservative Extensions

A rule for a silent transition typically consists of an operation of the base language applied to a computed value, e.g. seq skip $x \Longrightarrow x$. In Section 3 we had two kinds of signatures: the ingoing and the outgoing signature. We add a third signature functor F'', which consists of the operations of the original ingoing signature functor F, together with the computed values. Rules for silent transitions will be regarded as maps $T'' \to TT''$, where T'' is the free monad generated by F''. For example, the aforementioned rule has the corresponding mapping seq skip $x \longmapsto x$. We call these maps *unfolding rules* if they unfold variables in a trivial way:

Definition 4. *An* unfolding rule *is a natural transformation $r : T'' \to TT''$, subject to the condition $r \circ \eta'' = T\eta'' \circ \eta$.*

Set $v : T \to Id := [id, \perp] \circ \kappa$. This auxiliary morphism is called a *variable classifier*, used to query whether a given term is a variable. The infinite unfolding of r is $\bar{r} := \Phi_X^* (\eta_X \circ v_X'')$, the least fixpoint of Φ:

$$
\Phi \, \frac{T'' \xrightarrow{f} T}{T'' \xrightarrow{r} TT'' \xrightarrow{Tf} TT \xrightarrow{\mu} T}.
$$

One can show that this is a well-formed definition in a **CPPO**-enriched category, and that it is a natural transformation, see [7]. We compute a few examples:

- $\bar{r}$ (if true (if false x y) z) $= y$
- $\bar{r}$ (loop x) $=$ seq x (seq x (seq x ...))
- $\bar{r}$ (skip) $= \perp$

We also wish that $\bar{r}$ behaves as the identity on terms which have no silent transition rules acting on them, e.g. $\bar{r}$ (seq x y) $=$ seq x y. This is not warranted by Definition 4, but can be solved by requiring that r is based on a *decomposition structure* [7].

Definition 5. *Suppose that we have unfolding rules $r : T'' \to TT''$ and $r_+ : T''_+ \to T_+T''_+$. Then r_+ is an* unfolding rule extension *of r if the following condition is satisfied:*

$$
\begin{array}{ccc}
T'' & \xrightarrow{\quad\iota\quad} & T''_+ \\
{\scriptstyle r}\downarrow & & \downarrow{\scriptstyle r_+} \\
TT'' \xrightarrow[T\iota]{} TT''_+ & \xrightarrow[\iota_{T''_+}]{} & T_+T''_+
\end{array}
$$

Lemma 1. $\overline{r_+} \circ \iota_{T'',T''_+} = \iota_{T,T_+} \circ \bar{r}$.

4.2 An Open Distributive Law for Silent Transitions

We incorporate the infinite unfolding into a law of type $T''D \to DT'$ by setting $\Lambda^r := \Lambda \circ \bar{r}_D$. One can view Λ^r as an extension of Λ, in the sense of Definition 3. In this situation, the inclusion of the ingoing terms is $\bar{r}$, and since the behavior functors and outgoing signatures are equal, the inclusion of the outgoing terms is the identity. With $(\Lambda_+)^{r_+}$ being the usual extension counterpart, we can prove the following theorem.

Theorem 1. $op_{(\Lambda_+)^{r_+}}$ *is an extension of* op_{Λ^r}.

Proof. As in Proposition 3 we need to prove the statement for an arbitrary $h : X \to BX$. We show that everything in the following diagram commutes:

$$
\begin{array}{ccc}
T''X & \xrightarrow{\iota_X} & T''_+X \\
{\scriptstyle \bar{r}_X}\downarrow & & \downarrow{\scriptstyle \overline{r_+}_X} \\
TX & \xrightarrow{\iota_X} & T_+X \\
{\scriptstyle op_\Lambda h}\downarrow & & \downarrow{\scriptstyle op_{\Lambda_+} h_+} \\
BT'X \xrightarrow[B\iota_X]{} BT'_+X & \xrightarrow[\iota_{T'_+X}]{} & B_+T'_+X
\end{array}
$$

with $op_{\Lambda^r} h$ on the left and $op_{(\Lambda_+)^{r_+}} h_+$ on the right.

The top square commutes by Lemma 1, and the other regions commute by Proposition 3. Note that for the two side regions we instantiate $\iota_{T'',T}$ with $\bar{r}$ and $\overline{r_+}$. This is permitted, as the only requirement about $\iota_{T'',T}$ by Proposition 3 is that it is a natural transformation. $\square$

Lemma 2. Λ^r *is a natural transformation, and satisfies the first and third coherence condition of open distributive laws.*

If r contains "non-regular" rules such as seq skip $x \implies x$, then Λ^r fails to be compositional, i.e. it does not meet the second coherence condition. This can be seen by considering the layering of seq skip x as an instance of $TTDX$ into seq $(\eta \text{ skip}) (\eta\, x)$. Then the upper leg of the diagram results in $\perp$, since Λ_X^r skip $= \perp$, while the lower leg does not result in $\perp$. By requiring that r is regular, a notion due to Klin [7], we can show that Λ^r is an open distributive law.

Definition 6. *An unfolding rule r is* regular *if it can be generated by recursion from a rule $r_0 : F'' \to TT''$ such that $r_0 \circ \iota_{F,F''} = T\eta'' \circ \phi$.*

Thus, the previous rule is not regular, but the rule for loop (see Figure 1) is.

Proposition 4. *If r is a regular unfolding rule, then Λ^r is an open distributive law.*

Proof. What remains to verify is that Λ^r satisfies the second coherence condition, as the other conditions have already been proved in Lemma 2.

Theorem 30 in [7] says that when r is regular, then $\bar{r}$ is a monad morphism from T'' to T. Consider the following diagram in which we have unfolded the definition of Λ^r:

$$
\begin{array}{ccccccccc}
T''T''D & \xrightarrow{T''\bar{r}_D} & T''TD & \xrightarrow{T''\Lambda} & T''DT & \xrightarrow{\bar{r}_{DT'}} & TDT' & \xrightarrow{\Lambda_{T'}} & DT'T' \\
\downarrow{\mu''_D} & & {\bar{r}_{TD}}\downarrow & & & & \uparrow & & \downarrow{D\mu'} \\
& & TTD & & & \xrightarrow{T\Lambda} & & & \\
& & {\mu_D}\downarrow & & & & & & \\
T''D & \xrightarrow{\bar{r}_D} & TD & & & \xrightarrow{\Lambda} & & & DT'
\end{array}
$$

The region on the left commutes due to $\bar{r}$ being a monad morphism, the square commutes by the naturality of $\bar{r}$, and the remaining region commutes due to the second coherence condition of Λ.   □

5   Algebraic Laws

It is desirable that bisimulation relations remain intact under extensions of the language, so that bisimilarity proofs have to be checked only once. As it turns out, whether this holds depends on the precise definition of bisimulation one chooses to work with. In this section we consider a variant of the standard notion of bisimulations, called Formal-Hypothesis bisimulations, tailored to the fact that the state-space of the operational model consists of the terms. The perhaps most straightforward choice, also called Closed-Instance bisimilarity, demands that all substitutions of variables with closed terms are again bisimulations. However, CI-bisimulations are not preserved by language extensions [15]. The reason for this is that only substitutions with closed terms from the base language are considered by the hypotheses.

FH-bisimulations, introduced by De Simone [4], take into account that the variables of the terms in question may exhibit arbitrary behavior. CI- and FH-bisimulations have only been studied in the context of transition systems, and not of a generic B-coalgebra. We introduce FH-bisimulations here, adapted to our coalgebraic setting.

Definition 7 (FH-bisimulation). *A relation $R \subseteq TX \times TX$ is an FH-bisimulation relation on op_Λ if for every environment $h : X \to BX$, it holds that R is a bisimulation relation on $op_\Lambda h$.*

Since FH-bisimulations relate terms, we call a pair of such terms an *algebraic law*. Some obvious examples can be found by formulating silent transition rules as algebraic laws: seq skip $x = x$ and catch skip = skip. Note that if the terms are closed, then the definition coincides with standard bisimulations.

5.1   The Preservation of Algebraic Laws

We can prove that algebraic laws are preserved by conservative language extensions, by making use of the fact that the operational behavior is preserved from Theorem 1.

Theorem 2. *Suppose that $R \subseteq TX \times TX$ is an FH-bisimulation relation on op_Λ, and that $B = B_+$. Then*

$$R_+ := \{\langle (\iota_{T,T_+}) \times x, (\iota_{T,T_+}) \times y \rangle \mid x\,R\,y \}$$

is an FH-bisimulation on op_{Λ_+}.

Proof. First note that R_+ and R are isomorphic; we will denote the corresponding morphisms by $\pi_+ : R_+ \to R$ and $\iota_+ : R \to R_+$. Let $h : X \to BX$ be given. The assumption of the theorem says that for any h, there exists a morphism γ_h satisfying the bisimulation diagram in Section 2. We claim that the following composition is the required morphism to prove that R_+ is a bisimulation relation:

$$\frac{R \xrightarrow{\gamma_h} BR}{R_+ \xrightarrow{\pi_+} R \xrightarrow{\gamma_h} BR \xrightarrow{B\iota_+} BR_+}.$$

We verify this by the commuting diagram below for $i = 1, 2$, making use of Theorem 1.

Thus, the claimed bisimulation mapping is correct, which finishes the proof.　□

The premise of Theorem 2 essentially means that the extended language can not add any new effects. As a simple example to see how this fails without this premise, first consider the law catch $x = x$ in the absence of exceptions (i.e. for every state s, set $s.\mathsf{ex} = \mathsf{false}$) as the base language, and then add states with exceptions to the extended language.

5.2　Combining Algebraic Laws

Just as in the situation with standard bisimulations, there exists a greatest FH-bisimulation relation, notation $\overset{\text{FH}}{\leftrightarrow}$, which is the union of all FH-bisimulation relations. It is straightforward to show that $\overset{\text{FH}}{\leftrightarrow}$ itself is an FH-bisimulation relation, and that it is an equivalence relation.

Define the substitution of a function $f : X \to TX$ in a term t as $t[f] := \mu_X(Tf\,t)$. We will be concerned with proving that the following relation is an FH-bisimulation relation:

$$R := \{\langle t[f_1],\, u[f_2]\rangle \mid t \overset{\text{FH}}{\leftrightarrow} u\},$$

in which $f : X \to \overset{\text{FH}}{\leftrightarrow}$, a function which assigns to variables an FH-bisimilar pair of terms, and $f_i := \pi_i \circ f$ for $i = 1, 2$. Barring that this is valid, and knowing that loop $x = $ seq x (loop x) is a valid algebraic law, we can use the substitution $f : x \mapsto \langle$loop $x,$ seq x (loop x)$\rangle$ to derive that for example loop $x = $ seq x (seq x (loop x)). We call this property of FH-bisimulations *being substitutive* [16]. We prove this in two steps by considering the special cases preservation by *instantiation* ($t = u$) and preservation by *insertion* ($f_1 = f_2$).

The proofs below make essential use of the assumption that Λ is a distributive law. In the light of distributive laws obtained from mergings with unfolding rules as in Section 4, this section only applies to the situation where the unfolding rules are regular. This assumption provides a well-known property of bialgebraic semantics, which says that the operational model is compositional.

Lemma 3 (Compositionality). $B\mu_X \circ op_\Lambda\,(op_\Lambda\,h) = op_\Lambda\,h \circ \mu_X.$

Proof. Straightforward, making use of the naturality of μ and the second coherence condition of Λ.　□

Proposition 5. *The FH-bisimilarity relation is preserved by instantiation.*

Proof. We need to prove that $R' := \{\langle t[f_1], t[f_2]\rangle\}$ is an FH-bisimulation, in which $f : X \to \overset{\text{FH}}{\leftrightarrow}$. Remark that we have an isomorphism $R' \overset{\alpha}{\underset{\beta}{\rightleftarrows}} T \overset{\text{FH}}{\leftrightarrow}$, such that:

for $i = 1, 2$. Suppose that $h : X \to BX$ is arbitrary. The commuting diagram below in conjunction with the above remark shows that R' is an FH-bisimulation, with bisimulation mapping $B\beta \circ op_\Lambda \gamma_h \circ \alpha$.

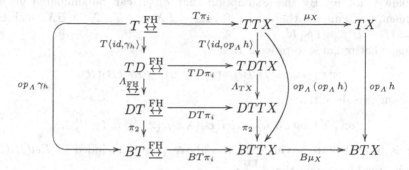

The region on the right is exactly compositionality of the operational model. The squares, from top to bottom respectively, make use of the fact that $\overset{FH}{\leftrightarrow}$ itself is an FH-bisimulation relation, and that Λ and π_2 are natural transformations. $\square$

Definition 8. *Given a coalgebra* $d : Y \to BY$ *and* $f : X \to Y$, d *can be simulated via* f *if there exists a coalgebra* $c : X \to BX$ *and a morphism* $f' : X \to Y$ *such that* $d \circ f = Bf' \circ c$.

For the next proposition, we will need to make the assumption that for any h, $op_\Lambda h$ can be simulated via f. To see that this is a reasonable assumption, as an example, for X take an infinitely large set of variables, and $BX := A \times X$, for some label set A. Gödel numberings provide a way to assign a unique number to each well-formed term [17]. This means that there exist enc : $TX \to X$ and dec : $X \to TX$, which form a bijection between X and TX. Then the validity of the assumption for this choice of B is witnessed by

$$h' x := B\mathsf{enc}\,(op_\Lambda h\,(f\,x)), \qquad f'\,x_B := B\mathsf{dec}\,(x_B).$$

We will need the following technical lemma to prove preservation by insertion.

Lemma 4. *If for every* $h : X \to BX$, $op_\Lambda h$ *can be simulated via* $f : X \to TX$, *then* $op_\Lambda h$ *can be simulated via* $[f]$ *by* $op_\Lambda h'$ *for some* $h' : X \to BX$, *in particular, the following diagram commutes:*

$$
\begin{array}{ccc}
TX & \xrightarrow{\;[f]\;} & TX \\
{\scriptstyle op_\Lambda h'}\downarrow & & \downarrow{\scriptstyle op_\Lambda h} \\
BT'X & \xrightarrow{\;B[f']\;} & BT'X
\end{array}
$$

Proposition 6. *The FH-bisimulation relation is preserved by insertion.*

Proof. We need to prove that $R' := \{\langle t[f], u[f]\rangle \mid t \overset{FH}{\leftrightarrow} u\}$ is an FH-bisimulation relation, where $f : X \to TX$. This means that we need to show that for any set of hypotheses $h : X \to BX$, and terms $t_0, u_0 : TX$ such that $t_0 \, R \, u_0$, it holds that $\langle op_\Lambda \, h \, t_0, op_\Lambda \, h \, u_0 \rangle \in Rel(B)(R')$.

It follows by the definition of R' that $op_\Lambda \, h \, t_0 = op_\Lambda \, h \, (t[f])$ for some t, and likewise for u_0. By the assumption that $op_\Lambda \, h$ can be simulated via any morphism, by Lemma 4 there exist $f' : X \to TX$ and $h' : X \to BX$, such that $op_\Lambda \, h \circ [f] = B[f'] \circ op_\Lambda \, h'$.

Thus, what remains to prove is that

$$\langle B[f'] \, (op_\Lambda \, h' \, t), B[f'] \, (op_\Lambda \, h' \, u) \rangle \in Rel(B)(R').$$

It is enough to show that

$$\langle op_\Lambda \, h' \, t, op_\Lambda \, h' \, u \rangle \in Rel(B)(\lambda \, x \, y, (x[f']) \, R' \, (y[f'])),$$

which is equivalent to saying that the above pair is included in $Rel(B)(R')$, which is true by the fact that $t \overset{\text{FH}}{\leftrightarrow} u$. ☐

Theorem 3. *The FH-bisimilarity relation is substitutive.*

Proof. By the previous two propositions, $t[f_1] \overset{\text{FH}}{\leftrightarrow} t[f_2] \overset{\text{FH}}{\leftrightarrow} u[f_2]$, and thus by transitivity of $\overset{\text{FH}}{\leftrightarrow}$ we can conclude that FH-bisimilarity is substitutive. ☐

6   Running the Operational Semantics

This section highlights another application of Theorem 1.

Final coalgebras, i.e. pairs $\langle Z, \zeta : Z \to BZ \rangle$, enjoy the property that there exists an operator $unfold : (X \to BX) \to X \to Z$ which takes a coalgebra as its argument and returns a morphism $X \to Z$ which maps the state-space of the argument to the final state-space. This morphism $unfold \, c$ is the unique coalgebra homomorphism from c to ζ. Here Z is the greatest solution to the equation $Z \cong BZ$.[1]

When the rules are closed, then $op_\Lambda \, h$ (where $h : X \to BX$) is a coalgebra and we can "run" the operational semantics by unfolding it, i.e. $run_\Lambda \, h :=$ $unfold(op_\Lambda \, h)$. Set $\iota_{Z,Z_+} := unfold((\iota_{B,B_+})_Z \circ \zeta)$. We can prove that running the extended operational model is faithful to running the base model.

Proposition 7. *Suppose that Λ and Λ_+ are closed distributive laws, and that Λ_+ is an extension of Λ. Then for all $h : X \to BX$ it holds that $\iota_{Z,Z_+} \circ run_\Lambda \, h = run_{\Lambda_+} \, h_+ \circ (\iota_{T,T_+})_X$.*

Proof. Both sides of the equation are coalgebra homomorphisms from the coalgebra $c := (\iota_{B,B_+})_{TX} \circ op_\Lambda \, h$ to the final coalgebra ζ_+. For the LHS this follows easily from the definitions, while for the RHS we make use of Theorem 1. By the fact that ζ_+ is final, there is at most one coalgebra homomorphism from c to ζ_+, and thus the equality holds. ☐

---

[1] For $BX := S \to 1 + S \times X$, as in Section 3, Z is given by the set of partial functions

$$\{f : S^* \to S^* \mid f \text{ is length and prefix preserving}\}.$$

7 Related Work

The results in this paper were developed within the bialgebraic semantics framework, a body of research initiated by Turi and Plotkin [18].

The theorems in Section 5, which prove that FH-bisimulations are preserved by conservative extensions, and that FH-bisimulations are substitutive, transfer the original results, obtained in the more traditional set-theoretic approach to SOS by Mosses et al. [15] and Rensink [16] respectively, to the bialgebraic framework. FH-bisimulations were originally introduced by De Simone [4].

The dichotomy between value terms and computational terms was emphasized by Churchill and Mosses [3], who introduce a rule format built on the tyft format, which has built-in rules to deal with silent transitions. They provide a variant of bisimilarity, and prove that it is a congruence in the resulting transition system. The distributive law Λ^τ of Section 4 has similar characteristics, through the infinite unfolding of silent transitions. This law is a variant of the one introduced by Klin [7].

An alternative to considering only free monads as in the present paper, is to quotient the term monad by the algebraic laws. Bonsangue et al. [2] prove that if Λ respects the algebraic laws, then there is a unique distributive law Λ' such that the quotient map is a well-behaved translation from Λ to Λ'.

A modular variant of GSOS has been provided by Jaskelioff et al. [6] as part of a HASKELL implementation of the bialgebraic framework. They distinguish ingoing from outgoing signatures, as in the present paper, but consider the outgoing signature as an abstract parameter of each modular rule, and add type-class constraints to ensure the inclusion of certain operations in the outgoing signature.

8 Conclusions

We have provided an operational rule format, tailored to the modular description of programming languages. The semantics supports truly unobservable transitions, as generated by rules for silent transitions. We have proved that algebraic laws are preserved by conservative extensions of the operational semantics, and that algebraic laws are substitutive. Our work has been developed within the bialgebraic framework [18], making it amenable to implementation in a theorem prover [11].

In future work we wish to ease the condition in Section 5.2 on the distributive law, enabling the substitutivity of algebraic laws for a wider range of silent transition rules. We would also like to explore applications to software verification.

Acknowledgments. The inspiration for this work arose from consultation with Peter D. Mosses by the author. Without his support this work would not have been possible. The authors also wish to thank the anonymous reviewers for their sharp comments.

References

1. Aceto, L., Fokkink, W., Verhoef, C.: Structural operational semantics. In: Bergstra, J., Ponse, A., Smolka, S. (eds.) Handbook of Process Algebra, pp. 197–292. Elsevier (1999)
2. Bonsangue, M.M., Hansen, H.H., Kurz, A., Rot, J.: Presenting distributive laws. In: Proceedings of CALCO 2013. LNCS, Springer (to appear, 2013)
3. Churchill, M., Mosses, P.D.: Modular bisimulation theory for computations and values. In: Pfenning, F. (ed.) FOSSACS 2013. LNCS, vol. 7794, pp. 97–112. Springer, Heidelberg (2013)
4. De Simone, R.: Higher-level synchronising devices in Meije-SCCS. Theor. Comp. Sci. 37, 245–267 (1985)
5. Jacobs, B.: Introduction to coalgebra: Towards mathematics of states and observations. in Preparation, version 2.0 (2012),
   http://www.cs.ru.nl/B.Jacobs/CLG/JacobsCoalgebraIntro.pdf
6. Jaskelioff, M., Ghani, N., Hutton, G.: Modularity and implementation of mathematical operational semantics. Elec. Notes in Theor. Comp. Sci. 229(5), 75–95 (2011)
7. Klin, B.: Adding recursive constructs to bialgebraic semantics. J. of Logic and Alg. Prog. 60, 259–286 (2004)
8. Klin, B.: Bialgebras for structural operational semantics: An introduction. Theor. Comp. Sci. 412(38), 5043–5069 (2011)
9. Lenisa, M., Power, J., Watanabe, H.: Distributivity for endofunctors, pointed and co-pointed endofunctors, monads and comonads. Elec. Notes in Theor. Comp. Sci. 33, 230–260 (2000)
10. Lenisa, M., Power, J., Watanabe, H.: Category theory for operational semantics. Theor. Comp. Sci. 327(1-2), 135–154 (2004)
11. Madlener, K., Smetsers, S.: GSOS formalized in Coq. In: Proceedings of TASE 2013, pp. 199–206. IEEE (2013)
12. Madlener, K., Smetsers, S., van Eekelen, M.: Modular bialgebraic semantics and algebraic laws. Technical Report ICIS–R13008, Radboud University Nijmegen (July 2013)
13. Mosses, P.D.: Modular structural operational semantics. J. of Logic and Alg. Prog. 60, 195–228 (2004)
14. Mosses, P.D.: Component-based semantics. In: Proceedings of SAVCBS 2009, pp. 3–10. ACM (2009)
15. Mosses, P.D., Mousavi, M.R., Reniers, M.A.: Robustness of equations under operational extensions. In: Fröschle, S., Valencia, F.D. (eds.) Proceedings of EXPRESS 2010, pp. 106–120. EPTCS (2010)
16. Rensink, A.: Bisimilarity of open terms. Inf. and Comp. 156(1), 345–385 (2000)
17. Sudkamp, T.A., Cotterman, A.: Languages and machines: An introduction to the theory of computer science, 3rd edn. Addison-Wesley (2006)
18. Turi, D., Plotkin, G.D.: Towards a mathematical operational semantics. In: Proc. of LICS 1997, pp. 280–291. IEEE (1997)
19. Watanabe, H.: Well-behaved translations between structural operational semantics. Elec. Notes in Theor. Comp. Sci. 65(1), 337–357 (2002)

A Double Effect λ-calculus
for Quantum Computation

Juliana Kaizer Vizzotto, Bruno Crestani Calegaro, and Eduardo Kessler Piveta

Programa de Pós Graduação em Informática
DELC/CT, Cidade Universitária
Universidade Federal de Santa Maria, RS/ Brazil

Abstract. In this paper we present a double effect version of the simply typed λ-calculus where we can represent both pure and impure quantum computations. The double effect calculus comprises a quantum arrow layer defined *over* a quantum monadic layer. In previous works we have developed the quantum arrow calculus, a calculus where we can consider just impure (or mixed) quantum computations. Technically, here we extend the quantum arrow calculus with a construct (and equations) that allows the communication of the monadic layer with the arrow layer of the calculus. That is, the quantum arrow is defined over a monadic instance enabling to consider pure and impure quantum computations in the same framework. As a practical contribution, the calculus allows to express quantum algorithms including reversible operations over pure states and measurements in the middle of the computation using a traditional style of functional programming and reasoning. We also define equations for algebraic reasoning of computations involving measurements.

1 Introduction

The last years have witnessed considerable efforts in the development of high level quantum programming languages, abstractions, and models, starting by the work of Selinger on the definition of functional quantum programming languages [1]. Since his work, many ideas have been proposed in this field, including the work of Altenkirch and Grattage, which introduces a functional programming language for pure quantum computations with quantum control [2], that uses a type system based on first order strict linear logic. Additionally, Andre van Tonder proposed a λ-calculus for pure quantum computations [3], and Arrighi and Dowek defined a linear-algebraic λ-calculus [4], which can be seen as a *purely quantum* programming language, dispensing the use of classical data and classical control structures. Following a series of works starting with [5], Selinger and Valiron ended up with the design of a typed λ-calculus for quantum computation [6] in which duplication is modeled by a comonad [7] and measurement is modeled by a monad [8].

We also have been working in this direction. First, we defined an interface for quantum computations inside Haskell [9] using monads and arrows [10].

A. Rauber Du Bois and P. Trinder (Eds.): SBLP 2013, LNCS 8129, pp. 61–74, 2013.
© Springer-Verlag Berlin Heidelberg 2013

We started with a monadic construction to model the superpositions in pure quantum state vectors, then we used arrows to model the probability distributions in quantum measurements (the mixed or impure states). This work was based on the use of density matrices to model general quantum states, pure and mixed, and superoperators to model general quantum computations, unitary and measurements.

Recently, motivated by the idea of having a version of a lambda calculus with effects and a traditional reasoning framework for quantum computation, we have proposed to use the arrow calculus [11] as a quantum programming language for *mixed* quantum computations [12]. However, in this last extension, some of the generality from our previous arrow interface was lost, as there is no construction to communicate the monadic layer of the calculus with the arrow layer (i.e. we can consider just pure or just mixed quantum computations). This restriction limits the expressiveness of the calculus as it is not possible, for instance, to represent quantum algorithms with measurements in the middle of the computation.

In this paper, we go one step further by proposing a new construction to allow the use of both pure and mixed quantum computations, obtaining a double effect λ-calculus with arrow computations built over a monadic instance. The construction is a lifting operation that builds arrows from monads of different types. As a practical contribution the calculus presented here allows to express quantum algorithms including reversible operations and measurements in the middle of the computation using a traditional style of functional programming and reasoning. Additionally, we provide equations for the measurement operation and investigate how these equations can be proved sound in the calculus. We believe our work can also contribute in the discussion about the categorical model of a general framework for quantum computation considering pure and mixed quantum computations.

This paper is structured as follows. We start presenting the quantum monadic λ-calculus for pure quantum computations in Section 2. Next, in Section 3, we briefly show the quantum arrow calculus for mixed quantum computation and discuss the limitations on the expressiveness of the calculus. Then, in Section 4, we propose to build the arrows constructions over a monadic instance. This gives the double effect λ-calculus for quantum computation. Finally, we conclude in Section 5.

2   Quantum Monadic λ-calculus

Quantum computation can be understood as the task of processing information using a quantum physical system. Then to study high level quantum programming capabilities and features we need to define a high level model for quantum operations and data.

Following the design and study of traditional programming languages, one starts with a core *pure* model and extends it with additional features to express computational effects like assignments, jumps, non-determinism, for instance.

Mainly motivated by simplicity and by the necessity of a framework for reasoning about quantum programs, we consider the λ-calculus as the core model.

2.1   Monadic λ-calculus

Extensions of the λ-calculus to model computational effects often refer to the idea introduced by Moggi [8] of using *monads*, a construction adopted from category theory. Intuitively monads separate the pure language from the effects, imposing minimal constraints on the language used to sequence effects. Extensions of the λ-calculus with monads retain much of the benefits of the original calculus, such as a formal algebraic system inspired by category theory.

Formally, the monadic λ-calculus extends the simply typed λ-calculus with an operation to *lift* pure values to monadic computations, $[\ ]_M$, and with a composition operator to sequence effects that is associative, let_M[1].

Beyond the basic monad laws for composition, some monads obey additional laws. Interesting extensions in the case of quantum computing are the monad *Plus*, which introduces a choice junction and a failure computation, and the monad *Minus*.

2.2   Quantum Monadic λ-calculus

The basic unit of information in quantum computation is the qubit, i.e., a binary *quantum* physical system. The first, say odd, characteristic of qubits is that they can be in a quantum *superposition* of basic values. Intuitively instead of being in a determinated state, say 0 or 1, a qubit can be in a superposition of 0 and 1, written in the Dirac notation as $\alpha|0\rangle + \beta|1\rangle$. The values α and β are complex numbers, called probability amplitudes for $|0\rangle$ and $|1\rangle$, respectivelly. Mathematically, a qubit can be a unit vector in the two-dimensional vector space spanned by $|0\rangle$ and $|1\rangle$ over the complex numbers.

As first noted by Mu and Bird [13] quantum superpositions can be elegantly encoded using a monad for non-determinism, that is, a monad that maintains a collection of possible values.

Consider *type* **Vec** $A = A \to \mathbb{C}$ the type of vectors over a computational basis A. Each basis element is maped to a complex number. Then the monadic lifting is used to build trivial vectors:

$$\frac{\Gamma \vdash M : A}{\Gamma \vdash [M]_M : \textbf{Vec } A}$$

The scalar multiplication allows to add probability amplitudes to the vectors:

$$\frac{\Gamma \vdash M : \textbf{Vec } A}{\Gamma \vdash \alpha * M : \textbf{Vec } A}$$

---

[1] Subscript M stands for *Monadic*. In following sections we will change only the subscript.

And the choice operator of the monad *Plus* extension is used to create quantum superpositions of basic vectors:

$$\frac{\Gamma \vdash M, N : \textbf{Vec } A}{\Gamma \vdash M + N : \textbf{Vec } A}$$

In Figure 1 we show the types for the quantum monadic λ-calculus. The ... stand for core types and terms of simply typed $\lambda - calculus$ in Appendix A.

Syntax
Probability Amplitudes $\alpha, \beta \in \mathbb{C}$
Typedef $\textbf{Vec } A \;\; = A \to \mathbb{C}$
Types $A, B, C \;\; ::= ... \mid \textbf{Vec } A$
Terms $L, M, N ::= ... \mid [M]_M \mid \text{let}_M \; x = M \text{ in } N \mid \text{vzero} \mid + \mid -$

Monadic Types

$$\frac{\Gamma \vdash M : A}{\Gamma \vdash [M]_M : \textbf{Vec } A} \qquad \frac{\Gamma \vdash M : \textbf{Vec } A \quad \Gamma, x : A \vdash N : \textbf{Vec } B}{\Gamma \vdash \text{let}_M \; x = M \text{ in } N : \textbf{Vec } B}$$

MonadPlus Types

$$\frac{\Gamma \vdash M, N : \textbf{Vec } A}{\Gamma \vdash M + N : \textbf{Vec } A} \qquad \frac{}{\Gamma \vdash \text{vzero} : \textbf{Vec } A}$$

MonadMinus Type   **Scalars Type**

$$\frac{\Gamma \vdash M, N : \textbf{Vec } A}{\Gamma \vdash M - N : \textbf{Vec } A} \qquad \frac{\Gamma \vdash M : \textbf{Vec } A}{\Gamma \vdash \alpha * M : \textbf{Vec } A}$$

Fig. 1. Quantum Monadic λ-calculus Types

The figure starts with the monadic types for simple vectors and for composition of vectors, and then shows the types for the extensions: monad *Plus*, monad *Minus* and scalar multiplication.

The equations for the quantum monadic λ-calculus are presented in Figure 2. The monad composition, let_M, takes care of propagating all the values in the superposition and summing up the different weights. The denotation of let_M is a matrix showing how to transform a quantum vector of type **Vec** A into a vector of type **Vec** B.

The intuition behind the laws of the extensions is that monad *Plus* is a disjunction of goals and the composition is a conjunction of goals. The conjunction evaluates the goals from left-to-right and is not symmetric.

Laws

(left$_M$)   let$_M$ $x = [L]_M$ in N $= N[x := L]$
(right$_M$) let$_M$ $x = L$ in $[x]$ $= L$
(assoc$_M$) let$_M$ $y = ($let$_M$ $x = L$ in $N)$ in $T =$ let$_M$ $x = L$ in (let$_M$ $y = N$ in T)

MonadPlus Laws

vzero $+ a$ $= a$
$a +$ vzero $= a$
$a + (b + c)$ $= (a + b) + c$
let$_M$ $x =$ vzero in T $=$ vzero
let$_M$ $x = (M + N)$ in $T =$ (let$_M$ $x = M$ in $T) + ($let$_M$ $x = N$ in T)

MonadMinus Laws

vzero $- a$ $= -a$
$a -$ vzero $= a$
let$_M$ $x = (M - N)$ in $T =$ (let$_M$ $x = M$ in $T) - ($let$_M$ $x = N$ in T)

Scalar Laws

let$_M$ $x = \alpha * M$ in T $= \alpha * ($let$_M$ $x = M$ in T)
$\alpha_1 * (\alpha_2 * M + \alpha_3 * N) = (\alpha_1 * \alpha_2) * M + (\alpha_1 * \alpha_3) * N$
$\alpha_1 * (\alpha_2 * M - \alpha_3 * N) = (\alpha_1 * \alpha_2) * M - (\alpha_1 * \alpha_3) * N$

Pairs Laws

$fst(\alpha_1 * [L_1]_M + \ldots + \alpha_n * [L_n]_M)$ $=$
   $\alpha_1 * [fst(L_1)]_M + \ldots + \alpha_n * [fst(L_n)]_M$
$snd(\alpha_1 * [L_1]_M + \ldots + \alpha_n * [L_n]_M)$ $=$
   $\alpha_1 * [snd(L_1)]_M + \ldots + \alpha_n * [snd(L_n)]_M$

Fig. 2. Quantum Monadic λ-calculus Equations

In this fairly simple quantum monadic λ-calculus we can model all pure quantum states and *reversible quantum computations*. In pure quantum computing all operations must be reversible, that is, they must avoid decoherence and loss of information.

Consider the type **Lin Bool Bool** as synonymous for **Bool** → **Vec Bool**. The name **Lin** stands for *linear* or unitary operator, which is reversible.

As an example of linear operation consider the hadamard quantum operation, which is the source of quantum superposition.

hadamard : **Lin Bool Bool**
   hadamard $= \lambda x.$if $x == True$ then $(1/\sqrt{2}) * [False]_M - (1/\sqrt{2}) * [True]_M$
                   else $(1/\sqrt{2}) * [False]_M + (1/\sqrt{2}) * [True]_M$

We can use the equations to prove that, for example, applying hadamard twice is the same as identity:

$$\text{hadmard}^2 = \lambda x.\text{let}_M \; y = \text{hadamard} \; x$$
$$\text{in hadamard} \; y$$

then

$$\text{hadamard}^2 False = False$$

However, there is another very important type of quantum operation called *measurement* which is not reversible, and that can be understood as a classical probabilistic view of quantum vectors. A measurement is an operation which outputs a probability distribution of quantum vectors. To deal with measurements we use a generalization of monads called arrows.

3   Quantum Arrow Calculus

Using the simple reversible model of quantum computation based on pure quantum vectors and reversible operations it is impossible to represent measurements. Hence to have a general model for quantum computation we based our work [9] on the idea of using density matrices to model general quantum states, pure and mixed, and superoperators to model general quantum computations, reversible and measurements. The appeal of using density matrix formalism is that we can represent both pure and mixed states. Pure vectors are those states which are intact. Mixed quantum states are those states which were subjected to observations, i.e, they are a classical probability distribution of pure quantum vectors.

Each pure vector $|\psi\rangle$ can be represented as a density matrix $|\psi\rangle\langle\psi|$ (multiplication of a column vector by its *dual* row vector). In addition we can represent classical probability distributions over pure vectors using this notation just setting some parts of the matrix to zero. The classical probabilities are maintained over the main diagonal.

Consider *type* **Dens** $A = (A, A) \to \mathbf{C}$ the type of density matrices over the basis A. Intuitivelly, the input (A, A) can be interpreted as a basis for a vector and its dual.

More recently, Hughes [10] introduced a generalization of monads, called *arrows*, to deal with a more general class of computational effects. Arrows include notions of computations with static components, independent of the input, as well as computations that consume multiple inputs.

Following the approach by Moggi [8] extending simply typed lambda calculus with monadic constructs and laws, the authors of the arrow calculus [11] extended the core lambda calculus with four new constructs satisfying five laws.

We define in [14,12] a quantum lambda calculus based on the core arrow calculus [11], which we call *quantum arrow calculus* for *mixed quantum computations*. As we will explain below, in the quantum arrow calculus it is just possible to write *mixed states*. The main constructs of the quantum arrow calculus are presented in Figure 3.

As in the monadic case, the first construct lifts basic values to density matrices.

$$\frac{\Gamma, \Delta \vdash M : A}{\Gamma; \Delta \vdash [M]_A \,!\, \mathbf{Dens}\, A}$$

Note that in the hypothesis we have an ordinary term judgment with one environment, Γ, Δ. However in the conclusion we have two environments, Γ and Δ (explicitly separated by the semicolon). That is an important feature of the arrow calculus: the command (for effectful computations) judgment has two environments, where variables in Γ come from ordinary lambda abstractions and variables in Δ come from *arrow abstractions*.

Having density matrices as commands in the calculus, we can define effectfull functions transforming density matrices into new density matrices, i.e. superoperators, using the arrow abstraction:

$$\frac{\Gamma; x : A \vdash Q \,!\, \mathbf{Dens}\, B}{\Gamma \vdash \lambda^{\bullet} x.Q : \mathbf{Super}\, A\, B}$$

The main point of using arrows is that computations mapping density matrices to new density matrices consume multiple inputs, that is, the basis of a vector and its dual.

The remaining two constructs: arrow application and composition are showed directly in Figure 3. Arrow application $L \bullet M$ allows the application of a superoperator to a density matrix, and composition, let_A [2] resembles the monadic composition.

The laws are the same of the arrow calculus, resembling the laws of the computational lambda calculus of Moggi. Arrow abstraction and application satisfy beta and eta laws, while arrow lifting and composition satisfy left unit, right unit and associativity.

Using the quantum arrow calculus it is possible to write mixed quantum states and superoperators acting on these states. One can note that we do not have an explicit measurement operation. That is because we are directly working with the observer perspective of the quantum system, i.e., just mixed states. Any operation in the quantum arrow calculus denotes a probabilistic function computed by quantum operations.

In [12], we add sum of arrows ($+\!\!+$), to represent the probability distribution generated by superpositions:

$$\frac{\Gamma; \Delta \vdash P, Q \,!\, \mathbf{Dens}\, A}{\Gamma; \Delta \vdash P +\!\!+ Q \,!\, \mathbf{Dens}\, A}$$

The equation for sums of arrows resembles the equation for the monadic sum:

$$P +\!\!+ (Q +\!\!+ R) \qquad = (P +\!\!+ Q) +\!\!+ R$$
$$\mathsf{let}_A\, x = P +\!\!+ Q \text{ in } R = (\mathsf{let}_A\, x = P \text{ in } R) +\!\!+ (\mathsf{let}_A\, x = Q \text{ in } R)$$

---

[2] Note here that we just changed de subscript from let_M to let_A (i.e., Arrow).

Syntax

Typedef	**Dens** A	$= (A, A) \to \mathbf{C}$
Typedef	**Super** $A\, B$	$= (A, A) \to \mathbf{Dens}\, B$
Types	A, B, C	$::= \ldots \mid \mathbf{Dens}\, A \mid \mathbf{Super}\, A\, B$
Terms	L, M, N	$::= \ldots \mid \lambda^{\bullet} x.Q$
Commands	P, Q, R	$::= L \bullet M \mid [M]_A \mid \mathrm{let}_A\ x = P\ \mathrm{in}\ Q$
Environments Γ, Δ		$::= x_1 : A_1, \ldots, x_n : A_n$

Arrow Types

$$\frac{\Gamma; x : A \vdash Q\,!\,\mathbf{Dens}\, B}{\Gamma \vdash \lambda^{\bullet} x.Q : \mathbf{Super}\, A\, B} \qquad \frac{\Gamma \vdash L : \mathbf{Super}\, A\, B \quad \Gamma, \Delta \vdash M : A}{\Gamma; \Delta \vdash L \bullet M\,!\,\mathbf{Dens}\, B}$$

$$\frac{\Gamma, \Delta \vdash M : A}{\Gamma; \Delta \vdash [M]_A\,!\,\mathbf{Dens}\, A} \qquad \frac{\Gamma; \Delta \vdash P\,!\,\mathbf{Dens}\, A \quad \Gamma; \Delta, x : A \vdash Q\,!\,\mathbf{Dens}\, B}{\Gamma; \Delta \vdash \mathrm{let}_A\ x = P\ \mathrm{in}\ Q\,!\,\mathbf{Dens}\, B}$$

Laws

$(\beta^{\leadsto})$	$(\lambda^{\bullet} x.Q) \bullet M$	$= Q[x := M]$
$(\eta^{\leadsto})$	$\lambda^{\bullet} x.(L \bullet [x]_A)$	$= L$
(left)	$\mathrm{let}_A\ x = [M]_A\ \mathrm{in}\ Q$	$= Q[x := M]$
(right)	$\mathrm{let}_A\ x = P\ \mathrm{in}\ [x]$	$= P$
(assoc)	$\mathrm{let}_A\ y = (\mathrm{let}\ x = P\ \mathrm{in}\ Q)\ \mathrm{in}\ R = \mathrm{let}_A\ x = P\ \mathrm{in}\ (\mathrm{let}_A\ y = Q\ \mathrm{in}\ R)$	

Fig. 3. Quantum Arrow Calculus

However, using the quantum monadic λ-calculus or the quantum arrow calculus we lose some generality from our previous arrow interface [9] as there is no construction to communicate the monadic layer of the calculus with the arrow layer of the calculus. That is, we can consider just pure or just mixed quantum computations.

4   The Double Effect λ-calculus for Quantum Computation

Unfortunately, using the quantum arrow calculus it is just possible to write mixed quantum states and superoperators acting on these states. Hence, using the quantum monadic λ-calculus or the quantum arrow calculus we lose some generality from our previous arrow interface [9] as there is no construction to communicate the monadic layer of the calculus with the arrow layer of the calculus. That is, we can consider just pure or just mixed quantum computations.

This restriction limits the expressiveness of the calculus as it is not possible, for instance, to represent quantum algorithms with measurements in the middle of the computation.

The main point is the arrow lifting operation, which just allows to lift ordinary values to arrows. Lifting only ordinary values we get just mixed states. In our Haskell interface for quantum computation [9] we implemented an operation to lift monadic *pure* quantum values to quantum arrows, as any pure quantum vector can be represented by its density matrix. Hence in the Haskell interface we can implement quantum algorithms using reversible quantum computations and measurements. However, this library uses classical arrows [10].

4.1   Constructions and Equations

So, with the purpose of having a calculus, based on the arrow calculus [11], for expressing quantum algorithms including pure quantum states and measurements in the middle of the computation, we first present a lifting construction of a pure quantum vector to its density matrix representation:

$$\frac{\Gamma \vdash [L]_M : \textbf{Vec } A}{\Gamma \vdash [[L]_M]_A : \textbf{Dens } A}$$

which allows to build mixtures of pure quantum states in the calculus. The denotation of this construct is given by a function:

$$pureD :: \textbf{Vec } A \to \textbf{Dens } A$$
$$pureD\ v = uncurry(v \rangle * \langle v)$$

exactly how presented in [9], where the function $\rangle * \langle$ produces the outer product of two vectors. This function embeds a pure quantum vector into its density matrix representation.

The calculus presented in this section inherits all the type rules and equations of simply typed λ-calculus, the monadic calculus, and arrow calculus.

We will just discuss the new equation implied by the new lifting. We need a new equations for arrow composition, as the terms to be composed can now be lifted monadic types:

$$(\text{left}_M^A)\text{let}_A\ x = [\alpha_1 * [L_1]_M + \ldots + \alpha_n * [L_n]_M]_A \text{ in } Q$$
$$= \text{let}_M\ x = \alpha_1 * [L_1]_M + \ldots + \alpha_n * [L_n]_M \text{ in } Q$$

The equation essentially shows that arrow composition can now be defined in terms of the monadic composition. This is the exact way we define arrow composition in [9]. Soundness of this equation can be proved using the translation o this construction of the calculus to classic arrows in [11], and then using the definition of arrow composition for superoperators presented in [9].

The translation of arrow composition to classic arrows is given by:

$$[[\text{let } x = P \text{ in } Q]]_\Delta = (arr\ id\ \&\&\& [[P]]_\Delta) \ggg [[Q]]_{\Delta,x}$$

where arr promotes a function to a pure arrow, $\ggg$ is arrow composition, Δ is the environment of variables that can be used in P, and f &&& g is a pairing function that applies arrows f and g to the same argument and pairs the result. The pairing is used to extend the environment with P. Then we can use the definition of arrow composition for superoperators:

$$f \ggg g = \lambda a.f\ a \ggg g$$

which says that superoperators' composition is defined in terms of the monadic composition, $\ggg\!=$, represented in the calculus as let_M.

We also add two operations for measurement: $meas ::$ **Super** $A\ B$, which measures a quantum state, i.e., obtains classical information from quantum data, and $trL ::$ Super $(A, B)\ B$, which measures the quantum state and then traces out (i.e., discharges) part of it, with the equations presented in Figure 5.

Now, we can also *measure* a pure quantum state and get, as the result, a density matrix representing the classical probability distribution denoted by that pure quantum state.

In Figures 4 and 5 we present all type rules, and laws of the modified calculus, respectively.

The equation $Meas_1$ shows that a measurement on a basic value simply returns the density matrix for the basic value. $Meas_2$ turns a monadic sum into an arrow sum. The denotation of this is to build a diagonal matrix, i.e., to set some parts of the density matrix to zero: a measurement. Equations trL_1 and trL_2 have the same meaning of the measurement equations, however they discharge the left part of the state. Equations α and $+$ show how to operate with the monadic scalars and sums in the arrow level, respectively. Finally, we present the equations for pairs. The use of pairs with monads and arrows constructions is an abstraction that allows to work on separated parts of the quantum values.

Simply-Typed Lambda Calculus
...
Monadic Types
...
Arrow Types
...
Types for measurements

$\Gamma, \Delta \vdash meas :$ **Super** $A\ B$ $\Gamma, \Delta \vdash trL :$ **Super** $(A, B)\ B$

Fig. 4. Double Effect λ-calculus Types

Simply-Typed Lambda Calculus Equations

...

Monadic Equations

...

Arrow Equations

...

New Arrow Equations

(left_M^A) $\text{let}_A\ x = [\alpha_1 * [L_1]_M + \ldots + \alpha_n * [L_n]_M]_A$ in Q $=$
$\phantom{(\text{left}_M^A)}$ $\text{let}_M\ x = \alpha_1 * [L_1]_M + \ldots + \alpha_n * [L_n]_M$ in Q

$(Meas_1)$ $\alpha * (meas \bullet L)$ $= [\alpha * [L]_M]_A$

$(Meas_2)$ $\alpha_1 * (meas \bullet L_1) + \ldots + \alpha_n * (meas \bullet L_n)$ $=$
 $\alpha_1 * (meas \bullet L) + \!+ \ldots + \!+ \alpha_n * (meas \bullet L_n)$

(trL_1) $\alpha * (trL \bullet (L, N))$ $= [\alpha * [N]_M]_A$

(trL_2) $\alpha_1 * (trL \bullet (L_1, N_1)) + \ldots + \alpha_n * (trL \bullet (L_n, N_n))$ $=$
 $\alpha_1 * (trL \bullet (L_1, N_1)) + \!+ \ldots + \!+ \alpha_n * (trL \bullet (L_n, N_n))$

(α) $\alpha * [\alpha_1 * [L_1]_M + \ldots + \alpha_n * [L_n]_M]_A$ $=$
 $[(\alpha * \alpha_1) * [L_1]_M + \ldots + (\alpha * \alpha_n) * [L_n]_M]_A$

$(+)$ $[M]_A + [N]_A$ $= [M + N]_A$

(fst_A) $fst * [\alpha_1 * [L_1]_M + \ldots + \alpha_n * [L_n]_M]_A$ $=$
 $[\alpha_1 * fst[(L_1)]_M + \ldots + \alpha_n * fst[(L_n)]_M]_A$

(snd_A) $snd * [\alpha_1 * [L_1]_M + \ldots + \alpha_n * [L_n]_M]_A$ $=$
 $[\alpha_1 * snd[(L_1)]_M + \ldots + \alpha_n * snd[(L_n)]_M]_A$

Fig. 5. Double Effect λ-calculus Equations

4.2   Examples

Consider the lifting of the hadamard example in section 2.2:

$$(\lambda^\bullet y.[\text{hadamard } y]_A) \bullet False$$

Then, applying the equation $(\beta^\leadsto)$ and the monadic equations on hadamard $False$ we get $[1/\sqrt{2} * [False]_M + 1/\sqrt{2} * [True]_M]_A$, which has a pure quantum vector, represented as a density matrix, as its denotation:

$$\begin{pmatrix} 1/2 & 1/2 \\ 1/2 & 1/2 \end{pmatrix}$$

Now, we can also *measure* this pure quantum state and get, as the result, a mixed state:

$$\mathsf{let}_A\ x = (\lambda^\bullet y.[\mathsf{hadamard}\ y]_A) \bullet False$$
$$\mathsf{in}\ meas \bullet x$$
$$\equiv^{\beta^\frown}\cdots$$
$$\mathsf{let}_A\ x = [1/\sqrt{2} * [False]_M + 1/\sqrt{2} * [True]_M]_A$$
$$\mathsf{in}\ meas \bullet x$$
$$\equiv^{\mathsf{left}_M^A}$$
$$1/\sqrt{2} * (meas \bullet False) + 1/\sqrt{2} * (meas \bullet True)$$
$$\equiv^{Meas_1 and Meas_2}$$
$$[1/\sqrt{2} * [False]_M]_A +\!\!+ [1/\sqrt{2} * [True]_M]_A$$

which denotes the following density matrix:

$$\begin{pmatrix} 1/2 & 0 \\ 0 & 1/2 \end{pmatrix}$$

Note that arrowplus, $+\!\!+$, just sum the density matrix for $[False]_M$ with the density matrix for $[True]_M$.

Now to illustrate the use of the double effect calculus to model quantum algorithms, which start with a pure quantum state and consider measurements in the middle of the computation, we model the quantum teleportation.

$$\begin{aligned} \mathsf{alice} \quad &= \lambda^\bullet(e, q).\mathsf{let}_A\ (q_1, e_1) = \lambda^\bullet(x, y).[\mathsf{cnot}(x, y)]_A \bullet (q, e) \\ &\quad \mathsf{in}\ \mathsf{let}_A\ q_2 = \lambda^\bullet y.[\mathsf{hadamard}\ y]_A \bullet q_1 \\ &\quad \mathsf{in}\ meas \bullet q_2 \end{aligned}$$

$$\begin{aligned} \mathsf{bob} \quad &= \lambda^\bullet(e, m_1, m_2).\mathsf{let}_A\ (m_2', m_1') = \lambda^\bullet(x, y).[\mathsf{cnot}(x, y)]_A \bullet (m_2, e) \\ &\quad \mathsf{in}\ \mathsf{let}_A\ (m_1', e_2) = \lambda^\bullet(x, y).[\mathsf{cz}\ (x, y)]_A \bullet (m_1, e) \\ &\quad \mathsf{in}\ trL \bullet ((m_1', m_2'), e_2) \end{aligned}$$

$$\begin{aligned} \mathsf{teleport} &= \lambda^\bullet(eL, eR, q).\mathsf{let}_A\ (m_1, m_2) = \mathsf{alice} \bullet (eL, q) \\ &\quad \mathsf{in}\ \mathsf{bob} \bullet (eR, eL, q) \end{aligned}$$

The example shows a conventional functional style of programming for quantum computation, considering pure quantum states and mixed quantum states together. In a previous work [12] we also model the teleportation using the quantum arrow calculus, however just considering mixed states, i.e., we modeled the user view of the quantum system. In the present work, due to the existence of the lifting operation we can work with unitary reversible operations acting on pure quantum values. The definition of the reversible operations: hadamard, controlled not, cnot, and controlled phase, cz is done at the monadic level. The definition of hadamard is given in Section 2.2. The controlled not can be defined as:

$$\mathsf{cnot} : \mathbf{Lin}\ (\mathbf{Bool}, \mathbf{Bool})\ (\mathbf{Bool}, \mathbf{Bool})$$
$$\mathsf{cnot} = \lambda(x, y).\mathsf{if}\ x == True\ \mathsf{then}\ (1/\sqrt{2}) * [(True, not\ y)]_M$$
$$\mathsf{else}\ (1/\sqrt{2}) * [(False, y)]_M$$

The controlled phase is defined in the same way. Moreover, we have an explicit measurement operation.

5   Conclusion

We have presented a quantum monadic λ-calculus as a quantum programming language. Our first contribution is a calculus with quantum reversible and measurement operations as well equations to make algebraic reasoning about quantum programs. As future work we intend to add types and other high level quantum data structures to the calculus. A prototype of an interpreter for this calculus is under development. A deep investigation of the relations of this categorical model with other important works like [15,16,17,18] is also a future work.

Acknowledgements. We thank the anonymous referee for useful comments and suggestions.

References

1. Selinger, P.: Towards a quantum programming language. Mathematical Structures in Computer Science 4(14), 527–586 (2004)
2. Altenkirch, T., Grattage, J.: A functional quantum programming language. In: 20th Annual IEEE Symposium on Logic in Computer Science (2005)
3. van Tonder, A.: A lambda calculus for quantum computation. SIAM Journal of Computing 33, 1109–1135 (2004)
4. Arrighi, P., Dowek, G.: Linear-algebraic λ-calculus: higher-order, encodings, and confluence. In: Voronkov, A. (ed.) RTA 2008. LNCS, vol. 5117, pp. 17–31. Springer, Heidelberg (2008)
5. Selinger, P., Valiron, B.: A lambda calculus for quantum computation with classical control. Mathematical Structures in Computer Science 16(3), 527–552 (2006)
6. Selinger, P., Valiron, B.: Quantum lambda calculus. In: Gay, S., Mackie, I. (eds.) Semantic Techniques in Quantum Computation, pp. 135–172. Cambridge University Press (2009)
7. Uustalu, T., Vene, V.: The essence of dataflow programming. In: Yi, K. (ed.) APLAS 2005. LNCS, vol. 3780, pp. 2–18. Springer, Heidelberg (2005)
8. Moggi, E.: Computational lambda-calculus and monads. In: Proceedings of the Fourth Annual Symposium on Logic in Computer Science, pp. 14–23. IEEE Press (1989)
9. Vizzotto, J.K., Altenkirch, T., Sabry, A.: Structuring quantum effects: Superoperators as arrows. Journal of Mathematical Structures in Computer Science: Special Issue in Quantum Programming Languages 16, 453–468 (2006)
10. Hughes, J.: Generalising monads to arrows. Science of Computer Programming 37, 67–111 (2000)
11. Lindley, S., Wadler, P., Yallop, J.: The arrow calculus. Journal of Functional Programming, 51–69 (2010)
12. Vizzotto, J.K., Librelotto, G.R., Sabry, A.: Reasoning about general quantum programs over mixed states. In: Oliveira, M.V.M., Woodcock, J. (eds.) SBMF 2009. LNCS, vol. 5902, pp. 321–335. Springer, Heidelberg (2009)
13. Mu, S.C., Bird, R.: Functional quantum programming. In: Second Asian Workshop on Programming Languages and Systems, KAIST, Korea (December 2001)
14. Vizzotto, J.K., Du Bois, A.R., Sabry, A.: The arrow calculus as a quantum programming language. In: Ono, H., Kanazawa, M., de Queiroz, R. (eds.) WoLLIC 2009. LNCS, vol. 5514, pp. 379–393. Springer, Heidelberg (2009)

15. Altenkirch, T., Chapman, J., Uustalu, T.: Relative monads formalised. Under consideration for Publication in Mathematical Structures in Computer Science (2010)
16. Abramsky, S.: High-level methods for quantum computation and information. In: LICS, pp. 410–414 (2004)
17. Selinger, P.: Dagger compact closed categories and completely positive maps. Electronic Notes in Theoretical Computer Science 170, 139–163 (2007)
18. Coecke, B.: Strongly compact closed semantics. Electronic Notes Theoretical Computer Science 155, 331–340 (2006)

A   Simply-Typed Lambda Calculus

The simply-typed lambda calculus with the type of booleans, and with let and if is shown in Figure 6. Let A, B, C range over types, L, M, N range over terms, and Γ, Δ range over environments. A type judgment $\Gamma \vdash M : A$ indicates that in environment Γ term M has type A.

Syntax

Types	$A, B, C ::= \mathbf{Bool} \mid A \times B \mid A \to B$
Terms	$L, M, N ::= x \mid \mathsf{True} \mid \mathsf{False} \mid (M, N) \mid \mathsf{fst}\ L \mid \mathsf{snd}\ L \mid \lambda x.N \mid L\ M$
	$\quad\quad\quad\ \mathsf{let}\ x = M\ \mathsf{in}\ N \mid \mathsf{if}\ L\ \mathsf{then}\ M\ \mathsf{else}\ N$
Environments Γ, Δ	$::= x_1 : A_1, \ldots, x_n : A_n$

Types

$$\frac{}{\emptyset \vdash \mathsf{False} : \mathbf{Bool}} \qquad \frac{}{\emptyset \vdash \mathsf{True} : \mathbf{Bool}} \qquad \frac{(x : A) \in \Gamma}{\Gamma \vdash x : A}$$

$$\frac{\Gamma \vdash M : A \quad \Gamma \vdash N : B}{\Gamma \vdash (M, N) : A \times B} \qquad \frac{\Gamma \vdash L : A \times B}{\Gamma \vdash \mathsf{fst}\ L : A} \qquad \frac{\Gamma \vdash L : A \times B}{\Gamma \vdash \mathsf{snd}\ L : B}$$

$$\frac{\Gamma, x : A \vdash N : B}{\Gamma \vdash \lambda x.N : A \to B} \qquad \frac{\Gamma \vdash L : A \to B \quad \Gamma \vdash M : A}{\Gamma \vdash L\ M : B}$$

$$\frac{\Gamma \vdash M : A \quad \Gamma, x : A \vdash N : B}{\Gamma \vdash \mathsf{let}\ x = M\ \mathsf{in}\ N : B} \qquad \frac{\Gamma \vdash L : \mathbf{Bool} \quad \Gamma \vdash M, N : B}{\Gamma \vdash \mathsf{if}\ L\ \mathsf{then}\ M\ \mathsf{else}\ N : B}$$

Laws

(β_1^x)	$\mathsf{fst}\ (M, N)$	$= M$
(β_2^x)	$\mathsf{snd}\ (M, N)$	$= N$
(η^x)	$(\mathsf{fst}\ L, \mathsf{snd}\ L)$	$= L$
$(\beta^\to)$	$(\lambda x.N) M$	$= N[x := M]$
$(\eta^\to)$	$\lambda x.(L\ x)$	$= L$
(let)	$\mathsf{let}\ x = M\ \mathsf{in}\ N$	$= N[x := M]$
(β_1^{if})	$\mathsf{if}\ \mathsf{True}\ \mathsf{then}\ M\ \mathsf{else}\ N$	$= M$
(β_2^{if})	$\mathsf{if}\ \mathsf{False}\ \mathsf{then}\ M\ \mathsf{else}\ N$	$= N$

Fig. 6. Simply-typed Lambda Calculus

Boilerplates for Reconfigurable Systems: A Language and Its Semantics

Alexandre Madeira[1,2,3], Manuel A. Martins[2], and Luís S. Barbosa[2]

[1] HASLab - INESC TEC and Universidade do Minho, Portugal
[2] CIDMA-Dep. of Mathematics, Universidade de Aveiro, Portugal
[3] Critical Software S.A., Portugal

Abstract. Boilerplates are simplified, normative English texts, intended to capture software requirements in a controlled way. This paper proposes a pallet of boilerplates as a requirements modelling language for reconfigurable systems, i.e., systems structured in different modes of execution among which they can dynamically commute. The language semantics is given as an hybrid logic, in an institutional setting. The mild use made of the theory of institutions, which, to a large extent, may be hidden from the working software engineer, not only provides a rigorous and generic semantics, but also paves the way to tool-supported validation.

1 Motivation and Overview

Requirements Engineering [9] is the branch of software engineering concerned with the precise identification of goals and constraints of the services provided by systems. Typically, this involves understanding, modelling and documenting not only the needs of potential users or customers, but also the deployment contexts in which such systems under development will be used. The deliverable of this stage in the software development process must be expressed in a form that is amenable to analysis, communication, and subsequent implementation.

In practice requirements engineers start with ill-defined, often conflicting, ideas of what the new system is expected to do. They are supposed to make progress towards a detailed, technical specification of the system. This entails the need for suitable support methodologies to record and structure the relevant information, as well as to express it in a clear, easy to understand notation.

The notion of a *boilerplate*, first introduced in [9], is a step in this direction: for each class of requirements, within a specific domain, a generic template is defined so that capturing requirements amounts to instantiated well-characterized textual schemes written in simplified, normative English. Informally, a boilerplate is a standardized scheme that can be reused over and over again, and is amenable to some form of computer-based simulation. The term derives from steel manufacturing, where it refers to steel rolled into large plates for use in steam boilers. The intuition is that a boilerplate has been time-tested and is 'strong as steel' suitable for repeated reuse. The use of 'controlled natural language' for requirements elicitation is a successful practice in industry and, despite

A. Rauber Du Bois and P. Trinder (Eds.): SBLP 2013, LNCS 8129, pp. 75–89, 2013.

of its informal character, does provide an interesting starting point towards more formal approaches.

Boilerplates are usually developed for specific business areas, classes of systems or typical design stages.This paper focus in *reconfigurable* systems. Those are systems whose form (i.e. resources involved, network topology, etc) changes along the computational process in response to varying context conditions.

The behavior of this kind of systems is indexed to a set of different run-time *configurations* between which the system commutes dynamically. Therefore, a specification takes the form of a *structured transition system*: transitions capture the evolution from one configuration to another, whereas each state corresponds to the full specification of data and services available at a particular configuration. Such local configurations can be described in different languages, ranging from, equational to first order logic or even to less conventional formalisms, e.g., fuzzy or multivalued logics. In the sequel we will refer to the logic used at the local level of configurations as the *base* logic.

If the base logic provides a language to express requirements relative to each configuration of the system, describing the reconfiguration dynamics itself requires a *modal* logic to express transition and change. Actually, we adopt an extension of ordinary modal logic in which dedicated propositional symbols, called *nominals*, each being true at exactly one possible state, are used to *name* states, i.e., the system's individual configurations. This extension is known as *hybrid* logic, whose roots go back Arthur N. Prior's work in the 1960s; see [1] for a detailed account and historic perspective. Along with nominals, it also introduces *satisfaction operators* $@_i\phi$, which formalise a statement ϕ being true at a specific configuration named i.

In such a context, the paper's contribution is twofold:

- first it introduces a collection of boilerplates for capturing typical requirements of reconfigurable systems;
- then, it takes seriously the challenge of providing a proper, unambiguous semantics for them.

Our perspective is that the methodological advantages of boilerplates, i.e. their conciseness and genericity, depends on the existence of a rigorous formal semantics for them, amenable to formal transformation and verification. On the other hand, the distinguishing feature of our approach is that boilerplates are parametric on whatever (*base*) logic is chosen for specifying the system's configurations.

The methodology proposed proceeds as follows: first a suitable base logic to express the properties of (local) configurations is chosen. Then, the requirements are collected into specific boilerplates which structure information on the relevant vocabulary, available configurations, events triggering reconfiguration and both local and global properties. Once instantiated, boilerplates are translated into specifications in (a suitable version of) *hybrid logic* (*e.g.* [2]) providing a formal description of requirements amenable to tool-supported validation. By the expression '*(suitable version of) hybrid logic*' we mean a language with enriches the base logic specific to each application with modalities and hybrid features to express reconfiguration and evolution. Such a language is derived in a formal and systematic way — the so-called *hybridisation process* whose theory was developed by the authors in [13,4].

Going generic entails a price to pay: to seek for a suitably generic notion of logical system encompassing syntax, semantics and satisfaction. Fortunately the concept is already well-established in the so-called theory of institutions of Goguen and Burstall [6,3]. At expenses of some extra (and a bit heavy) notation, institutions offer an abstract representation of a logic, and their theory provides modular structuring and parameterization mechanisms which are defined 'once and for all', abstracting from the concrete particularities of the each specification logic [5]. The formal semantics for boilerplates proposed in this paper is framed in this setting: each logic (base and hybridised) is regarded as an *institution*.

Another advantage of the institutional framework is its ability to relate logics and transport results from one to another [14], which means that a theorem prover for the latter can be used to reason about specifications written in the former. Our approach takes advantage of this to provide 'for free' suitable tool support through a translation of collections of boilerplates to first-order logic and their validation in the HETS [16] tool.

The paper is organized as follows: Section 2 introduces a pallet of boilerplates for reconfigurable systems and illustrates their use through a small example. A formal semantics for this pallet of boilerplates is addressed in Section 3. Finally, Section 4 proposes a methodology for engineering requirements of reconfigurable systems, from their elicitation and expression in boilerplates until their validation and prototyping within the HETS framework.

The semantic framework used in the sequel is based on the theory of institutions and a method to generate hybrid from arbitrary logics. Part of it, namely the background formalism and notation, can be skipped at first reading without compromising a broader understanding of the paper's ideas. For the interested reader, details and examples are given in the Appendix.

2   A Language of Boilerplates for Reconfigurability

As sketched in the previous section, requirements for reconfigurable systems are captured in a collection of boilerplates which, taken jointly, specify a structured transition system. Its states, corresponding to different *configurations*, or *modes of execution*, are endowed with a specific description of the functionality available locally. The boilerplates proposed below define globally the relevant modes of execution and the transition structure, as well as, at the local level of each mode, the interface of services available and their properties.

Basic Boilerplates

Five classes of boilerplates are introduced to register requirements, structuring them as a (structured) transition system. The choice of the *base* logic $\mathcal{I}$ is made within the boilerplates concerned with the system's interface. A concrete instantiation of these boilerplates requires such a choice: notation $BP(\mathcal{I})$

stands therefore, for the set of boilerplates in which the requirements for local configurations are given in $\mathcal{I}$. The basic boilerplates proposed are as follows:

1. Identification of the relevant configurations:

> *System plays the configurations* <set of configurations>
> <Mode> *is a execution mode*

2. Definition of event sets able to trigger a mode transition, i.e., a system's reconfiguration:

> *System has events* <set of Event>
> <Event> *is an event*

3. Definition of the basic transition structure:

> *System changes from* <Mode> *to* <Mode> *through the event* <Event>
> *System may change from* <Mode> *to* <Mode> *through the event* <Event>

4. Definition of the system's interface:

> *System interface is defined by* <InterfaceExp>

5. Local specification, i.e., relative to the system's functionality at each configuration (stated in the chosen *base* logic):

> *Property* <Prop> *holds in all modes*
> *Property* <Prop> *holds in* <Mode>

6. Definition of possible transitions (i.e., reconfigurations) emerging from local properties (e.g., a certain limit value for a parameter is achieved).

> <Event> *changes modes satisfying* <Prop> *into modes satisfying* <Prop>
> <Event> *changes* <Mode> *to modes satisfying* <Prop>

An Example

For example let us consider a small, self-contained example. Other examples appeared in the first author's PhD thesis [10]. For the moment, consider the following requirements for a quite peculiar, 'plastic' buffering structure:

> *A 'plastic' buffer is a versatile data structure with two distinct modes of execution: in one of them it behaves as a stack; in the other as a queue. The reconfiguration is triggered by by an external event 'shift'.*

We start fixing the transition structure between the buffer's (two) modes of execution.

Modes and events:

> − **fifo** *is a mode*
> − **lifo** *is a mode*
> − **Shift** *is an event*

Transition structure:

> *System changes from* <**lifo**> *to* <**fifo**> *through the event* <**shift**>
> *System changes from* <**fifo**> *to* <**lifo**> *through the event* <**shift**>

For the specification of each execution mode, or configuration, one may resort to propositional logic $\mathcal{PL}$, the buffer requirements are expressed in $BP(\mathcal{PL})$. The following boilerplate fixes the local behaviour: the proposition *stack_bh* is to hold in configurations in which the buffer behaves like a stack; proposition *queu_bh* when it behaves as a queue.

> *System interface is defined by* <{**stack_bh,queu_bh**}>

Hence,

> − *Property queu_bh holds in* **fifo**
> − *Property stack_bh holds in* **lifo**

In practice, however, the propositional setting may not be enough: most properties are better expressed in *equational* logic $\mathcal{EQ}$. Thus, one my state

> *System interface is defined by* < Σ_{Pbuffer} >

where Σ_{Pbuffer} is the classical first-order signature of a stack/queue data type with *write*, *read* and *del* operations together with a constant *new* to denote the empty buffer. Hence, local properties are expressed by

> − *Property* **read**(**write**(m, e)) = e *holds in* **lifo**
> − *Property* m = **new** ⇒ **read**(**write**(m, e)) = e *holds in* **fifo**
> − *Property* ¬(m = **new**) ⇒ **read**(**write**(m, e)) = **read**(m) *holds in* **fifo**
> − *Property* **del**(**write**(m, e)) = m *holds in* **lifo**
> − *Property* ¬(m = **new**) ⇒ **del**(**write**(m, e)) = **write**(**del**(m), e) *holds in* **fifo**
> − *Property* m = **new** ⇒ **del**(**write**(m, e)) = **new** *holds in* **lifo, fifo**

A precise semantics for this sort of boilerplates is given in the following section by their transformation into a proper formal specifications in suitable hybrid logics.

3   A Formal Semantics for $BP(\mathcal{I})$

If the collection of boilerplates proposed here for reconfigurable systems leads naturally to models based on structured transition systems, the choice of (a variant of) hybrid logic for their semantics comes as no surprise. Reactive systems are classically expressed in modal languages; on the other hand, a naming mechanism for states makes easier to distinguish between properties valid in some, but not all, configurations.

The semantic framework is as follows: Once the system's requirements are captured in a collection $BP(\mathcal{I})$ of boilerplates instantiated over a *base* logic $\mathcal{I}$, its semantics is given by a systematic translation to a hybrid logic over $\mathcal{I}$. I.e, a logic whose language extends that of $\mathcal{I}$ with a set Λ of *modalities*, the corresponding *eventually* ($\langle \lambda \rangle$) and *henceforth* ([λ]) operators, for each $\lambda \in \Lambda$, a set *Nom* of *nominals* to name configurations, and, for each $i \in Nom$ a satisfaction operator $@_i$ enforcing the validity of its argument in configuration i. Formally, the collection of boilerplates gives rise to a proper specification in the hybrid logic $\mathcal{HI}$ corresponding to $\mathcal{I}$. The generation of $\mathcal{HI}$ from $\mathcal{I}$, i.e., the *hybridisation* of $\mathcal{I}$, is also a systematic process whose technical details are summarised in the Appendix.

For the moment we shall concentrate in the process of generating a $\mathcal{HI}$-specification from a collection of boilerplates. Note the introduction of nominals to refer to local configurations and of modalities to state properties of the overall transition structure. This is better illustrated through an example. Let us, thus, revisit the buffer example.

In Section 2 two collections of boilerplates were considered for this example. The first one resorted to *propositional* logic $\mathcal{PL}$. Its semantics is, therefore, a generated specification in hybrid propositional logic $\mathcal{HPL}$:

spec RECONFBUFFER1 =
    nominal *fifo, lifo*
    modalities *shift*
    propositions *stack_bh, queue_bh*
    • $@_{fifo}\,stack\_bh$
    • $@_{lifo}\,queue\_bh$
    • $@_{lifo}< shift > fifo$
    • $@_{fifo}< shift > lifo$

The models M for this specification are standard Kripke structures. For instance, the structure defined over a set of two states $\{s_{lifo}, s_{fifo}\}$ and whose accessibility relation is $W_{shift} = \{(s_{lifo}, s_{fifo}), (s_{fifo}, s_{lifo})\}$. The value of propositions $stack\_bh$ and $queue\_bh$ is each state is as follows: $M_{s_{lifo}}(stack\_bh) = M_{s_{fifo}}(queue\_bh) = \top$ and $M_{s_{lifo}}(queue\_bh) = M_{s_{fifo}}(stack\_bh) = \bot$.

The second, richer set of boilerplates resorted to *equational* logic $\mathcal{EQ}$ to capture local requirements equationally. The resulting specification is now expressed in hybrid equational logic $\mathcal{HEQ}$, as follows.

spec RECONFBUFFER2 =
    nominal *fifo, lifo*
    modalities *shift*
    sorts *mem, item*
    op   *new* : *mem*;   *write* : *mem* × *item* → *mem*; *del* : *mem* → *mem*; *read* : *mem* → *item*
    ∀ *m* : *mem*; *e* : *item*;
    • $read(write(new, e)) = e$
    • $del(write(new, e)) = new$
    • $@_{lifo}\,read(write(m, e)) = e$
    • $@_{fifo}(m{=}new) \Rightarrow read(write(m, e)) = e$
    • $@_{fifo}\neg\,(m{=}new) \Rightarrow read(write(m, e)) = read(m)$
    • $@_{lifo}\,del(write(m, e)) = m$
    • $@_{fifo}(m{=}new) \Rightarrow del(write(m, e)) = new$
    • $@_{fifo}\neg\,(m{=}new) \Rightarrow del(write(m, e)) = write(del(m), e)$
    • $@_{lifo}< shift > fifo$
    • $@_{fifo}< shift > lifo$

A model M for this second specification is given by a Kripke structure as above but realising, in each state, $M_{s_{lifo}}$ and $M_{s_{fifo}}$ as the classical (initial) models for the stack and queue data types, respectively.

Boilerplates for LTS components specification:	
•*System has modes* <set of Mode>	• Nom := Nom ⊎ set of Mode
•*<Mode> is a mode*	• Nom := Nom ⊎ {Mode}
•*System has events* <set of Event>	• Λ := Λ ⊎ set of Event
•*<Event> is an event*	• Λ := Λ ⊎ {Event}
• *System's interface is defined by*<InterfaceExp>	• Σ := InterfaceExp
Boilerplates for simple transitions:	
•*System changes from* <Mode1> *to* <Mode2> *through event* <Event>	• @$_{\text{Mode1}}$⟨Event⟩Mode2
• *System may change from* <Mode1> *to* <Mode2> *through event* <Event>	• @$_{\text{Mode1}}$[Event]Mode2
• *<Event> changes system to* <Mode>	• [Event]$Mode$
•*There are no transitions into* <Mode> *through* <Event>	• ¬⟨Event⟩$Mode$
Boilerplates for transitions tagged by properties:	
• *<Event> changes modes satisfying* <Prop1> *into modes satisfying* <Prop2>	• Prop1 ⇒ [Event]Prop2
• *<Event> changes* <Mode> *to modes satisfying* <Prop>	• Mode ⇒ [Event]Prop
• *<Event>changes modes satisfying* <Prop> *to mode* <Mode>	• Prop ⇒ [Event] Mode
Boilerplates for properties:	
• *Property* <Prop> *holds in all modes*	• Prop
• *Property* <Prop> *holds in* <Mode>	• @$_{\text{Mode}}$Prop
• *There is no mode satisfying* <Prop>	• ¬ Prop
• *There is at least one mode satisfying* <Prop>	• Ew Prop
• *There is exactly one mode satisfying* <Prop>	• $\forall w, v \in W$ [@$_v$Prop $\wedge$ @$_w$Prop] ⇒ $v = w$

4   The Specification Process

We have seen how to go from a collection of boilerplates to a formal specification in a suitable hybrid logic. The latter not only provides a precise semantics to the requirements gathered, but also paves the way to their *validation*. Actually, a central ingredient for the successful integration of a formal methodology in the industrial practice is the existence of effective tool support.

In order to prototype requirements captured by a collection of boilerplates or to validate their internal consistency, the hybrid specifications are translated into *first-order* logic ($\mathcal{FOL}$), so that the software engineer can take advantage of several provers already available for $\mathcal{FOL}$.

The institution-based framework underlying the hybridisation process, which provides a whole pallet of (hybrid) logics for translating requirements, also offers for free the conceptual machinery for this translation to $\mathcal{FOL}$, whenever

it exists. Then, the prover toolset HETS [16], a framework specifically designed
to support specifications expressed in different institutions, offers suitable tool
support. Using a metaphor of [15], HETS may be seen as a "motherboard" where
different "expansion cards" can be plugged. These pieces are individual logics
(with their particular analysers and proof tools) as well as logic translations,
suitably encoded in the theory of institutions.

HETS already integrates parsers, static analyzers and provers for a wide set
of individual logics and manages heterogeneous proofs resorting to the so-called
graphs of logics, i.e., graphs whose nodes are logics and, whose edges, are comorphisms between them. Note that hybrid logic, namely its propositional variant,
has already a number of implementations (see e.g. HTAB [8], HYLOTAB [19]
and SPARTACUS [7]). Our approach, however, provides a uniform first order logical framework for analysis and verification supporting the whole methodology.
Moreover, to the best of our knowledge, richer versions of hybrid logic do lack
effective tool support, which makes our approach by translation the only option
available.

We can now explain, step-by-step, the overall methodology for requirements
elicitation and validation, as depicted in Fig. 1.

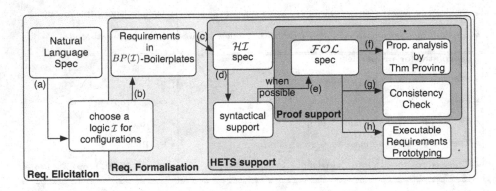

Fig. 1. Tool support

(a),(b) As usual, requirements start from a set of basic facts about what is
perceived as the system's goals and constraints. Typically, this determines
the choice of a *base* logic $\mathcal{I}$ for expressing properties of local configurations.
Examples in propositional and equational logic were discussed above. Often,
however, more complex languages are required. One can, for example, specify configurations as *multialgebras* to cope with non determinism, in which
case a multi-valued logic would be the obvious choice. Another possibility to
explore is resorts to *partial equational logic* to deal with exceptions, or *observational logics* to specify systems whose configurations encapsulate hidden
state-spaces. Finally, if each configuration is itself presented as a transition
system, one may choose a *modal logic* as a base, ending up with a (global)
modal language to express evolution of modal (local) specifications. This

freedom of choosing a base logic for each application is in line with a basic engineering concern which recommends that the choice of a specification framework depends on the nature of the requirements one has to deal with. Once $\mathcal{I}$ is fixed, the systems requirements are captured in $BP(\mathcal{I})$ instantiation of boilerplates. Note that the set of boilerplates proposed enforces a specification organised in terms of a structured transition system.

(c),(d) The next stage is the translation of the collection of boilerplates $BP(\mathcal{I})$ into a specification in the corresponding hybrid logic $\mathcal{HI}$ according to Boilerplates Table. This specification can be recognized as a HETS specification using the HCASL package recently introduced by the authors in [17].

(e) The existence of a suitable translation, technically a *comorphism* [3], from $\mathcal{HI}$ to $\mathcal{FOL}$ gives, for free, access to a number of provers integrated in HETS in which requirements can be validated. Such a translation, as noticed above, is not available for all logics. References [13,4], however, do provide a roadmap for addressing this issue: [13] shows that the hybridisation of an institution with a comorphism to $\mathcal{FOL}$ also has a comorphism to $\mathcal{FOL}$. Then reference [4] extends this result and characterizes conservativity of those translations to define in which cases it is possible to borrow, in an effective way, proof support from $\mathcal{FOL}$. Note that the proof of this result is is constructive, offering a method to implement such translations. In practice, this is a very general, broadly applicable result since several specification logics do have a comorphism to $\mathcal{FOL}$. Such is the case, for example, of propositional, equational, first-order, modal or even hybrid logic among many others.

Once framed in HETS, the requirement specifications can be validated resorting to several provers for $\mathcal{FOL}$ already "plugged" into HETS [15], e.g., SOFTFOL, SPASS and MATHSERVE BROKER, among others. Additionally, one may also to take advantage of a number of other provers borrowed from other institutions through comorphisms with source in $\mathcal{FOL}$.

(f),(g) Several other features of HETS can be explored in the context of the methodology proposed here. For instance, the model finder of Darwin, which is already integrated in the platform, may be used as a consistency checker for specifications derived from requirements. On the other hand, encodings of $\mathcal{FOL}$ into HASCASL[18], a specification language for functional programs, open new perspectives for prototyping $BP(\mathcal{I})$ generated specifications in a standard programming language as HASKELL.

5   Concluding

The paper proposes a pallet of boilerplates requirements elicitation of reconfigurable systems, as a first step to the definition of a *domain specific language* for this domain of software technology. The pallet is, obviously, not closed, provided that every extension comes equipped with a translation scheme. The combination of different sets of requirements expressed in hybridised versions $\mathcal{HI}$ of different base logics $\mathcal{I}$ is also an interesting strategy to take.

The hybridisation method introduced in [13], which, underlies the construction of suitable specification languages is also able to cope with quantification modalities (i.e., the system's events), a feature which may lead to an enrichment of the boilerplates pallet available at the time of writing. This may provide semantics for boilerplates able to express deadlock situations or to specify more than one-step (ir)-reversibility transition properties. Unfortunately the introduction of nominal quantification rules out the possibility of a suitable first order encoding for the logic, thus reducing the method tool support. Encodings to second-order-logic are, however, being developed.

A known limitation of the method proposed in this paper concerns interface reconfiguration. Technically, service functionality and behaviour exhibited in all system's configurations need to be specified over a common first-order signature. This difficulty was overcome, to a large extent, in a recent publication [12].

Acknowledgements. This work is funded by ERDF - European Regional Development Fund through the COMPETE Programme and by National Funds through FCT, the Portuguese Foundation for Science and Technology, project FCOMP-01- 0124-FEDER-028923.

References

1. Blackburn, P.: Arthur Prior and hybrid logic. Synthese 150(3), 329–372 (2006)
2. Brauner, T.: Hybrid Logic and its Proof-Theory. Applied Logic Series. Springer (2010)
3. Diaconescu, R.: Institution-independent Model Theory. Studies in Universal Logic. Birkhäuser Basel (2008)
4. Diaconescu, R., Madeira, A.: Encoding hybridized institutions into first order logic (submitted, 2013)
5. Diaconescu, R., Tutu, I.: On the algebra of structured specifications. Theor. Comput. Sci. 412(28), 3145–3174 (2011)
6. Goguen, J.A., Burstall, R.M.: Institutions: Abstract model theory for specification and programming. J. ACM 39(1), 95–146 (1992)
7. Götzmann, D., Kaminski, M., Smolka, G.: Spartacus: A tableau prover for hybrid logic. Electr. Notes Theor. Comput. Sci. 262, 127–139 (2010)
8. Hoffmann, G., Areces, C.: Htab: a terminating tableaux system for hybrid logic. Electr. Notes Theor. Comput. Sci. 231, 3–19 (2009)
9. Hull, M.E.C., Jackson, K., Dick, J.: Requirements engineering, 2nd edn. Springer (2005)
10. Madeira, A.: Foundations and techniques for software reconfigurability. PhD thesis, University of Minho, Portugal (Joint MAP-i Doctoral Program) (2013)
11. Madeira, A., Faria, J.M., Martins, M.A., Barbosa, L.S.: Hybrid specification of reactive systems: An institutional approach. In: Barthe, G., Pardo, A., Schneider, G. (eds.) SEFM 2011. LNCS, vol. 7041, pp. 269–285. Springer, Heidelberg (2011)
12. Madeira, A., Neves, R., Martins, M.A., Barbosa, L.S.: When even the interface evolves. In: Wang, H., Banach, R. (eds.) Proceedings of TASE the 7th IEEE Symp. on Theoretical Aspects of Software Engineering, TASE, Birmingham, pp. 79–82. IEEE Computer Society (July 2013)

13. Martins, M.A., Madeira, A., Diaconescu, R., Barbosa, L.S.: Hybridization of institutions. In: Corradini, A., Klin, B., Cîrstea, C. (eds.) CALCO 2011. LNCS, vol. 6859, pp. 283–297. Springer, Heidelberg (2011)
14. Mossakowski, T.: Foundations of heterogeneous specification. In: Wirsing, M., Pattinson, D., Hennicker, R. (eds.) WADT 2003. LNCS, vol. 2755, pp. 359–375. Springer, Heidelberg (2003)
15. Mossakowski, T., Maeder, C., Codescu, M., Lucke, D.: HETS User Guide - Version 0.99. Technical report, DFKI Lab Bremen (April 2013)
16. Mossakowski, T., Maeder, C., Lüttich, K.: The heterogeneous tool set, HETS. In: Grumberg, O., Huth, M. (eds.) TACAS 2007. LNCS, vol. 4424, pp. 519–522. Springer, Heidelberg (2007)
17. Neves, R., Madeira, A., Martins, M.A., Barbosa, L.S.: Hybridisation at work. In: CALCO TOOLS. LNCS. Springer (to appear, 2013)
18. Schröder, L., Mossakowski, T.: Hascasl: Towards integrated specification and development of functional programs. In: Kirchner, H., Ringeissen, C. (eds.) AMAST 2002. LNCS, vol. 2422, pp. 99–116. Springer, Heidelberg (2002)
19. van Eijck, J.: Hylotab-tableau-based theorem proving for hybrid logics. Technical report, CWI, Amsterdam (2002)

Appendix: The Hybridisation Process

This appendix provides a brief overview of the hybridisation method which allows for the systematic construction of hybrid languages from arbitrary logics. The method is framed in the theory of institutions whose basic definitions are recalled.

Institutions

An *institution* is a category theoretic formalisation of a logical system, encompassing syntax, semantics and satisfaction. The concept was put forward by Goguen and Burstall, in the end of the seventies, in order to *"formalise the formal notion of logical systems"*, in response to the *"population explosion among the logical systems used in Computing Science"* [6]. Formally,

$$\mathcal{I} = (\text{Sign}^{\mathcal{I}}, \text{Sen}^{\mathcal{I}}, \text{Mod}^{\mathcal{I}}, (\models^{\mathcal{I}}_{\Sigma})_{\Sigma \in |\text{Sign}^{\mathcal{I}}|})$$

- a category $\text{Sign}^{\mathcal{I}}$ of *signatures* and *signature* morphisms,
- a functor $\text{Sen}^{\mathcal{I}} : \text{Sign}^{\mathcal{I}} \to \mathbb{S}\text{et}$ giving for each signature a set whose elements are called *sentences* over that signature,
- a functor $\text{Mod}^{\mathcal{I}} : (\text{Sign}^{\mathcal{I}})^{op} \to \mathbb{C}AT$, giving for each signature Σ a category whose objects are called Σ-*models*, and whose arrows are called Σ-*(model) homomorphisms*, and
- a relation $\models^{\mathcal{I}}_{\Sigma} \subseteq |\text{Mod}^{\mathcal{I}}(\Sigma)| \times \text{Sen}^{\mathcal{I}}(\Sigma)$ for each $\Sigma \in |\text{Sign}^{\mathcal{I}}|$, called the *satisfaction relation*,

such that for each morphism $\varphi : \Sigma \to \Sigma' \in \text{Sign}^{\mathcal{I}}$, the satisfaction condition

$$M' \models^{\mathcal{I}}_{\Sigma'} \text{Sen}^{\mathcal{I}}(\varphi)(\rho) \text{ if and only if } \text{Mod}^{\mathcal{I}}(\varphi)(M') \models^{\mathcal{I}}_{\Sigma} \rho \qquad (1)$$

holds for each $M' \in |\text{Mod}^{\mathcal{I}}(\Sigma')|$ and $\rho \in \text{Sen}^{\mathcal{I}}(\Sigma)$.

Example 1 (Propositional Logic).

A signature $Prop \in |\text{Sign}^{PL}|$ is a set of propositional variables symbols and a signature morphism is just a function $\varphi : Prop \to Prop'$ Therefore, Sign^{PL} coincides with the category $\mathbb{S}et$.

Functor Mod maps each signature $Prop$ to the category $\text{Mod}^{PL}(Prop)$ and each signature morphism φ to the reduct functor $\text{Mod}^{PL}(\varphi)$. Objects of $\text{Mod}^{PL}(Prop)$ are functions $M : Prop \to \{\top, \bot\}$ and, its morphisms, functions $h : Prop \to Prop$ such that $M(p) = M'(h(p))$. Given a signature morphism $\varphi : Prop \to Prop'$, the reduct of a model $M' \in |\text{Mod}^{PL}(Prop')|$, say $M = \text{Mod}^{PL}(\varphi)(M')$ is defined, for each $p \in Prop$, as $M(p) = M'(\varphi(p))$.

The sentences functor maps each signature $Prop$ to the set of propositional sentences $\text{Sen}^{PL}(Prop)$ and each morphism $\varphi : Prop \to Prop'$ to the sentences' translation $\text{Sen}^{PL}(\varphi) : \text{Sen}^{PL}(Prop) \to \text{Sen}^{PL}(Prop')$. The set $\text{Sen}^{PL}(Prop)$ is the usual set of propositional formulae defined by the grammar

$$\rho ::= p \mid \rho \vee \rho \mid \rho \wedge \rho \mid \rho \Rightarrow \rho \mid \neg\rho$$

for $p \in Prop$. The translation of a sentence $\text{Sen}^{PL}(\varphi)(\rho)$ is obtained by replacing each proposition of ρ by the respective φ-image. Finally, for each $Prop \in \text{Sen}^{PL}$, the satisfaction relation $\models^{PL}_{Prop}$ is defined as usual:

- $M \models^{PL}_{Prop} p$ iff $M(p) = \top$, for any $p \in Prop$;
- $M \models^{PL}_{Prop} \rho \vee \rho'$ iff $M \models^{PL}_{Prop} \rho$ or $M \models^{PL}_{Prop} \rho'$,

and similarly for the other connectives.

Example 2 (Equational logic).

Signatures in the institution EQ of equational logic are pairs (S, F) where S is a set of sort symbols and $F = \{F_{\underline{\text{ar}} \to s} \mid \underline{\text{ar}} \in S^*, s \in S\}$ is a family of sets of operation symbols indexed by arities $\underline{\text{ar}}$ (for the arguments) and sorts s (for the results). *Signature morphisms* map both components in a compatible way: they consist of pairs $\varphi = (\varphi^{\text{st}}, \varphi^{\text{op}}) : (S, F) \to (S', F')$, where $\varphi^{\text{st}} : S \to S'$ is a function, and $\varphi^{\text{op}} = \{\varphi^{\text{op}}_{\underline{\text{ar}} \to s} : F_{\underline{\text{ar}} \to s} \to F'_{\varphi^{\text{st}}(\underline{\text{ar}}) \to \varphi^{\text{st}}(s)} \mid \underline{\text{ar}} \in S^*, s \in S\}$ a family of functions mapping operations symbols respecting arities.

A model M for a signature (S, F) is an algebra interpreting each sort symbol s as a carrier set M_s and each operation symbol $\sigma \in F_{\underline{\text{ar}}} \to s$ as a function $M_\sigma : M_{\underline{\text{ar}}} \to M_s$, where $M_{\underline{\text{ar}}}$ is the product of the arguments' carriers. Model morphism are homomorphisms of algebras, i.e., S-indexed families of functions $\{h_s : M_s \to M'_s \mid s \in S\}$ such that for any $m \in M_{\underline{\text{ar}}}$, and for each $\sigma \in F_{\underline{\text{ar}} \to s}$, $h_s(M_\sigma(m)) = M'_\sigma(h_{\underline{\text{ar}}}(m))$. For each signature morphism φ, the *reduct* of a model M', say $M = \text{Mod}^{EQ}(\varphi)(M')$ is defined by $(M)_x = M'_{\varphi(x)}$ for each sort and function symbol x from the domain signature of φ. The models functor maps signatures to categories of algebras and signature morphisms to the respective reduct functors.

Sentences are universal quantified equations $(\forall X) t = t'$. Sentence translations along a signature morphism $\varphi : (S, F) \to (S', F')$, i.e., $\text{Sen}^{EQ}(\varphi) :$

$\text{Sen}^{EQ}(S, F) \to \text{Sen}^{EQ}(S', F')$, replace symbols of (S, F) by the respective φ-images in (S', F'). The sentences functor maps each signature to the set of first-order sentences and each signature morphism to the respective sentences translation. The satisfaction relation is the usual Tarskian satisfaction defined recursively on the structure of the sentences as follows:

- $M \models_{(S,F)} t = t'$ when $M_t = M_{t'}$, where M_t denotes the interpretation of the (S, F)-term t in M defined recursively by $M_{\sigma(t_1,\dots,t_n)} = M_\sigma(M_{t_1}, \dots, M_{t_n})$.
- $M \models_{(S,F)} (\forall X)\rho$ when $M' \models_{(S,F+X)} \rho$ for any $(S, F + X)$-expansion M' of M.

The Hybridisation Method

Having recalled the notion of an institution, we shall now briefly review the core of the *hybridisation* method proposed in [13,4]. For the sake of brevity, we shall restrict ourselves to a simplified (quantifier-free and non-constrained) version of the general method.

As explained in the paper, the method enriches a base (arbitrary) institution $\mathcal{I} = (\text{Sign}^{\mathcal{I}}, \text{Sen}^{\mathcal{I}}, \text{Mod}^{\mathcal{I}}, (\models_{\Sigma}^{\mathcal{I}})_{\Sigma \in |\text{Sign}^{\mathcal{I}}|})$ with hybrid logic features and the corresponding Kripke semantics. The result is still an institution, $\mathcal{HI}$, called the *hybridisation of $\mathcal{I}$*.

The category of $\mathcal{HI}$-signatures. The base signature is enriched with nominals and polyadic modalities. Therefore, the category of $\mathcal{I}$-*hybrid signatures*, denoted by $\text{Sign}^{\mathcal{HI}}$, is defined as the direct (cartesian) product of categories:

$$\text{Sign}^{\mathcal{HI}} = \text{Sign}^{\mathcal{I}} \times \text{Sign}^{REL}.$$

Thus, signatures are triples $(\Sigma, \text{Nom}, \Lambda)$, where $\Sigma \in |\text{Sign}^{\mathcal{I}}|$ and, in the *REL*-signature (Nom, Λ), Nom is a set of constants called *nominals* and Λ is a set of relational symbols called *modalities*; Λ_n stands for the set of modalities of arity n. Morphisms $\varphi \in \text{Sign}^{\mathcal{HI}}((\Sigma, \text{Nom}, \Lambda), (\Sigma', \text{Nom}', \Lambda'))$ are triples $\varphi = (\varphi_{\text{Sig}}, \varphi_{\text{Nom}}, \varphi_{\text{MS}})$ where $\varphi_{\text{Sig}} \in \text{Sign}^{\mathcal{I}}(\Sigma, \Sigma')$, $\varphi_{\text{Nom}} : \text{Nom} \to \text{Nom}'$ is a function and $\varphi_{\text{MS}} = (\varphi_n : \Lambda_n \to \Lambda'_n)_{n \in \mathbb{N}}$ a $\mathbb{N}$-family of functions mapping nominals and $n - ary$-modality symbols, respectively.

$\mathcal{HI}$-sentences functor. The second step is to enrich the base sentences accordingly. The sentences of the base institution and the nominals are taken as atoms and composed with the boolean connectives, modalities, and satisfaction operators as follows: $\text{Sen}^{\mathcal{HI}}(\Sigma, \text{Nom}, \Lambda)$ is the least set such that

- $\text{Nom} \subseteq \text{Sen}^{\mathcal{HI}}(\Delta)$;
- $\text{Sen}^{\mathcal{I}}(\Sigma) \subseteq \text{Sen}^{\mathcal{HI}}(\Delta)$;
- $\rho \star \rho' \in \text{Sen}^{\mathcal{HI}}(\Delta)$ for any $\rho, \rho' \in \text{Sen}^{\mathcal{HI}}(\Delta)$ and any $\star \in \{\vee, \wedge, \Rightarrow\}$,
- $\neg\rho \in \text{Sen}^{\mathcal{HI}}(\Delta)$, for any $\rho \in \text{Sen}^{\mathcal{HI}}(\Delta)$,
- $@_i\rho \in \text{Sen}^{\mathcal{HI}}(\Delta)$ for any $\rho \in \text{Sen}^{\mathcal{HI}}(\Delta)$ and $i \in \text{Nom}$;
- $[\lambda](\rho_1, \dots, \rho_n), \langle\lambda\rangle(\rho_1, \dots, \rho_n) \in \text{Sen}^{\mathcal{HI}}(\Delta)$, for any $\lambda \in \Lambda_{n+1}, \rho_i \in \text{Sen}^{\mathcal{HI}}(\Delta), i \in \{1, \dots, n\}$.

Given a morphism $\varphi = (\varphi_{\text{Sig}}, \varphi_{\text{Nom}}, \varphi_{\text{MS}}) : (\Sigma, \text{Nom}, \Lambda) \to (\Sigma', \text{Nom}', \Lambda')$, the translation of sentences $\text{Sen}^{\mathcal{HI}}(\varphi)$ is defined as follows:

- $\text{Sen}^{\mathcal{HI}}(\varphi)(\rho) = \text{Sen}^{\mathcal{I}}(\varphi_{\text{Sig}})(\rho)$ for any $\rho \in \text{Sen}^{\mathcal{I}}(\Sigma)$;
- $\text{Sen}^{\mathcal{HI}}(\varphi)(i) = \varphi_{\text{Nom}}(i)$;
- $\text{Sen}^{\mathcal{HI}}(\varphi)(\neg\rho) = \neg\text{Sen}^{\mathcal{HI}}(\varphi)(\rho)$;
- $\text{Sen}^{\mathcal{HI}}(\varphi)(\rho \star \rho') = \text{Sen}^{\mathcal{HI}}(\varphi)(\rho) \star \text{Sen}^{\mathcal{HI}}(\varphi)(\rho')$, $\star \in \{\vee, \wedge, \Rightarrow\}$;
- $\text{Sen}^{\mathcal{HI}}(\varphi)(@_i\rho) = @_{\varphi_{\text{Nom}}(i)}\text{Sen}^{\mathcal{HI}}(\rho)$;
- $\text{Sen}^{\mathcal{HI}}(\varphi)([\lambda](\rho_1, \ldots, \rho_n)) = [\varphi_{\text{MS}}(\lambda)](\text{Sen}^{\mathcal{HI}}(\rho_1), \ldots, \text{Sen}^{\mathcal{HI}}(\rho_n))$;
- $\text{Sen}^{\mathcal{HI}}(\varphi)(\langle\lambda\rangle(\rho_1, \ldots, \rho_n)) = \langle\varphi_{\text{MS}}(\lambda)\rangle(\text{Sen}^{\mathcal{HI}}(\rho_1), \ldots, \text{Sen}^{\mathcal{HI}}(\rho_n))$.

$\mathcal{HI}$-models functor. Models of the hybridised logic $\mathcal{HI}$ can be regarded as $(\Lambda\text{-})$Kripke structures whose worlds are $\mathcal{I}$-models. Formally $(\Sigma, \text{Nom}, \Lambda)$-*models* are pairs (M, W) where

- W is a (Nom, Λ)-model in REL;
- M is a function $|W| \to |\text{Mod}^{\mathcal{I}}(\Sigma)|$.

In each world (M, W), $\{W_n \mid n \in \text{Nom}\}$ provides interpretations for *nominals* in Nom, whereas relations $\{W_\lambda \mid \lambda \in \Lambda_n, n \in \omega\}$ interprete *modalities* in Λ. We denote $M(w)$ simply by M_w. The reduct definition is lifted from the base institution: the reduct of a Δ'-model (M', W') along a signature morphism $\varphi = (\varphi_{\text{Sig}}, \varphi_{\text{Nom}}, \varphi_{\text{MS}}) : \Delta \to \Delta'$, denoted by $\text{Mod}^{\mathcal{HI}}(\varphi)(M', W')$, is the Δ-model (M, W) such that

- W is the $(\varphi_{\text{Nom}}, \varphi_{\text{MS}})$-reduct of W'; i.e.
  - $|W| = |W'|$;
  - for any $n \in \text{Nom}, W_n = W'_{\varphi_{\text{Nom}}(n)}$;
  - for any $\lambda \in \Lambda, W_\lambda = W'_{\varphi_{\text{MS}}(\lambda)}$;

  and
- for any $w \in |W|, M_w = \text{Mod}^{\mathcal{I}}(\varphi_{\text{Sig}})(M'_w)$.

Satisfaction. Let $(\Sigma, \text{Nom}, \Lambda) \in |\text{Sign}^{\mathcal{HI}}|$ and $(M, W) \in |\text{Mod}^{\mathcal{HI}}(\Sigma, \text{Nom}, \Lambda)|$. For any $w \in |W|$ we define:

- $(M, W) \models^w \rho$ iff $M_w \models^{\mathcal{I}} \rho$; when $\rho \in \text{Sen}^{\mathcal{I}}(\Sigma)$,
- $(M, W) \models^w i$ iff $W_i = w$; when $i \in \text{Nom}$,
- $(M, W) \models^w \rho \vee \rho'$ iff $(M, W) \models^w \rho$ or $(M, W) \models^w \rho'$,
- $(M, W) \models^w \rho \wedge \rho'$ iff $(M, W) \models^w \rho$ and $(M, W) \models^w \rho'$,
- $(M, W) \models^w \rho \Rightarrow \rho'$ iff $(M, W) \models^w \rho$ implies that $(M, W) \vdash^w \rho'$,
- $(M, W) \models^w \neg\rho$ iff $(M, W) \not\models^w \rho$,
- $(M, W) \models^w [\lambda](\xi_1, \ldots, \xi_n)$ iff for any $(w, w_1, \ldots, w_n) \in W_\lambda$ we have that $(M, W) \models^{w_i} \xi_i$ for some $1 \leq i \leq n$.
- $(M, W) \models^w \langle\lambda\rangle(\xi_1, \ldots, \xi_n)$ iff there exists $(w, w_1, \ldots, w_n) \in W_\lambda$ such that and $(M, W) \models^{w_i} \xi_i$ for any $1 \leq i \leq n$.
- $(M, W) \models^w @_j\rho$ iff $(M, W) \models^{W_j} \rho$.

We write $(M, W) \models \rho$ iff $(M, W) \models^w \rho$ for any $w \in |W|$.

Theorem 1 ([13]). *Let $\Delta = (\Sigma, \text{Nom}, \Lambda)$ and $\Delta' = (\Sigma', \text{Nom}', \Lambda')$ be two $\mathcal{HI}$-signatures and $\varphi : \Delta \to \Delta'$ a morphism of signatures. For any $\rho \in \text{Sen}^{\mathcal{HI}}(\Delta)$, $(M', W') \in |\text{Mod}^C(\Delta')|$, and $w \in |W|$,*

$$\text{Mod}^{\mathcal{HI}}(\varphi)(M', W') \models^w \rho \text{ iff } (M', W') \models^w \text{Sen}^{\mathcal{HI}}(\varphi)(\rho).$$

The method can be illustrated through its application to the two institutions described above and used in the paper: those of propositional and equational logics.

Example 3 ($\mathcal{HPL}$). The hybridisation of the propositional logic institution *PL* is an institution where signatures are triples $(Prop, \text{Nom}, \Lambda)$ and sentences are generated by

$$\rho ::= \rho_0 \mid i \mid @_i\rho \mid \rho \odot \rho \mid \neg\rho \mid \langle\lambda\rangle(\rho, \ldots, \rho) \mid [\lambda](\rho, \ldots, \rho) \tag{2}$$

where $\rho_0 \in \text{Sen}^{PL}(Prop)$, $i \in \text{Nom}$, $\lambda \in \Lambda_n$ and $\odot = \{\vee, \wedge, \Rightarrow\}$. Note there is a double level of connectives in the sentences: the one coming from base *PL*-sentences and another introduced by the hybridisation process. However, they "semantically collapse" and, hence, no distinction between them needs to be done (see [4] for details). A $(Prop, \text{Nom}, \Lambda)$-model is a pair (M, W), where W is a transition structure with a set of worlds $|W|$. Constants $W_i, i \in \text{Nom}$ stand for the named worlds and $(n+1)$-ary relations W_λ, $\lambda \in \Lambda_n$ are the accessibility relations characterising the structure. For each world $w \subset |W|$, $M(w)$ is a (local) *PL*-model, assigning propositions in *Prop* to the world w.

Restricting the signatures to those with just a single unary modality (i.e., where $\Lambda_1 = \{\lambda\}$ and $\Lambda_n = \emptyset$ for the remaining $n \neq 1$), results in the usual institution for classical hybrid propositional logic [2].

Example 4 ($\mathcal{HEQ}$). Signatures of $\mathcal{HEQ}$ are triples $((S, F), \text{Nom}, \Lambda)$ and the sentences defined as in (2), but taking (S, F)-equations $(\forall X)t = t'$ as atomic base sentences. Models are Kripke structures with a (local)-(S, F)-algebra per state. Distinct configurations are therefore modeled by distinct algebras and reconfigurations expressed by transitions over a graph of algebras (cf., [11,10]).

Contextual Abstraction in a Type System for Component-Based High Performance Computing Platforms

Francisco Heron de Carvalho Junior, Cenez Araújo Rezende,
Jefferson de Carvalho Silva, and Wagner Guimarães Al-Alam

Pós-Graduao em Ciência da Computação,
Universidade Federal do Ceará, Brazil
{heron,cenezaraujo,jeffersoncarvalho,alalam}@lia.ufc.br

Abstract. This paper presents the formalization of HTS (Hash Type
System), a type system for component-based high performance computing (CBHPC) platforms. HTS aims at supporting an automated
approach for dynamic discovering, loading and binding of parallel components. HTS gives support for building multiple implementations of
abstract components, the performance of which are tuned according to
the specific features of high-end distributed-memory parallel computing
platforms and the application requirements, through context abstraction.

1 Introduction

Grids [16] and clouds [4] have introduced a new class of large-scale HPC platforms formed by heterogeneous collections of computational *resources*. Such
platforms aim at enabling applications with outstanding impact in scientific
discovery and technological innovation, leading to an ever-increasing scale and
complexity of software in HPC. At the same time, the hardware complexity has
increased due to heterogeneous parallel computing [18], making the tuning of the
software performance according to the particular characteristics of each target
parallel computing architecture important. So, there is an increasing need of new
programming models, techniques and abstractions to face these challenges.

Components are independent units of software composition with well-defined
interfaces, subject to independent deployment and third-party composition [23].
The research on component-based high performance computing (CBHPC) platforms investigate how to use components in dealing with scale and complexity of
modern HPC software, subject to the heterogeneity of parallel computing platforms [18]. CCA (Common Component Architecture) [5], Fractal [8], and GCM
(Grid Component Model) [7] are the most prominent CBHPC initiatives, which
have presented successful case studies using real applications.

Our main contribution to CBHPC is the Hash component model, which faces
the lack of both expressive and efficient models of parallel components and their
connectors [11]. HPE (Hash Programming Environment) is the reference implementation of Hash, as a platform for managing the life-cycle of parallel components, so-called #-components, in cluster computing platforms [13,15].

A. Rauber Du Bois and P. Trinder (Eds.): SBLP 2013, LNCS 8129, pp. 90–104, 2013.
© Springer-Verlag Berlin Heidelberg 2013

In a parallel computing system, the best algorithms and parallelism strategies for implementing its software parts is highly dependent on the architecture of the target parallel computing platform [17]. In the context of CBHPC platforms, we are interested in addressing the problem of selecting the best implementation for each component of a parallel computing system according to a *context*, from a set of alternative implementations cataloged in a library. A context is an abstraction for the characteristics of parallel computing systems that influence their performance. The relevance of this problem has increased with the emerging of heterogeneous parallel computing platforms [18] as resources of grids and clouds. For addressing it, this paper introduces HTS (Hash Type System), the type system developed for HPE. HTS aims at minimizing the end-user intervention by delegating the decisions in the implementation of components to parallel computing specialists. For that, it is based on a kind of contractual interface, so-called *abstract component*, which represents a set of components that address a well-defined concern. The implementation of each component is tuned according to a set of context parameters. The contextual abstraction distinguishes HTS from the other component adaptability approaches of CBHPC platforms.

Following this introduction, Section 2 presents the Hash Component model and its reference implementation, HPE, where HTS has been implemented and validated, followed by an overview of related works. Section 3 provides an intuitive introduction to the abstractions behind HTS, such as *abstract components*, *contexts* and *resolution*, also presenting a case study with simulated applications from NPB (NAS Parallel Benchmarks). Section 4 presents a mathematical formalization of HTS on top of a composition calculus, with the purpose of proving its relevant safety properties. Finally, Section 5 concludes this paper, by discussing its contributions, limitations, and lines for further works with HTS.

2 Background

The Hash component model brings to CBHPC a general concept of parallel component - the so-called *#-component*, formed by a set of *units* that represent processes running at distinct processing nodes of a parallel computing platform. Like Fractal, a #-component may be composed from other #-components, the so-called *inner components*, by *overlapping composition* [12]. For that, an *overlapping function* maps the units of the inner components to the units of the #-component. Each mapping defines a *slice* of the target unit.

A *configuration* specifies the units, inner components and overlapping function of a #-component, using an architecture description language (ADL).

As a consequence of overlapping composition, the slices of a unit belongs to the same process, communicating with each other directly through the same address space. Thus, a #-component may coordinate its inner components through local procedure calls (*inter-component interactions*), whereas the units of a #-component may communicate through message-passing (*intra-component interactions*). In doing so, #-components may encapsulate patterns of parallel computation and communication, also minimizing the cost of component bindings.

A component platform that complies with the Hash component model supports distributed units, overlapping composition and a set of *component kinds*.

Component kinds group #-components that comply with the same component model. They are like *meta-components* of SCIJump [21], but also used for introducing new programming abstractions to a CBHPC platform, possibly oriented to specific application domains. For example, it provides support for libraries of reusable connectors [10] and the distinction of #-components according to the kind of HPC resources they represent in a cloud-based CBHPC platform. Other component platforms support a single component kind and a pre-defined set of connectors, making it difficult dealing with the heterogeneity and evolution of parallel computing platforms. For that, they often deal with non-functional concerns by introducing orthogonal abstractions, such as controllers (Fractal), indirect bindings and cohorts (CCA) and collective ports (GCM).

HPE (*Hash Programming Environment*)[1] is a general purpose CBHPC platform which complies with CCA and the Hash component model, targeted at cluster computing platforms [13,9]. It supports eight component kinds: *computations, data structures, synchronizers, topologies, platforms, environments, applications*, and *features*. HPE faces the problem of supporting a fully expressive and simple definition of parallel component in a CBHPC platform, with minimal intrinsic performance overhead compared to monolithic code [15].

HPE is a choreography of services of three types: the FRONT-END, from which a programmer build configurations and implementations of #-components, and control their life cycle; the CORE, for cataloging #-components in a distributed library; and the BACK-END, for managing a parallel computing platform where #-components are deployed and execute.

The FRONT-END accesses the services of the CORE for cataloging user-defined configurations and retrieving configurations for overlapping composition. Also, it accesses the services of the BACK-END for executing #-components of kind application, retrieved from the CORE. From the CORE, when loading an application, the BACK-END discovers and retrieves the implementation of each #-component of the application which is the best tuned to its parallel computing platform, and also according to the application requirements.

In CBHPC, the works on dynamic adaptation of components have relation with HTS [14,2,19]. The relevance of this topic in grid platforms [3] has motivated GCM designers to support general *autonomic computing* capabilities. These works address the problem of supporting runtime changes in component configuration and/or implementation according to the evolving conditions of the parallel system. In general, they require monitoring a set of pre-defined parameters of system evolution, and reconfiguration actions must be known a priori. However, the autonomic computing capabilities of GCM make possible ad-hoc reconfigurations, by supporting appropriate non-functional controllers. *Behavioural skeletons* have proposed the idea of capturing adaptation patterns in common patterns of parallel computations [1].

---

[1] The HPE code is hosted at http://hash-programming-environment.googlecode.com

P-COM^2 [24], a CBHPC platform developed in a research work outside CCA and GCM initiatives, has a closer relation with HTS. It proposes a compile-time solution based on self-describing components with *associative interfaces*. They are contractual interfaces that carry information used for selection and matching of components (*profile*) and formal descriptions of their interactions, behaviour and safety properties (*state machine* and *protocol*) through ASL (Architecture Specification Language). The profiles are related to HTS contexts. P-COM^2 focuses on the problems of encapsulating legacy code and formal analysis of components behavior and interactions. Both are subject to dynamic reconfiguration through orthogonal mechanisms, but HTS provides more flexibility for tuning components, since it is not restricted to a fixed set of possible assumptions, like that ones supported by ASL.

$$\langle context\_signature \rangle := \text{COMPONENT\_ID} \ [\langle param_1 \rangle, \langle param_2 \rangle, \cdots, \langle param_n \rangle]$$
$$\langle param \rangle := \boldsymbol{parameter\_id} = CTX\_VAR : \langle instantiation\_type \rangle$$
$$\langle instantiation\_type \rangle := \text{COMPONENT\_ID} \ [\langle arg_1 \rangle, \langle arg_2 \rangle, ..., \langle arg_n \rangle]$$
$$\langle arg \rangle := \boldsymbol{parameter\_id} = \langle instantiation\_type \rangle \ | \ \boldsymbol{parameter\_id} = CTX\_VAR$$

Fig. 1. Abstract Syntax of Abstract Component Signatures and Instantiation Types

3 Contextual Abstraction through Abstract Components

An *abstract component* is the type of a set of #-components representing distinct implementations of a given concern. It is abstracted away, through the so-called *contextual abstraction*, from a set of assumptions about how each #-component must be implemented according to the features of the target parallel computing platform and the application to which it will be bound.

The configuration of an abstract component describes the units, inner components and the overlapping function of the #-components it represents. Also, it describes a *context signature*. Figure 1 presents a simple syntax for representing context signatures ($\langle context\_signature \rangle$). They are defined by the *name* of the abstract component (COMPONENT_ID) and a set of *context parameters* ($\langle param \rangle$), each one having a *name* (**parameter_id**), a *context variable* (CTX_VAR) and a *bound*, defined by an instantiation type ($\langle instantiation\_type \rangle$).

An *instantiation type* is recursively defined by a pair of a name of an abstract component and a set of *context arguments* ($\langle arg \rangle$), each one defined by an instantiation type and associated to a context parameter of the abstract component though its name. The context argument must be a subtype of the *bound* of the context parameter.

An instantiation type is *open* if it has at least one context parameter which is not associated neither with a context argument nor with a variable identifier of the enclosing configuration, so-called a *free context parameter*. Otherwise, it is *close*. We say that two free context parameters are *binded* if they have the same variable identifier.

The inner components of a configuration and #-components are typed by instantiation types. Different combinations of context arguments lead to distinct contexts. In execution time, a #-component whose instantiation type is *closer* to the instantiation type of each inner component of a #-component instantiated from a configuration will be chosen by a *resolution algorithm*, constrained by the the subtyping relation. The resolution algorithm will be presented in Section 3.2. Before it, the next section presents an example that provide more intuition for abstract components and contextual abstraction.

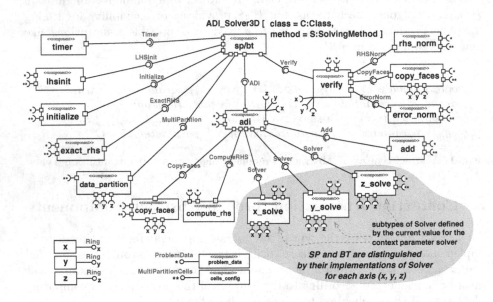

Fig. 2. **SP/BT** Configuration Architecture [15]

3.1   Case Study: SP and BT from the NAS Parallel Benchmarks

The NAS Parallel Benchmarks (NPB) [6] is a software package for evaluating the performance of parallel computers, comprising 8 programs. **SP** (Scalar-Pentadiagonal Linear System Solver), **BT** (Block-Tridiagonal Linear System Solver), **LU** (LU factorization) and **FT** (Fourier Transform) have been translated to C#/MPI.NET and refactored into components for evaluating the performance of HPE [15]. **SP** and **BT** demonstrate the ability of changing the component architecture of an application through dynamic context changing.

SP and **BT** are alternative implementations of the alternating direct implicit (ADI) method for solving three sets of uncoupled 3D systems of equations. Thus, they have similar architectures, as depicted in Figure 2. HTS captures the similarities between them, which are not clear in the original versions. Automated resolution and binding have made it possible to configure an abstract component ADI_SOLVER3D of kind *application*, which can be instantiated to **SP** or **BT**

according to the choices of its context arguments in instantiation types, isolating their differences in the *solver* components as depicted in Figure 2.

ADI_SOLVER3D has two context parameters: **method**, bound by SOLVING-METHOD, defining the solving method; and **class**, bound by CLASS, specifying the problem class. SPMETHOD and BTMETHOD are the subtypes of SOLVING-METHOD that distinguish the solvers of **SP** and **BT**, by supplying **method**. In turn, the subtypes of CLASS are CLASS_W and CLASS_A, representing default workloads of NPB. A generic #-component ADI_Solver3DImpl implements the instantiation type ADI_SOLVER3D[**method** = SOLVINGMETHOD, **class** = CLASS]. For instance, one may run **SP** on the problem class A by submitting ADI_SOLVER3D[**method** = SPMETHOD, **class** = CLASS_A] to the BACK-END of HPE. The resolution algorithm will find ADI_Solver3DImpl and instantiate it by applying the context arguments of the submitted instantiation type, which are recursively passed to the inner components.

During execution, one may change **method** from SPMETHOD to BTMETHOD, causing disconnection of all the #-components binded to inner components whose instantiation types depends on **method** and whose available #-components are distinguished by it, such as **adi**, **x_solve**, **y_solve** and **z_solve** (Figure 2).

x_solve, **y_solve** and **z_solve** are inner components of **adi**, typed by ADI with the argument to **method**. The #-components of ADI may be ADIImpl, if **method**=BTMETHOD, and SP_ADIImpl, if **method**=SPMETHOD. SP_ADIImpl is a #-component of SP_ADI, which is derived from ADI by adding the inner component **txinvr** and freezing the context parameter **method** to SP-METHOD (see inheritance operations in Section 4.3), not shown in Figure 2. Thus, a change of **method** from BTMETHOD to SPMETHOD reconfigures **adi** from an instance of ADIImpl to an instance of SP_ADIImpl, to which the existing **copy_faces**, **compute_rhs** and **add** are reconnected and **txinvr** is instantiated and connected. Finally, **x_solve**, **y_solve** and **z_solve** are changed from impl.sp.solve.SolverImpl to impl.bt.solve.SolverImpl, by keeping the old instances of **problem_data** and **cells_info** since they do not depend on **method**. They represent the data structures processed by the application, i. e. its state.

3.2   Resolution Algorithm

The *resolution algorithm* looks for a #-component that matches an instantiation type, by traversing the its subtypes in a certain order. Subtypes are determined at each step by generalizing the next non-free context parameter, in the order they are declared in the instantiation type. Thus, by controlling the order in which context parameters are specified in an instantiation type, a programmer may give priority to the most critical assumptions about the implementation of the given abstract component, according to the application needs. This is the reason for using names, instead of the position, to refer to context parameters.

Let $C\left[par_1 = X_1 : B_1^X, par_2 = X_2 : B_2^X, \cdots, par_m = X_m : B_m^X\right]$ represent the abstract component C, where $\{X_1, X_2, \ldots, X_m\}$ are context variables and $\{B_1^X, B_2^X, \ldots, B_m^X\}$ are instantiation types (bounds). Let $\{Y_1, Y_2, \ldots, Y_q\}$ be the free context variables in $B_1^X, B_2^X, \ldots, B_n^X$, bounded by $\{B_1^Y, B_2^Y, \ldots, B_q^Y\}$, respectively. Finally, let $\mathcal{T} \equiv C\left[par_{i_1} = A_1, par_{i_2} = A_2, \cdots, par_{i_n} = A_n\right]$, where $\{par_{i_1}, par_{i_2}, \cdots, par_{i_n}\} \subseteq \{par_1, par_2, \cdots, par_m\}$ and $A_k <: B_{i_k}^X$, for $k \in \{1, 2, \ldots, n\}$, be the instantiation type of an inner component ι of some configuration. The following resolution algorithm will look for a #-component for matching the instantiation type $\mathcal{T}$, which will be bound to ι:

1. Let C_i be the abstract component of A_i, for $i \in \{1, \ldots, n\}$;
2. For $i \in \{1, 2, \ldots, n\}$, let C_i^j be the j-th supertype of C_i, where $C_i^0 \equiv C_i$ and C_i^j is the direct supertype of C_i^{j-1} by inheritance, if it exists;
3. Let $\mathcal{R}$ be a *resolution tree*, whose root is labeled C_0^0. For $i \in \{1, 2, \ldots, n-1\}$, a node labeled C_i^j has sons with labels $C_{i+1}^0, C_{i+1}^1, \ldots, C_{i+1}^{k_i}$, where $C_{i+1}^{k_i}$ is the top-level supertype of C_{i+1}^0;
4. Do a pre-order depth-first traversing of $\mathcal{R}$. At each visit to a leaf node, $\{C_1^{j_1}, C_2^{j_2}, \ldots, C_n^{j_n}\}$ include the labels of the nodes in the path from the root to the leaf. By construction, they are valid context arguments for $par_{i_1}, par_{i_2}, \ldots, par_{i_n}$, respectively, which are the non-free context parameters of $\mathcal{T}$. Then, perform the following operations:
   (a) Build an instantiation type $\mathcal{T}'$ from $\mathcal{T}$, by defining the instantiation types $A_1', A_2', \ldots, A_n'$ by replacing $C_1^{j_1}, C_2^{j_2}, \ldots, C_n^{j_n}$ for $C_1, C_2, \ldots, C_n$ in $A_1, A_2, \ldots, A_n$, respectively, and then by replacing $A_1', A_2', \ldots, A_n'$ for $A_1, A_2, \ldots, A_n$ in $\mathcal{T}$, in such a way that the occurrences of the context variables $X_{i_1}, X_{i_2}, \ldots, X_{i_n}$ of the signature of C have $A_1', A_2', \ldots, A_n'$ as context arguments in $\mathcal{T}'$;
   (b) Look at the environment of #-components for a #-component whose instantiation type matches $\mathcal{T}'$ in their closed context arguments.
   (c) If a #-component is found, abort the traversal and return it;
5. If all nodes have been visited, and no #-component has been found, an exception is raised informing that a #-component that fits the instantiation type of the ι does not exist in the environment of #-components.

The resolution algorithm assumes that a #-component of an abstract component C is also registered as a #-component of any abstract component C', such that C' is a supertype of C. By subtyping inheritance, this is a valid assumption, since C implements the concern of C'. Using this approach, the inner component **adi** of ADI_SOLVER3D, typed by ADI, may be supplied by a #-component of its subtype SP_ADI, derived by inheritance from ADI as pointed out in the previous section. This occurs when instantiating **SP**, when the context parameter *method* of ADI in the type of **adi** is supplied with SPMETHOD. This is possible because SP_ADIImpl is registered as a subtype of both ADI and SP_ADI. Inheritance derivation is formally discussed in Section 4.3.

4   Formalization and Safety Properties

This section presents τHOC^3 (Hash Overlapping Component Composition Calculus), a calculus for hierarchical composition of #-components, where they are

$$
\begin{aligned}
\mathtt{t} \longrightarrow\ & x && \textit{variable}\\
& \mathtt{t\ t} && \textit{application}\\
& \lambda x.\mathtt{t} && \textit{untyped \#-component functor}\\
& \left(\mathtt{u}_i{}^{\,i=1...k}\right) && \textit{\#-component instance}\\
\mathtt{u} \longrightarrow\ & l \dashrightarrow \langle \mathtt{u}_i{}^{\,i=1...k}\rangle && \textit{slice composition}\\
& l && \textit{base slice}\\
& x.l && \textit{slice projection variable}\\
\mathtt{v} \longrightarrow\ & \lambda x.\mathtt{t} && \textit{untyped \#-component functor}\\
& \left(\mathtt{u}_i{}^{\,i=1...k}\right) && \textit{\#-component instance}
\end{aligned}
$$

Fig. 3. $\tau\mathsf{HOC}^3$ - Untyped Fragment (Syntax)

functions whose arguments are inner components combined, by overlapping composition, for defining their units. It is aimed at reasoning about HTS.

Figure 3 and 5 show the syntax and composition semantics of terms (t) of $\tau\mathsf{HOC}^3$, respectively. The composition semantics presents reduction rules for mapping terms to non-reducible terms, which may be either a *stuck term* or a *value* (v). A value represents a *#-component instance*. A well-formed term, i. e. a term that can be reduced to a value, represents a configuration. HPE uses a second-order fragment of $\tau\mathsf{HOC}^3$, since inner components (parameters) of #-components are always supplied with *#-component instances* (value arguments).

A *#-component instance* is defined by a non-empty set of units. Each unit is a rooted labeled directly acyclic graph (DAG), the so-called *unit graph*, whose label is defined by the label of the root. The other nodes represent the slices of the unit, whose labels are labels of units of overlapped inner components. In a unit graph of a *#-component functor*, a *slice projection variable* $x.l$ refers to the unit labeled l of the #-component in the argument x. After an application, if x is a *#-component instance* with a unit labeled l, $x.l$ refers to its *unit graph*, i. e. $\left(\mathtt{u}_i{}^{\,i=1...k}\right).l \equiv u_j$, for some $j \in \{1, \cdots, k\}$ such that $label\,(u_j) = l$, where $label\,(l) = l$ and $label\,\left(l \dashrightarrow \langle s_i{}^{\,i=1...k}\rangle\right) = l$.

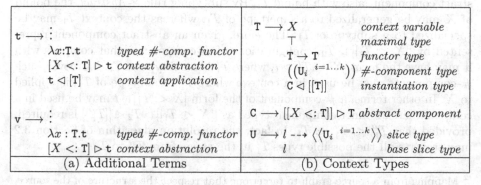

Fig. 4. $\tau\mathsf{HOC}^3$ - Typed Fragment (Syntax)

Figure 4 presents the typed fragment of $\tau\mathsf{HOC}^3$, aimed at reasoning about *abstract components* and *instantiation types*. *Context abstraction* terms represent configurations that abstract away from the types of its constituent terms through context parameters. The context arguments may be supplied by means of *context application* terms (reduction rules *E-TApp* and *E-TAppTAbs*). Typing and subtyping relations are defined in Figures 6 and 7, respectively. For type variables and functor types, typing and subtyping rules are inherited from the specifications of the typed λ-calculus [22].

$$\frac{\Sigma \vdash t_1 \to t_1'}{\Sigma \vdash t_1 \; t_2 \to t_1' \; t_2} \qquad \frac{\Sigma \vdash t_2 \to t_2'}{\Sigma \vdash v_1 \; t_2 \to v_1 \; t_2'} \qquad \Sigma \vdash (\lambda x{:}T.t_1) \; v_2 \to [x \longmapsto v_2] \; t_1$$
$$\text{(E-App1)} \qquad\qquad \text{(E-App2)} \qquad\qquad\qquad \text{(E-AppAbs)}$$

$$\frac{\Sigma \vdash t_1 \to t_1'}{\Sigma \vdash t_1 \lhd [T_1] \to t_1' \lhd [T_1]} \qquad \Sigma \vdash ([X <: T_1] \rhd t_1) \lhd [T_2] \to [X \longmapsto T_2] \; t_1$$
$$\text{(E-TApp)} \qquad\qquad\qquad\qquad \text{(E-TAppTAbs)}$$

Fig. 5. $\tau\mathsf{HOC}^3$ (Reduction Rules - Composition Semantics)

According to the typing rule *T-Max*, any type is a subtype of $\top$, representing the *maximal type* of HTS. Therefore, a term $\lambda x.t$ is equivalent to $\lambda x{:}\top.t$.

Types of #-*component instances* are also represented by rooted DAG's of labeled units, excepting for *slice projection variables*. Therefore, in the subtyping rule *S-Hash*, $U_i \overset{hom}{\longmapsto} U_i'{}^{\;i=1\ldots k}$ means that there is a graph homomorphism [2] from the unit type U_i to the unit type U_i', for each $i \in \{1, \cdots, n\}$, i. e. a unit typed as U_i' has the slices and the same root of a unit typed as U_i.

An *instantiation type* has two parts, separated by $\lhd$: an *abstract component*, represented by the syntax variable C, and a type, representing the *context argument*. The typing rule *T-TAbs* defines that a term $[X <: T_1] \rhd t$ represents a configuration of a #-component of an *abstract component* $[[X <: T_1]] \rhd T_2$ for the *context* defined by T_1, where X denotes the context parameter of the abstract component, also with bound T_1. By subtyping rule *S-Abstract*, the bound of X may be generalized to a supertype of T_1, whereas the context T_1 may be specialized to a subtype of T_1. Therefore, given an abstract component represented by $[[X <: T_1]] \rhd T_2$, configurations of #-components that complies with it may have the form $[X <: T_1'] \rhd t$, where T_1' is a subtype of T_1. Moreover, such #-components may be used in a context where T_1'', a subtype of T_1', is applied to X. In other terms, a #-component of the form $[X <: T_1'] \rhd t$ may be used in a context where an inner component typed as $[[X <: T_1]] \rhd T_2 \lhd [[T_1'']]$ is required, provided that $T_1'' <: T_1' <: T_1$. In fact, the resolution algorithm of Section 3.2 may traverse all the possible types T_1' in the range from T_1'' to T_1.

---

[2] Mapping from a source graph to target one that respect the structure of the source, i. e. adjacent vertices of the source are mapped to adjacent vertices of the target.

$$\frac{\Gamma_i \vdash u_i : U_i \quad ^{i=1...n}}{\Gamma \vdash (u_i\ ^{i=1...n}) : ((U_i\ ^{i=1...n}))}$$
$$(T\text{-}Base1)$$

$$\frac{l_1 = l_2 \quad \Gamma_i \vdash u_i : U_i \quad ^{i=1...k}}{\Gamma \vdash l_1 \dashrightarrow \langle u_i\ ^{i=1...k}\rangle : l_2 \dashrightarrow \langle U_i\ ^{i=1...k}\rangle}$$
$$(T\text{-}Base2)$$

$$\Gamma \vdash l : l \qquad \frac{\Gamma \vdash x : ((U_i\ ^{i=1...n})) \quad label(U) = l \quad U \in \{U_1,\dots,U_n\}}{\Gamma \vdash x.l : U} \qquad \frac{x : T \in \Gamma}{\Gamma \vdash x : T}$$
$$(T\text{-}Base3) \hspace{4cm} (T\text{-}Base4) \hspace{4cm} (T\text{-}Var)$$

$$\frac{\Gamma, x : T_1 \vdash t : T_2}{\Gamma \vdash \lambda x{:}T_1.t : T_1 \to T_2} \qquad \frac{\Gamma \vdash t_1 : T_{11}\to T_{12} \quad \Gamma \vdash t_2 : T_{11}}{\Gamma \vdash t_1\ t_2 : T_{12}} \qquad \frac{\Gamma \vdash t : T' \quad \Gamma \vdash T' <: T}{\Gamma \vdash t : T}$$
$$(T\text{-}Abs) \hspace{3.5cm} (T\text{-}App) \hspace{3.5cm} (T\text{-}Sub)$$

$$\frac{\Gamma, X <: T_1 \vdash t : T_2}{\Gamma \vdash [X <: T_1] \triangleright t : [[X <: T_1]] \triangleright T_2 \triangleleft [[T_1]]} \qquad \frac{\Gamma \vdash t : [[X <: T_1]] \triangleright T_2 \triangleleft [[T_1]]}{\Gamma \vdash t \triangleleft [T_1] : T_2}$$
$$(T\text{-}TAbs) \hspace{5cm} (T\text{-}TApp)$$

Fig. 6. $\tau\mathsf{HOC}^3$ (Typing Relation)

4.1 Representation of Abstract Components and Instantiation Types in $\tau\mathsf{HOC}^3$

Let $C\left[par_1 = X_1 : B_1, par_2 = X_2 : B_2, \cdots, par_m = X_m : B_m\right]$ be the signature of the abstract component C. It can be represented as $C \equiv [[X_1 <: B_1, X_2 <: B_2, \cdots, X_m <: B_m]] \triangleright U_{body}$, where $B_1, B_2, \dots, B_m$ are the $\tau\mathsf{HOC}^3$ representation of the bounds and U_{body} represents the specification of the abstract component in terms of the context variables $X_1, X_2, \dots, X_m$.

Let $C\left[par_1 = B'_1, par_2 = B'_2, \cdots, par_m = B'_m\right]$ be a closed instantiation type of C, represented as $C \triangleleft [[B'_1, B'_2, \cdots, B'_m]]$. Moreover, let $\mathsf{C_{Impl}}$ be a #-component typed with this instantiation type. In $\tau\mathsf{HOC}^3$, it has the form $\mathsf{C_{Impl}} \equiv [X_1 <: B'_1, X_2 <: B'_2, \cdots, X_m <: B'_m] \triangleright v_{body}$, where the term v_{body} represents the implementation of the #-component under the assumptions represented by $B'_1, B'_2, \cdots B'_m$. If $\mathsf{C_{Impl}}$ is chosen for an inner component typed as $C\left[par_1 = B''_1, par_2 = B''_2, \cdots, par_m = B''_m\right]$, where $B''_i < B'_i$ for $i = 1, 2, \cdots, m$, it is applied to the context arguments by the term $\mathsf{C_{Impl}} \triangleleft [B''_1, B''_2, \cdots, B''_m]$.

If $\mathsf{C_{Impl}}$ has inner components typed by *instantiation types* $T_1, T_2, \dots, T_n$, the term v_{body} may be $v_{body} \equiv ?x_1{:}T_1. (?x_2{:}T_2. (\cdots . (?x_n{:}T_n. v)))$, where $?x{:}T.t$ is a *resolution term*. Let $T_i \equiv [[X_1 <: B_1, \dots, X_n <: B_n]] \triangleright U \triangleleft [[B''_1, \dots, B''_n]]$ be the instantiation type of the i-th inner component. The rule *E-Resolution* says that $\Sigma, \Delta \vdash ?x_i{:}T_i.t \to (\lambda x_i{:}U.t)\,(t' \triangleleft [B''_1, \dots, B''_n])$, where t' represents the #-component found by the *resolution algorithm* (Section 3.2) for T_i, in the environment Δ of cataloged #-components. For this extension, it is necessary to add Δ to the other reduction rules.

Note that the types of inner components $(T_1, T_2, \dots, T_n)$ may be defined in terms of $X_1, X_2, \dots, X_m$. Also, U_{body} is a *#-component instance type*, since

$$\Gamma \vdash S <: S \quad \Gamma \vdash S <: \top \quad \frac{\Gamma \vdash S <: U \quad \Gamma \vdash U <: T}{\Gamma \vdash S <: T} \quad \frac{\Gamma \vdash T_1' <: T_1 \quad \Gamma \vdash T_2' <: T_2}{\Gamma \vdash T_1 \rightarrow T_2' <: T_1' \rightarrow T_2} \quad \frac{X <: T \in \Gamma}{\Gamma \vdash X <: T}$$

$$\text{(S-Refl)} \qquad \text{(S-Max)} \qquad\qquad \text{(S-Trans)} \qquad\qquad\qquad \text{(S-Arrow)} \qquad\qquad \text{(S-TVar)}$$

$$\frac{U_i \overset{hom}{\longmapsto} U_i' \quad i=1...k}{((U_i' \ ^{i=1...k})) <: ((U_i \ ^{i=1...k}))} \qquad \frac{\Gamma \vdash T_0' <: T_0 \quad \Gamma, X <: T \vdash T_1' <: T_1 \quad \Gamma \vdash T_2' <: T_2}{\Gamma \vdash [[X <: T_0']] \rhd T_1' \lhd [[T_2]] <: [[X <: T_0]] \rhd T_1 \lhd [[T_2']]}$$

$$\text{(S-Hash)} \qquad\qquad\qquad\qquad\qquad \text{(S-Abstract)}$$

Fig. 7. τHOC^3 (Subtyping Relation)

v_{body} evaluates to a *#-component instance* if $x_1, x_2, \ldots, x_n$ are resolved in $C_{Impl} \lhd$ $[B_1'', B_2'', \cdots, B_m'']$, i.e. $X_i = B_i''^{i=1...m}$.

4.2 Progress and Preservation in HTS

In what follows, the proofs of two important theorems about τHOC^3 are outlined. By *progress*, an HPE configuration must always define a well structured #-component instance or a parallel program, since it is a well-typed term of τHOC^3. By *preservation*, the type of a #-component instance or parallel program is completely defined by its HPE configuration. For brevity, since τHOC^3 is defined as an extension of the typed lambda calculus with subtyping, some results and proof fragments presented in Benjamin Pierce's book [22] are reused in the following proofs.

Lemma 1. CANONICAL FORMS FOR CONTEXT ABSTRACTION TERMS. *If v is a value of type $[[X <: T_1]] \rhd T_2 \lhd [[T_1]]$, then $v \equiv [X <: T_1] \rhd t$.*

Proof. By the syntax of τHOC^3 (figures 3 and 4), a value may be either an *abstraction*, a *#-component instance*, or a *context abstraction*. By the typing relation, only a context abstraction of the form $[X <: T_1] \rhd t$ may be v.

Theorem 1. PROGRESS. *Suppose t is a closed, well-typed term (i. e. $\vdash t : T$ for some T). Then either t is a value or else there is some t' with $t \rightarrow t'$.*

Proof. By induction on a derivation of $t : T$. The cases for *T-Var*, *T-Abs*, *T-App*, and *T-Sub* come from the proof for the simply typed lambda calculus. The cases for *T-TAbs* and *T-Basc1* are trivial, since t is a value in the rule. In the case of *T-TApp*, $t \equiv t_1 \lhd [T_1]$ and $T \equiv T_2$, where $\Gamma \vdash t_1 : [[X <: T_1]] \rhd T_2 \lhd [[T_1]]$. By the induction hypothesis, t_1 is a value or t_1 can make a step of derivation towards t_1' ($\Sigma \vdash t_1 \rightarrow t_1'$). If t_1 is a value, by Lemma 1, it has the form $[X <: T_1] \rhd t_2$, yielding $t' \equiv [X \rightarrow T_1] t_2$. Therefore, *E-TAppTAbs* applies. Otherwise, it is possible to apply *E-TApp*, yielding $t' \equiv t_1' \lhd [T_1]$.

Lemma 2. TYPE SUBSTITUTION PRESERVES TYPING *[22]. If $\Gamma, X <: Q, \Delta \vdash t : T$ and $\Gamma \vdash P <: Q$, then $\Gamma, [X \longmapsto P]\Delta \vdash [X \longmapsto P] t : [X \longmapsto P] T$.*

Theorem 2. PRESERVATION. *if $\Gamma \vdash t : T$ and $t \to t'$, then $\Gamma \vdash t' : T$.*

Proof. Also, by induction on a derivation of $t : T$. The cases for *T-Var*, *T-Abs*, *T-App*, and *T-Sub* come from the proof for the typed lambda calculus with subtyping. For *T-TAbs* and *T-Base1*, where t is a value, and so t does not reduce to t', the theorem is vacuously satisfied. For *T-TApp*, where $t \equiv t_1 \triangleleft [T_1]$, t_1 may be either a value or a derivable term for which there is a t_1' such that $\Sigma \vdash t_1 \to t_1'$. In the former case, by Lemma 1, $t_1 \equiv [X <: T_1] \triangleright t_2$, and $T \equiv [[X <: T_1]] \triangleright T \triangleleft [[T_1]]$. Thus, by the antecedent of *T-TApp*, conclude that $\Gamma, X <: T_1 \vdash t_2 : T$. Since the application of *E-TAppTAbs* yields $[X \longmapsto T_1] t_2$, it is possible to conclude, by using the Lemma 2, that $\Gamma \vdash [X \longmapsto T_1] t_2 : T$. In the latter case, by induction hypothesis, $\Sigma \vdash t_1 \to t_1'$ and $\Gamma \vdash t_1' : [[X <: T_1]] \triangleright T \triangleleft [[T_1]]$ too, since $\Gamma \vdash t_1 : [[X <: T_1]] \triangleright T \triangleleft [[T_1]]$. Therefore, by letting $t' \equiv t_1' \triangleleft [T_1]$, it is possible to conclude that $\Gamma \vdash t' : T$.

4.3   Type Safety of Inheritance Derivation of HPE Configurations

HPE supports the derivation of abstract components from other ones through inheritance of their configurations. In the example of Section 3.1, this is used for introducing particular restrictions of **SP** to the abstract component ADI, which is common to **SP** and **BT**. Due to these additional restrictions, the #-component ADIImpl, of ADI, is only appropriate to **BT**, but not to **SP**. For including the restrictions of **SP**, by reusing ADI, an abstract component SP_ADI was derived by inheritance from ADI, by freezing the context parameter **method** to SP-METHOD and by adding the required inner component **txinvr**. From SP_ADI, a #-component SP_ADIImpl is derived for attending the needs of **SP**.

Inheritance derivation leads to safety issues. Formally, let C_{abs} be an arbitrary abstract component, where $C_{abs} \equiv [[X_1 <: B_1, X_2 <: B_2, \cdots, X_m <: B_m]] \triangleright U_{body}$. Is it safe to use a #-component of an abstract component derived by inheritance from C_{abs} in the context of an inner component typed with an instantiation type $C_{abs} \triangleleft [[B_1'', B_2'', \cdots, B_m'']]$? For responding it, let $\mathsf{C_{Impl}} \equiv [X_1 <: B_1', X_2 <: B_2', \cdots, X_m <: B_m'] \triangleright ?i_1{:}T_1. (?i_2{:}T_2. (\cdots . (?i_n{:}T_n. v)))$ be a #-component of $C_{abs} \triangleleft [[B_1', B_2', \cdots, B_m']]$ applied to the context of $C_{abs} \triangleleft [[B_1'', B_2'', \cdots, B_m'']]$, where $B_i'' <: B_i'^{\;i=1\ldots m}$, where $B_i'' <: B_i'^{\;i=1\ldots m}$, i. e. it is instantiated as $\mathsf{C_{Impl}} \triangleleft [B_1'', B_2'', \cdots, B_m'']$. In what follows, the four inheritance operations for deriving a configuration from other configuration in HPE are introduced, followed by a proof that the abstract component represented by the former is a subtype of the abstract component represented by the latter.

Case 1 - Adding a Context Parameter. Let $C_{abs}' \equiv [[X_1 <: B_1, X_2 <: B_2, \cdots, X_m <: B_m, X_{m+1} <: B_{m+1}]] \triangleright U_{body}$ be the abstract component inherited from C_{abs} by adding a context parameter X_{m+1} bounded by B_{m+1}. Note that X_{m+1} is not referred to in the body of C_{abs}', which is the same body U_{body} of C_{abs}. Now, let $\mathsf{C_{Impl}'} \equiv [X_1 <: B_1', X_2 <: B_2', \cdots, X_m <: B_m', X_{m+1} <: B_{m+1}'] \triangleright ?i_1{:}T_1. (?i_2{:}T_2. (\cdots . (?i_n{:}T_n. v)))$ be an arbitrary #-component derived from

C_{Impl}, typed as $C'_{abs} \lhd [[B'_1, B'_2, \cdots, B'_m, B'_{m+1}]]$. Now, suppose $C'_{Impl} \lhd [B'_{m+1}]$, i.e. the result of an application of C'_{Impl} that supplies the context parameter X_{m+1} with B'_{m+1}, its argument in the instantiation type of C'_{Impl}. By $E\text{-}TAppTAbs$, $C'_{Impl} \lhd [B'_{m+1}]$ evaluates to $[X_{m+1} \longmapsto B'_{m+1}][X_1 <: B'_1, X_2 <: B'_2, \cdots, X_m <: B'_m] \rhd ?i_1{:}T_1.(?i_2{:}T_2.(\cdots.(?i_n{:}T_n.\, v)))$. Since X_{m+1} is not referenced in the right side of the substitution, it is possible to conclude that $C'_{Impl} \lhd [B'_{m+1}] \equiv C_{Impl}$. Also, by construction of HPE configurations, C'_{Impl} represents all the possible #-components of C'_{abs}, since there are no points where references to the additional type variable X_{m+1} might appear in the configurations of the #-components of C'_{abs}. Therefore, it is always possible to apply a #-component of the derived abstract component by taking the bound of the additional context parameter as its argument in the instantiation type of the #-component.

Case 2 - Adding an Inner Component. In this case, let $C'_{abs} \equiv [[X_1 <: B_1, X_2 <: B_2, \cdots, X_m <: B_m]] \rhd U'_{body}$ be the inherited abstract component, with an additional inner component, which change U_{body} to U'_{body}. Thus, a #-component of C'_{abs} has the form $C'_{Impl} \equiv [X_1 <: B'_1, X_2 <: B'_2, \cdots, X_m <: B'_m] \rhd ?i_1{:}T_1.(?i_2{:}T_2.(\cdots.(?i_n{:}T_n.(?i_{n+1}{:}I_{n+1}.\, v'))))$. By construction, the type U'_{body}, of v', derives from the type U_{body}, of v, by adding the slices of i_{n+1}. Therefore, let $U_{body} \equiv ((U_1, U_2, \ldots, U_k))$ and $U'_{body} \equiv ((U'_1, U'_2, \ldots, U'_k))$. For some i, either $U_i = U'_i$ or $U'_i - U_i = \langle S \rangle$, where S is the graph of a unit of the #-component typed as I_{n+1}. In both cases, $U_i \xmapsto{hom} U'_i$ for any i. Therefore, by $S\text{-}Hash$, $U'_{body} <: U_{body}$.

Case 3 - Narrowing the Bound of a Context Parameter. Let $C'_{abs} \equiv [[X_1 <: B_1, X_2 <: B_2, \cdots, X_i <: B^\star_i, \cdots, X_m <: B_m]] \rhd U'_{body}$ be the inherited abstract component, with the bound of the context parameter X_i restricted from B_i to $B^\star_i$, where $B^\star_i <: B_i$. Thus, any #-component of C'_{abs} is also a #-component of C_{abs}, since any context argument for X_i in the instantiation type of a #-component of C'_{abs}, say B'_i, is also a subtype of B_i, since $B'_i <: B^\star_i <: B_i$.

Case 4 - Freezing a Context Parameter. Let $C'_{abs} \equiv [[X_1 <: B_1, X_2 <: B_2, \cdots, X_{i-1} <: B_{i-1}, X_{i+1} <: B_{i+1}, \cdots, X_m <: B_m]] \rhd \to U'_{body}$ be the inherited abstract component, where the context parameter X_i is frozen to the value $B^\star_i$, where $B^\star_i <: B_i$, so that all the occurrences of X_i in the instantiation types of the inner components of #-components of C'_{abs} are replaced by $B^\star_i$. Using the same argument of *Case 3*, any #-component of C'_{abs} is a #-component of C_{abs}.

5   Conclusions

HTS is a type system for addressing the problem of automated discovering and binding of parallel components tuned to the architecture of target parallel computing platforms and fitting the requirements of applications. It is relevant due to the dissemination of cloud computing platforms that offer the performance of heterogeneous parallel computing platforms as services, where the choice of the best implementation of a component may be a cumbersome task, yet essential for taking advantage of the power of the computational resources.

This paper is concerned with relevant formal properties of HTS, on top of a calculus of overlapping composition of #-components, which show that HTS may be implemented safely, i.e. a #-component derived from a well-formed configuration always exist, it is unique and it can be discovered from a proper abstract specification (instantiation type) and its super-types. Also, it has been shown that operations used to derive abstract components from other ones are safe.

HTS has been implemented in HPE, following the Hash component model. Since HPE complies with CCA, HTS might be introduced to other CBHPC platforms, including Fractal/GCM compliant ones, since the essential differences between CCA and Fractal/GCM platforms are well-known [20].

HTS may be also applied to the design of other kinds of programming systems, such as usual programming languages. For instance, in an object-oriented programming language, context parameters may be introduced to classes, leading to a concept of class augmented with contextual abstraction, for instantiating objects from one in a set of classes according to some specified context, possibly taking into consideration dynamic properties of the execution environment.

References

1. Aldinucci, M., Campa, S., Danelutto, M., Vanneschi, M., Kilpatrick, P., Dazzi, P., Laforenza, D., Tonellotto, N.: Behavioural Skeletons in GCM: Autonomic Management of Grid Components. In: Proceedings of the 16th Euromicro Conference on Parallel, Distributed and Network-Based Processing (PDP 2008), pp. 54–63. IEEE Computer Society (2008)

2. André, F., Buisson, J., Pazat, J.-L.: Dynamic Adaptation of Parallel Codes: Toward Self-Adaptable Components for the Grid. In: Proceedings of the Workshop on Component Models and Systems for Grid Applications (in ICS 2004), pp. 143–156. Springer, US (June 2004)

3. Andrzejak, A., Reinefeld, A., Schintke, F., Schtt, T.: On Adaptability in Grid Systems. In: Getov, V., Laforenza, D., Reinefeld, A. (eds.) Future Generation Grids, pp. 29–46. Springer, US (2006)

4. Antonopoulos, N., Gillam, L.: Cloud Computing: Principles, Systems and Applications. Computer Commmunications and Networks. Springer (2011)

5. Armstrong, R., Kumfert, G., McInnes, L.C., Parker, S., Allan, B., Sottile, M., Epperly, T., Tamara, D.: The CCA Component Model For High-Performance Scientific Computing. Concurrency and Computation: Practice and Experience 18(2), 215–229 (2006)

6. Bailey, D.H., Harris, T., Shapir, W., van der Wijngaart, R., Woo, A., Yarrow, M.: The NAS Parallel Benchmarks 2.0. Technical Report NAS-95-020, NASA Ames Research Center (December 1995), http://www.nas.nasa.org/NAS/NPB

7. Baude, F., Caromel, D., Dalmasso, C., Danelutto, M., Getov, W., Henrio, L., Prez, C.: GCM: A Grid Extension to Fractal for Autonomous Distributed Components. Annals of Telecommunications 64(1), 5–24 (2009)

8. Bruneton, E., Coupaye, T., Stefani, J.B.: Recursive and Dynamic Software Composition with Sharing. In: European Conference on Object Oriented Programming (ECOOP 2002). Springer (2002)
9. Carvalho Junior, F.H., Correa, R.C.: The Design of a CCA Framework with Distribution, Parallelism, and Recursive Composition. In: Workshop on Component-Based High Performance Computing (CBHPC 2010), pp. 339–348. IEEE (2010)
10. Carvalho Junior, F.H., Correa, R.C., Lins, R.D., Silva, J.C., Araújo, G.A.: High Level Service Connectors for Components-Based High Performance Computing. In: Proceedings of the 19th International Symposium on Computer Architecture and High Performance Computing, pp. 237–244. IEEE (October 2007)
11. Carvalho Junior, F.H., Lins, R.D.: Separation of Concerns for Improving Practice of Parallel Programming. INFORMATION, An International Journal 8(5), 621–638 (2005)
12. Carvalho Junior, F.H., Lins, R.D.: An Institutional Theory for #-Components. Electronic Notes in Theoretical Computer Science 195, 113–132 (2008)
13. Carvalho Junior, F.H., Lins, R.D., Correa, R.C., Araújo, G.A.: Towards an Architecture for Component-Oriented Parallel Programming. Concurrency and Computation: Practice and Experience 19(5), 697–719 (2007)
14. Courtrai, L., Guidec, F., Le Sommer, N., Maheo, Y.: Resource management for parallel adaptive components. In: Proceedings of the 2003 International Parallel and Distributed Processing Symposium (IPDPS 2003), p. 7. IEEE (April 2003)
15. de Carvalho Junior, F.H., Rezende, C.A.: A Case Study on Expressiveness and Performance of Component-Oriented Parallel Programming. Journal of Parallel and Distributed Computing 73(5), 557–569 (2013)
16. Foster, I., Kesselman, C.: The Grid 2: Blueprint for a New Computing Infrastructure. M. Kauffman (2004)
17. Grama, A., Gupta, A., Karypis, J., Kumar, V.: Introduction to Parallel Computing. Addison-Wesley (1976)
18. Hall, M.W., Gil, Y., Lucas, R.F.: Self-Configuring Applications for Heterogeneous Systems: Program Composition and Optimization Using Cognitive Techniques. Proceedings of the IEEE 96(5), 849–862 (2008)
19. Liu, H., Parashar, M.: Enabling self-management of component-based high-performance scientific applications. In: Proceedings of the 14th IEEE International Symposium on High Performance Distributed Computing (HPDC-14), pp. 59–68. IEEE (July 2005)
20. Malawski, M., Bubak, M., Baude, F., Caromel, D., Henrio, L., Morel, M.: Interoperability of Grid Component Models: GCM and CCA Case Study. In: Priol, T., Vanneschi, M. (eds.) CoreGRID, pp. 95–105. Springer (2007)
21. Parashar, M., Li, X., Parker, S.G., Damevski, K., Khan, A., Swaminathan, A., Johnson, C.R.: Advanced Computational Infrastructures for Parallel/Distributed Adaptive Applications. In: The SCIJump Framework for Parallel and Distributed Scientific Computing. Wiley Press (2009)
22. Pierce, B.: Types and Programming Languages. The MIT Press (2002)
23. Wang, A.J.A., Qian, K.: Component-Oriented Programming. Wiley-Interscience (2005)
24. Yoon, Y., Browne, J.C., Crocker, M., Jain, S., Mahmood, N.: Productivity and performance through components: the ASCI Sweep3D application. Concurrency and Computation: Practice and Experience 19(5), 721–742 (2007)

Towards a Domain-Specific Language for Patterns-Oriented Parallel Programming

Dalvan Griebler and Luiz Gustavo Fernandes

Pontifícia Universidade Católica do Rio Grande do Sul (PUCRS),
GMAP Research Group (FACIN/PPGCC), Brazil
Av. Ipiranga, 6681 - Prédio 32, 90619-900 - Porto Alegre, RS, Brazil
dalvan.griebler@acad.pucrs.br, luiz.fernandes@pucrs.br

Abstract. Pattern-oriented programming has been used in parallel code development for many years now. During this time, several tools (mainly frameworks and libraries) proposed the use of patterns based on programming primitives or templates. The implementation of patterns using those tools usually requires human expertise to correctly set up communication/synchronization among processes. In this work, we propose the use of a Domain Specific Language to create pattern-oriented parallel programs (DSL-POPP). This approach has the advantage of offering a higher programming abstraction level in which communication/synchronization among processes is hidden from programmers. We compensate the reduction in programming flexibility offering the possibility to use combined and/or nested parallel patterns (*i.e.*, parallelism in levels), allowing the design of more complex parallel applications. We conclude this work presenting an experiment in which we develop a parallel application exploiting combined and nested parallel patterns in order to demonstrate the main properties of DSL-POPP.

1 Introduction

In recent years, High Performance Computing (HPC) has become a wide spread research field which is no more restricted to highly specialized research centers. The use of HPC is crucial to achieve significant research goals in many segments of the modern Computer Science. In this scenario, multi-core processors are now a mainstream approach to deliver higher performance to parallel applications and they are commonly available in workstations and servers.

Although these architectures present a high computing power, developers still have to acquire technical skills to take advantage of the available parallelism. This can lead developers to deal with complex mechanisms, which in addition may result in very specialized solutions [1]. In this sense, programmers may prefer to stay away from parallel programming due to the required efforts to learn how to correctly use it. For that reason, it becomes necessary to investigate alternatives to face this complexity offering to developers different ways to create efficient scalable parallel applications for current architectures.

In the HPC literature, many libraries and frameworks based on the pattern-oriented approach or similar were proposed to make parallel programming easier.

A. Rauber Du Bois and P. Trinder (Eds.): SBLP 2013, LNCS 8129, pp. 105–119, 2013.

As recent successful examples, it is possible to cite FastFlow [2], Muesli [3], SkeTo [4] and Skandium [5] (among many others that will be discussed in Section 2). This scenario is an evidence that parallel patterns, initially known as skeletons [6], provide a high-level abstraction to develop algorithms while taking advantage of the benefits of parallel architectures. Thus, besides improving the productivity of expert parallel code developers, the use of specific patterns or combinations of them can help less experienced parallel code developers to create efficient and scalable applications [7].

Most part of the pattern-oriented environments proposed so far were designed for clusters and computational grids [8]. With the advance of multi-core platforms, this tendency is changing. Pattern-oriented libraries and frameworks for shared memory systems are becoming more and more necessary. In this context, we believe that parallel patterns along with an expert code generation can guide developers to efficiently create parallel applications for those kind of platforms.

In this paper, we intend to explore the use of patterns an their features through a Domain-Specific Language for Patterns-Oriented Parallel Programming (DSL-POPP) designed for multi-core platforms. By doing that, we intend to hide from developers low level mechanisms such as load balance, flow control schemes and synchronization operations needed to implement parallel applications using patterns. Additionally, we want to provide a way for developers to easily combine patterns in different levels of parallelism (nested and fused patterns). One of the main reasons of using the DSL approach is because it allows minimal changes in a general purpose language (such as the C language for instance, which is familiar to many programmers). Besides, it is crucial for our goal because it makes it easier to change code to experiment different nesting of parallel patterns. Summarizing, the main contributions of our paper are the following:

- we introduce a Domain-Specific Language for Patterns-Oriented Parallel Programming;
- we propose a programming model to achieve nested parallelism through different combinations of patterns based on routines and code blocks structures;
- we show an experimental image processing scenario in which we carry out implementations and tests with the combination of pipeline and master/slave patterns.

The rest of this paper is organized as follows. Section 2 presents the related work. Section 3 discusses the Pattern-Oriented Parallel Programming paradigm (POPP). The DSL-POPP environment is introduced in Section 4. Section 5 presents performance evaluation experiments of parallel code developed using DSL-POPP. Finally, Section 6 concludes this work.

2   Related Work

Since the emergence of the structured programming concept with parallel skeletons introduced by Murray Cole [6], several libraries, frameworks and languages employed this approach on parallel and distributed systems. Murray proposed eSkel, an environment that allows skeletons constructions of parallel programming using similar MPI primitives in C code [9]. More recently, the SkeTo parallel skeleton library (a C++ library coupled with MPI) implements two-stage dynamic task scheduling to support multi-core clusters [4]. The nestable parallelism pattern is not an objective, but SkeTo provides data structures (lists, trees and matrices) implemented using templates, and parallel skeletons operations (map, reduce, scan and several others) can be invoked on them.

Muesli is a C++ template library that uses MPI and OpenMP to support multi-processor and multi-core architectures [3]. Contrary to SkeTo, Muesli supports nesting data and task parallel skeletons. Also, Lithium [10] and its successor Muskel [11] are skeletons libraries for clusters and both support the nestable skeletons using the macro data-flow model. Inspired on Lithium and Muskel frameworks, Skandium is a Java library for shared memory systems that provides task and data nested skeletons, instantiated via parametric objects [5].

FastFlow is a programming framework for shared memory systems which implements a stack of C++ template libraries using lock-free synchronization mechanisms [2]. However, in FastFlow, developers must implement the pattern through framework routines as in others frameworks and libraries previously mentioned. Differently, we propose the use of a Domain Specific Language to abstract the low level parallel mechanisms necessary to implement parallel patterns, such as load balance, control flow, tasks splitting and synchronization operations. In DSL-POPP user interface environment, programmers develop sequential code in code blocks inside the pattern predefined structure. Our language offers the possibility of nesting (parallelism in levels) and combining parallel patterns.

Finally, there are research works that focus on pattern-oriented parallel languages. These languages and domain-specific languages share similar features such as the existence of a compiler and automatic code generation. P3L is an explicit parallel language that provides skeletons constructions to explore parallelism [12]. In other words, P3L defines skeletons constructions with input/output and sequential modules. More recently, Skil [13] offers a subset of C language (high order functions, curring and polymorphic types) which should be used to implement patterns. Skil does not offer pre-implemented patterns and does not allow nested patterns. In contrast to those languages, we have designed DSL-POPP to explore different combinations of patterns and levels of parallelism in shared memory systems. Additionally, we have introduced an alternative way to implement patterns in user level interface through routines and code blocks directly integrated in the C language code.

3   Patterns-Oriented Parallel Programming

Parallel skeletons have been an alternative to create parallel programming interfaces since the early 90s. As the name implies, they are algorithms skeletons to develop structured parallel programs. Skeletons are similar to Software Engineering concept of Design Patterns [14]. Patterns became popular in parallel programming with object-oriented programming. One of the main reasons to use parallel patterns, is because they allow the programming environment designers to generate parallel codes freely from the parametrization of the abstractions and from the addition of sequential code [1,7]. Also, a pattern-oriented approach can help programmers to develop complex parallel applications since a pattern provide the structure of the program implementation. This reduces considerably the efforts to learn how to use parallelism techniques to take advantage from high performance architectures [1,14].

We propose the use of POPP (Patterns-Oriented Parallel Programming) generic model to create an interface programming environment based on the patterns approach. This model is potentially designed to explore different levels and combinations of patterns implementations. We chose to offer the POPP model through a domain-specific language programming interface what allow us to automatically generate parallel code. Our objective is not to create a new and independent parallel language, but extend a general purpose language offering a higher abstraction layer over it in which we intend to make low level parallelism mechanisms as abstract as possible for developers.

The POPP model relies on a combination of patterns routines conceptually defined and code blocks corresponding to the parallel pattern. Since programs can be composed by different types of computations (routines), the parallelism may not be expressed by a single routine. For that reason, our model allows the inclusion of subroutines which can be used to compose patterns in a hierarchical way offering different parallelism levels. A representation of the POPP generic model is illustrated in Figure 1.

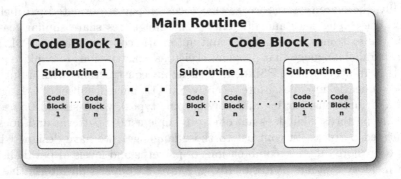

Fig. 1. The POPP model

In order to illustrate how to implement a parallel pattern in the POPP model, we describe two examples of classical parallel patterns: master/slave and pipeline (Figure 2). In master/slave pattern, the master is responsible for sending the computational tasks for all slaves. Then, once all tasks have been computed, results are sent back to the master to finalize the whole computation. For this pattern, both POPP routine and subroutines can implement their own master and slaves code blocks. For instance, it is possible to have inside a slave code block a subroutine composed of other master and slaves code blocks.

Differently, the pipeline pattern is based on a line of stages, in which each stage performs part of the computational workload. The output of each stage is the input of the next one [1]. The POPP model allows the creation of a pipeline in which stages can be implemented as subroutines with their own stages. The final composition can be represented by several pipeline stages.

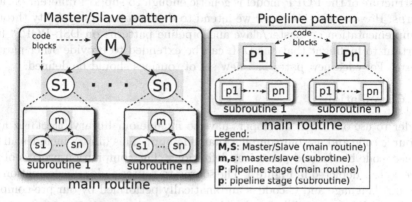

Fig. 2. Master/slave and pipeline patterns

As previously mentioned, patterns can be combined in the POPP model using main routine and subroutines combinations. We present a version of hybrid patterns in Figure 3. In this example, the main routine uses the pipeline pattern and two of its stage blocks parallelize their operations using the master/slave pattern. This configuration is only an example. Others combinations of patterns can be also implemented such as a master/slave pattern in which slaves apply the pipeline pattern as subroutines.

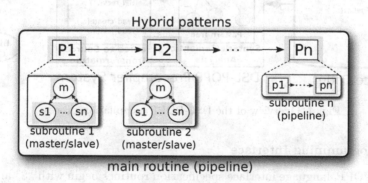

Fig. 3. An example of combined patterns

In this section we presented the abstract idea of the POPP model, which includes different levels of patterns implementation and their combination. These features became clearer in the next section, in which a domain-specific language is proposed based on this programming model.

4 DSL-POPP in a Nutshell

The structure of the POPP model is generic enough to support different parallel patterns. However, in this paper we intend to demonstrate its usability through the implementation of master/slave and pipeline patterns on DSL-POPP. It is important to highlight that our DSL can be extended to provide other parallel patterns. For each new pattern, a new set of routines should be defined.

4.1 Compilation

In order to use our DSL, developers have to include our library (poppLinux.h) in the source code and use our compiler (named popp). This library includes all the routines, code blocks and primitives definitions. The compilation process of the source code is depicted in Figure 4. The source-to-source code transformation between our language and C code is automatically performed by our pre-compiler system, which is responsible for checking syntax and semantic errors. Then, the pre-compiler systems generates the C parallel code using the Pthreads library based on the parallel patterns used. Besides, for the source-to-source code transformation, we created a Shared Memory Message Passing Interface (SMMPI) to carry out threads communication. Finally, we use the GNU C compiler to generate binary code for the target platform.

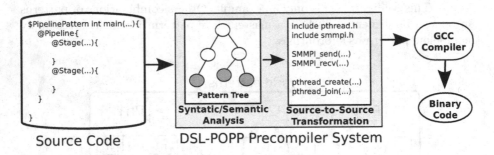

Fig. 4. Overview of the DSL-POPP compilation process

4.2 Programming Interface

In DSL-POPP, language interface specification routines begin with "$" and code blocks with "@". The pattern routine should be declared in a function followed by the return data type and its name. Code blocks should be used inside of the pattern routine and they contain full C code. Figure 5 describes the syntax and logical structure of DSL-POPP constructions.

As we can see in Figure 5(a) at the left side, a $PipelinePattern routine supports two code blocks: pipeline block (@Pipeline{}) and stage block (@Stage(...){}). The pipeline block should be declared at least once and it is responsible for coordinating the pipeline flow. Each stage block corresponds to a stage in the pipeline and can be declared as many times as necessary inside the pipeline code block. In stage blocks, parameters are the number of threads, the buffer to be sent to the next stage and the buffer size.

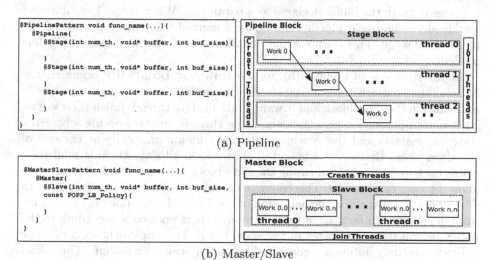

(a) Pipeline

(b) Master/Slave

Fig. 5. Syntax and logical structure of the DSL-POPP

In Figure 5(b) also at the left side, we show how a $MasterSlavePattern routine implements algorithms using master and slave blocks (@Master{} and @Slave(...){}). The master coordinates all computation flow and starts the slave blocks. The slave blocks must be used to obtain parallelism inside of the master. Additionally, it is necessary to inform the number of slave threads, the buffer to be sent to the master, the size of the buffer and the load balance policy.

4.3   Patterns Implementation

Still in Figure 5, we show how DSL-POPP organizes routines and code blocks and implements the pattern-oriented parallelism. Basic parallel patterns such as Master/Slave or Pipeline are structured based on data exchange through messages. Aiming at simplifying the Pthreads code generation phase for multi-core platforms, we created a Shared Memory Message Passing Interface (SMMPI) which implements threads communication through semaphore routines. The send and receive operations are carried out based on threads identification. For instance, when a thread send a buffer to another thread, in reality it is using sem_post to unblock the destination thread which is waiting on a `sem_wait` to receive the buffer and start its work. In the pipeline pattern code generation, we use SMMPI routines to perform send and receive through pipeline stages transferring data through the buffer defined as a parameter of the stage block.

A pipeline routine can be implemented in several ways. The example presented at the right side of Figure 5(a) shows the classic scenario in which all stages blocks have only one thread per stage. In this scenario, the pipeline block creates all necessary threads and wait them all to finish their works. This procedure is repeated transparently from the first up to the last stage block declaration. As it is possible to notice, communication between stages is also implicit and it happens through the buffer declared as a parameter. When stages have different workloads, a non-linear pipeline can be implemented using more threads on the unbalanced stage. This feature avoids significant performance losses in pipeline implementations.

At the right side of Figure 5(b), we illustrate how DSL-POPP organizes the Master/Slave pattern implementation. The master block creates as many threads as defined in the slave block and it waits until all slave threads finish their works. This is transparent for programmers, since threads creation occurs where the slave block starts and the synchronization occurs automatically at the end of the slave block. Besides, at the end of slave block, all slave threads send their works back to master thread (using the slave block parameter buffer) in order to allow it to merge all results. This communication procedure is also transparent to developers. Finally, the implementation of the load balance policy is also hidden from developers. In fact, slave threads receive their workloads according to the policy informed by parameter in the slave block. The implementation of these policies is entirely automatic generated by our pre-compiler system. Three load balance policies are available:

- `POPP_LB_STATIC`: the workload is divided by the number of threads. The resulting chunks are then statically assigned to slave threads as they start their computation;
- `POPP_LB_DYNAMIC`: the workload is divided in chunks, each one containing a number of tasks defined by the number of slave threads (finer task grain). When a thread finishes a task, it dynamically asks for another one to the master thread until there are no more tasks to be computed;
- `POPP_LB_COST`: the workload is divided in chunks, each one containing a number of tasks defined by the number of slave threads. Tasks are reorganized in such a way chunks have similar computational costs. Chunks are dynamically assigned to slave threads during execution time.

4.4   Levels of Parallelism

In the DSL-POPP, we use nested and combined patterns to achieve sub-level parallelism and hybrid patterns combination. It is important to mention that our implementation allows the use of nested patterns only inside slave (Master/Slave) and stage (Pipeline) blocks, not in the master block. Figure 6 shows the threads flow control graph for possible uses of nested and combined patterns implementations for a two level parallelism.

In Figure 6(a), we illustrate the use of nested pipeline patterns. Figure 6(b) and (d) present combination of pipeline and master/slave patterns (hybrid versions). Finally, Figure 6(c) shows how is the control flow when nested master/slave patterns are used inside of the slave block. ·

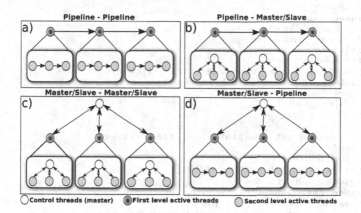

Fig. 6. Overview of thread graph in DSL-POPP

Also, it is possible to notice through an analysis of the control flows in Figure 6 what are the active threads during the execution time of a given application (taken in account for performance evaluation measurements). Control threads (representing the master thread) do not perform significant computation and appear only to facilitate the comprehension of the abstract representation of the master/slave pattern control flow. An example demonstrating the use of nested and combined patterns over a real application is presented in the next section.

5   Experimental Evaluation

In order to carry out an experimental evaluation of DSL-POPP and its features, we use it to parallelize an image processing application which applies a sequence of filters in a set of input images. In this section, we start briefly describing how we parallelize the application using DSL-POPP (Section 5.1). After, we introduce our experimental scenario in terms of platform and set of tests (Section 5.2). Finally, we present and discuss the performance results (Section 5.3).

5.1   Application Description and Implementation

We chose an image processing application because it allows us to explore parallelism combining both patterns available in DSL-POPP. The input is a list of bitmap images over which three different edge detection filters are applied (Prewitt, Sobel and Roberts) sequentially.

```
1#include<poppLinux.h>
2int list_size , num_th;
3char **list_buffer;
4$MasterSlavePattern unsigned char *do_sobel(unsigned char *image,
5int width,int height){
6 @Master{
7  unsigned char *filter_sobel=(unsigned char*) malloc(height*width);
8  @Slave(num_th,filter_sobel ,height*width,POPP_LB_STATIC){
9   unsigned char *filter_sobel=(unsigned char*)malloc(height*width);
10   int x,y,u,v;
11   unsigned char image_buffer[3][3];
12   for(y=1;y<height-1;y++)
13    for(x=1;x<width-1;x++)
14     for(v=0;v<3;v++)
15      for(u=0;u<3;u++)
16       image_buffer[v][u]=image[(((y+v-1)*width)+(x+u-1))];
17      filter_sobel[((y*width)+x)]=sobel(image_buffer);
18   } //slave
19  return filter_sobel;
20 } //master
21}
22$PipelinePattern int main(int argc, char **argv){
23 @Pipeline{
24  //....pre processing...
25  @Stage(1, filter , height * width){
26   int width, height, row;
27   unsigned char *image, *filter;
28   for(row=0; row<list_size; row++){
29    getImageSize(list_buffer[row],&width,&height);
30    image=(unsigned char *) malloc(height*width);
31    filter=(unsigned char *) malloc(height*width);
32    memcpy(image,save_bmp2binary(list_buffer[row],image,width,height),
33    width*height);
34    memcpy(filter ,do_prewitt(image,width,height),width*height);
35   }
36  }//stage
37  @Stage(1, filter , height * width){
38   int width, height, row;
39   unsigned char *filter;
40   for(row=0; row<list_size; row++){
41    getImageSize(list_buffer[row], &width, &height);
42    filter = (unsigned char *) malloc(height * width);
43    memcpy(filter , do_sobel(filter , width, height), width*height);
44   }
45  }//stage
46  @Stage(1, filter , height * width){
47   int width, height, row;
48   unsigned char *filter;
49   for(row=0; row<list_size; row++){
50    getImageSize(list_buffer[row], &width, &height);
51    filter = (unsigned char *) malloc(height * width);
52    memcpy(filter ,do_roberts(filter ,width,height),width*height);
53    save_bmp(convertName_bmp2filter(list_buffer[row]),filter ,width,
54    height);
55   }
56  }//stage
57  //pos processing
58 }
59}
```

Listing 1.1. Overview of DSL-POPP Image Processing Algorithm Implementation

In Listing 1.1, we present one possible way to parallelize the application using patterns available in DSL-POPP. Only parts of the application code are shown in order to evaluate the use DSL-POPP key features. In this example, we implemented the sequence of filter as a pipeline and each filter was individually parallelized using master/slave pattern.

In line 4, the Sobel filter function is implemented using the master/slave pattern. We do not show here, but both Prewitt and Roberts filters apply the same master/slave pattern since the base edge detection algorithm is quite similar. Readers can notice that the use of the master/slave routines does not require significant changes in the sequential code. We only declare the Sobel function using master/slave syntax routines, and the `filter_sobel` variable (line 7) defined in the master block receives the slave results. The double declaration of `filter_sobel` is necessary because variables are private in each code block. Moreover, we used the static load balance policy (`POPP_LB_STATIC`) in the slave block (line 8). In this implementation, the outermost for-loop (line 12) will be automatically split among the slave threads during the automatic code generation.

For the main function (line 22), a pipeline routine (lines 23 to 54) performs all pre-processing instructions (e.g., input images list allocation and organization) in the pipeline block and introduces the declaration of all pipelines stages (lines 25, 36 and 45). Again, no significant changes in the sequential code were necessary. We kept the same for-loop construction for all stage blocks. The course of a single input image through the pipeline stages is transparent for the developer since DSL-POPP analyzes the code blocks declarations and automatically generates a code in which the image is moved to the next stage through the buffer parameter. Once again, all internally declared code blocks variables are private.

5.2   Tests Scenario

We created a set of different implementations of the image processing application intending to highlight how patterns can be easily combined in different ways using DSL-POPP. Evidently, some of the pattern combinations presented better results than the others and many others combinations were possible. What is important in our point of view is that DSL-POPP make it easier to create those parallel versions offering a way to compare parallel solutions for the same problem with less development effort. The following implementations were evaluated:

- **Test-1**: implements just one level of parallelism using master/slave for the image filter functions. In this scenario, we employed 3 to N slave threads;
- **Test-2**: achieves parallelism using pipeline in the main function and master/slave for filter functions. Tests in this implementation were carried out using one thread per stage combined with 1 to N slaves threads;
- **Test-3.1**: both main and filter functions were implemented using master/slave. For this test, we used 3 slaves threads in the main function with 1 to N slaves in the filter functions;
- **Test-3.2**: implements the same patterns routines that Test-3.1, but the main function combines from 1 to N slaves threads and the filter functions only execute with 3 slave threads;

- **Test-4**: the main function is implemented using pipeline in which each stage employs 1 to N threads;
- **Test-5**: just implements master/slave in the main function in which 3 to N slaves threads are used.

Our results were obtained by computing the average execution time of 40 executions for each thread count. We fixed the number of necessary samples using a 95% confidence interval. For our experimental evaluation, we used 40 input images of size 3000×2550. The target architecture is composed of two Intel Xeon E7-2850 (ten cores each) at 2.0GHz and 80GB of main memory running Ubuntu-Linux-10.04-server-64bits. It is important to mention that experiments with more than 20 threads were possible due to virtual nodes (hyper-threading).

5.3 Performance Results

For the performance evaluation, we calculate the speedup as well as the efficiency through an average of 40 executions. We plotted the performance results in Figure 7.

The experiments results show that Test-1 does not achieve acceptable performance when the number of threads increases. This occurs in this scenario because we are doing the parallelism only in the image filters and the grain becomes too small as the number of threads grows. A better performance is achieved in the Test-2, in which we also explore parallelism in the main function with a pipeline routine at the same time as the filter functions with master/slave routine. Nevertheless, Test-2 does not scale well after 15 threads.

Test-3.1, which uses nested master/slave patterns, has similar performance to Test-2 even though the main routine in that case was implemented using the pipeline pattern. Test 3.2 presented the best results due to a better match between the number of active slave threads used and the static load balance policy applied. In fact, the limitation of the slave threads to 3 in the second level helped to avoid the computation of very fine grain tasks.

In Test-4, only the main routine was parallelized using the pipeline pattern. In this case, as the number of threads grows, pipeline stages become multi-threaded. Results indicate a better performance with less threads than Test-2 and Test-3.1, but they are not better than Test-3.2 possibly due to slightly different computational costs in each pipeline stage. Finally, Test-5 which implements just a one level master/slave pattern, presented loss of performance in some threads configuration (12, 18 and 24) due to a larger grain that does not match well with the static load balance policy we used.

At this point, it is important to stress out that all six implementations were carried out with very few modifications in the original source code. The essence of the algorithms itself was not changed, only the structure of the parallel solutions were inserted in the code. Even for more complex hybrid implementations, the effort to modify the code was minimum. Thus, we could test different solutions very quickly and find one with satisfactory performance and scalability.

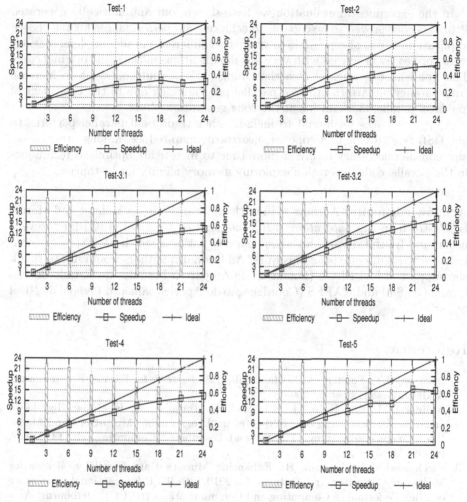

Fig. 7. DSL-POPP Results

6   Conclusions

In this paper, we proposed a Domain Specific Language for Patterns-Oriented Parallel Programming (DSL-POPP) that automatically generates parallel code for multi-core platforms. DSL-POPP offers primitives and programming environments to implement parallel code based on patterns with the C programming language. The main idea is to completely hide from developers low level mechanisms necessary to implement flow control, threads synchronization and load balance in parallel programs. Additionally, structured patterns may be easily nested or combined to create more complex parallel solutions with more than one level of parallelism.

In the experimental evaluation we have shown, our automatically generated Pthreads code proved to be capable to achieve good performances for the chosen application. It was also possible to verify that different parallel implementations were very easily produced with very few modifications in the same original code. This confirms our original idea that using a DSL would allow us to increase transparency in pattern-oriented parallel programming due to the treatment of low level parallel mechanisms at the code generation phase.

As future works we intend to include other traditional parallel patterns to our DSL (*e.g.*, divide and conquer, heartbeat, map-reduce, among others). We also consider necessary to invest more time to investigate optimized techniques in the parallel code generation exploring memory affinity for instance.

Acknowledgments. Authors wish to thank Jean-François Méhaut and Márcio B. Castro from the *Laboratoire d'Informatique de Grenoble* (LIG) for the very useful and fruitful discussions about parallel patterns which have strongly contributed to set directions for this work. Additionally, authors would like to thank the support of FAPERGS (Fundação de Amparo à Pesquisa do Estado do Rio Grande do Sul) and CAPES (Coordenação de Aperfeiçoamento Pessoal de Nível Superior).

References

1. Mattson, G.T., Sanders, A.B., Massingill, L.B.: Patterns for Parallel Programming. Addison-Wesley, Boston (2005)
2. Aldinucci, M., Danelutto, M., Kilpatrick, P., Torquati, M.: FastFlow: High-Level and Efficient Streaming on Multi-core. In: Programming Multi-Core and Many-Core Computing Systems. Parallel and Distributed Computing, ch. 13. Wiley, Boston (2013)
3. Ciechanowicz, P., Kuchen, H.: Enhancing Muesli's Data Parallel Skeletons for Multi-core Computer Architectures. In: 2010 12th IEEE International Conference on High Performance Computing and Communications (HPCC), Melbourne, Australia, pp. 108–113 (September 2010)
4. Karasawa, Y., Iwasaki, H.: A Parallel Skeleton Library for Multi-core Clusters. In: International Conference on Parallel Processing (ICPP 2009), Vienna, Austria, pp. 84–91 (September 2009)
5. Leyton, M., Piquer, J.M.: Skandium: Multi-core Programming with Algorithmic Skeletons. In: 2010 18th Euromicro International Conference on Parallel, Distributed and Network-Based Processing (PDP), Pisa, Italy, pp. 289–296 (February 2010)
6. Cole, M.: Algorithmic Skeletons: Structured Management of Parallel Computation. MIT Press, Cambridge (1989)
7. Intel Mccool, D.M.: Structured Parallel Programming with Deterministic Patterns. In: HotPar-2nd USENIX Workshop on Hot Topics in Parallelism, Berkeley, CA, pp. 1–6 (June 2010)
8. González-Vélez, H., Leyton, M.: A Survey of Algorithmic Skeleton Frameworks: High-Level Structured Parallel Programming Enablers. Softw. Pract. Exper. 40(12), 1135–1160 (2010)

9. Benoit, A., Cole, M., Gilmore, S., Hillston, J.: Flexible Skeletal Programming with eSkel. In: Cunha, J.C., Medeiros, P.D. (eds.) Euro-Par 2005. LNCS, vol. 3648, pp. 761–770. Springer, Heidelberg (2005)
10. Aldinucci, M., Danelutto, M., Teti, P.: An Advanced Environment Supporting Structured Parallel Programming in Java. Future Gener. Comput. Syst. 19(5), 611–626 (2003)
11. Aldinucci, M., Danelutto, M., Kilpatrick, P.: Skeletons for Multi/Many-core Systems. In: Proc. of the Parallel Computing: From Multicores and GPU's to Petascale (Proc. of PARCO 2009), Lyon, France, pp. 265–272 (September 2009)
12. Bacci, B., Danelutto, M., Orlando, S., Pelagatti, S., Vanneschi, M.: P3L: A Structured High-Level Parallel Language, and its Structured Support. Concurrency: Practice and Experience 7(3), 225–255 (1995)
13. Botorog, G.H., Kuchen, H.: Skil: An Imperative Language with Algorithmic Skeletons for Efficient Distributed Programming. In: Proceedings of 5th IEEE International Symposium on High Performance Distributed Computing, Syracuse, NY, USA, pp. 243–252 (August 1996)
14. Gamma, E., Helm, R., Jonhson, R., Vlissides, J.: Design Patterns: Elements of Reusable Object-Oriented Software. Addison-Wesley, Boston (2002)

Multiple Intermediate Structure Deforestation by Shortcut Fusion*

Alberto Pardo[1], João Paulo Fernandes[2,3], and João Saraiva[2]

[1] Instituto de Computación, Universidad de la República, Uruguay
pardo@fing.edu.uy
[2] HASLab / INESC TEC, Universidade do Minho, Portugal
{jpaulo,jas}@di.uminho.pt
[3] Reliable and Secure Computation Group ((Rel)ease),
Universidade da Beira Interior, Portugal

Abstract. Shortcut fusion is a well-known optimization technique for functional programs. Its aim is to transform multi-pass algorithms into single pass ones, achieving deforestation of the intermediate structures that multi-pass algorithms need to construct. Shortcut fusion has already been extended in several ways. It can be applied to monadic programs, maintaining the global effects, and also to obtain circular and higher-order programs. The techniques proposed so far, however, only consider programs defined as the composition of a single producer with a single consumer. In this paper, we analyse shortcut fusion laws to deal with programs consisting of an arbitrary number of function compositions.

1 Introduction

Shortcut fusion [1] is an important optimization technique for functional programs. It was proposed as a technique for the elimination of intermediate data structures generated in function compositions $fc \circ fp$, where a producer $fp :: a \to t$ builds a data structure t, which is then traversed by a consumer $fc :: t \to b$ to produce a result. When some conditions are satisfied, we may transform these programs into equivalent ones that do not construct the intermediate structure t.

Extended forms of shortcut fusion have also been proposed to eliminate intermediate structures in function compositions in which the producer and the consumer share some additional context information. These extensions transform compositions $fc \circ fp$, where $fp :: a \to (t, z)$ and $fc :: (t, z) \to b$, into circular [2,3] and higher-order [3,4] equivalent programs, and have increased the applicability of shortcut fusion. Nevertheless, they consider programs consisting of the composition between two functions only. As a consequence, it is not possible to (straightforwardly) apply such techniques to programs that rely on multiple traversal strategies, like compilers and advanced pretty-printing algorithms [5].

---

* This work is funded by ERDF - European Regional Development Fund through the COMPETE Programme (operational programme for competitiveness) and by National Funds through the FCT - Fundação para a Ciência e a Tecnologia (Portuguese Foundation for Science and Technology) within projects FCOMP-01-0124-FEDER-020532 and FCOMP-01-0124-FEDER-022701.

A. Rauber Du Bois and P. Trinder (Eds.): SBLP 2013, LNCS 8129, pp. 120–134, 2013.
© Springer-Verlag Berlin Heidelberg 2013

The main contribution of this paper is to present generalized forms of shortcut fusion which apply to an arbitrary number of function compositions of the form $f_n \circ \cdots \circ f_1$, for $n > 2$. We establish sufficient conditions on each f_i that guarantee that consecutive fusion steps are applicable when following both a left-to-right and a right-to-left strategy. By means of what we call *chain laws*, we show how to obtain the intermediate fused definitions in such a way that further fusion steps apply. The formulation of the chain laws is the result of combining two fusion approaches: that of shortcut fusion and the one used in the formulation of fusion laws known as *acid rain* [6]. Our fusion method, characterised by requiring certain conditions on the functions involved in the compositions, differs from that employed by *warm fusion* [7].

We analyse two cases of multi-traversal programs: a) the standard case where only a data structure is passed between producer and consumer, and b) programs where in each composition, besides a data structure, some additional information is passed. Case b) is particularly interesting because it is the case where circular and higher-order programs are derived by applying fusion. The type of circular programs we derive are the natural representation of Attribute Grammars (AG) in a lazy setting [8,9]. In the AG community, however, a multi-pass program is usually derived from an AG (i.e., from a circular program) [10,11]. In this paper we study and prove correctness of the opposite transformation, that is, we study how a circular program (i.e., an AG) is derived from a multi-pass one.

Throughout the paper we will use Haskell notation, assuming a cpo semantics in terms of pointed cpos, but without the presence of the *seq* function [12]. For the sake of presentation, we will focus on definitions, laws, and examples over the list datatype only. A generic formulation of all concepts and laws developed in the paper, as well as their proofs, valid for a wide range of datatypes, is presented in an extended version of the paper.

The paper is organized as follows. In Section 2 we review shortcut fusion while in Section 3 we do so with the laws that serve for the derivation of circular and higher-order programs. In Section 4 we analyse the problem of fusing multi-traversal programs and present laws that give conditions for the derivation of circular and higher-order programs in those cases. Section 5 concludes the paper.

2   Shortcut Fusion

Shortcut fusion [1] is a program transformation technique for the elimination of intermediate data structures generated in function compositions. This technique is a consequence of parametricity properties, known as "free theorems" [13], associated with polymorphic functions. For its application, shortcut fusion requires the consumer to process all the elements of the intermediate data structure in a uniform way. This condition is established by requiring that the consumer is expressible as a *fold* [14], a program scheme that captures function definitions by structural recursion. For example, for lists, *fold* is defined as:

$$
\begin{array}{ll}
\textit{fold} & :: (b, a \rightarrow b \rightarrow b) \rightarrow [a] \rightarrow b \\
\textit{fold } (\textit{nil}, \textit{cons}) \; [\,] & = \textit{nil} \\
\textit{fold } (\textit{nil}, \textit{cons}) \; (a : \textit{as}) = \textit{cons } a \; (\textit{fold } (\textit{nil}, \textit{cons}) \; \textit{as})
\end{array}
$$

This function is equivalent to the well-known *foldr* function [14]. It traverses the list and replaces [] by the constant *nil* and the occurrences of (:) by function *cons*. The pair (*nil*, *cons*) is called an algebra. We denote by $in_L = ([], (:))$ the algebra composed by the list constructors. For example, the function that selects the elements of a list that satisfy a given predicate:

filter   :: $(a \rightarrow Bool) \rightarrow [a] \rightarrow [a]$
filter pr []   = []
filter pr $(a : as)$ = **if** *pr a* **then** $a : filter\ pr\ as$ **else** *filter pr as*

can be written in terms of *fold* as follows:

filter pr = *fold* (*fnil*, *fcons*) **where** *fnil*   = []
                                              fcons a r = **if** *pr a* **then** $a : r$ **else** *r*

On the other hand, the producer must be a function such that the computation that builds the output data structure consists of the repeated application of the data type constructors. To meet this condition the producer is required to be expressible in terms of a function, called *build* [1], which carries a "template" (a polymorphic function) that abstracts the occurrences of the constructors of the intermediate data type. In the case of lists:

build   :: $(\forall b . (b, a \rightarrow b \rightarrow b) \rightarrow c \rightarrow b) \rightarrow c \rightarrow [a]$
build $g = g\ in_L$

The polymorphic type of *g* ensures that it can only construct its result of type *b* by using the operations of its argument algebra of type $(b, a \rightarrow b \rightarrow b)$. As a result, *build* returns a list that is uniformly constructed by the repeated application of the list constructors [] and (:). For example, the function that constructs the list of numbers between *n* and 1:

down   :: $Int \rightarrow [Int]$
down 0 = []
down n = $n : down\ (n - 1)$

can be written in terms of *build* as follows:

down = *build gd* **where** *gd* (*nil*, *cons*) 0 = *nil*
                              gd (*nil*, *cons*) *n* = *cons n* (*gd* (*nil*, *cons*) $(n - 1)$)

The essential idea behind shortcut fusion is then to replace, in the producer, the occurrences of the intermediate datatype's constructors (abstracted in the "template" of the build) by appropriate values/functions specified within the consumer (the algebra carried by the fold). As a result, one obtains a definition that computes the same as the original composition but without building the intermediate data structure. This transformation is usually referred to as the *fold/build* law.

Law 1 (FOLD/BUILD FOR LISTS) *fold* (*nil*, *cons*) ∘ *build g* = *g* (*nil*, *cons*)

To see an example of application of this law, let us consider the function that computes the factors of a number:

factors   :: $Int \rightarrow [Int]$
factors n = *filter* ('*isFactorOf*' *n*) (*down* (*n* '*div*' 2))

where x '$isFactorOf$' $n = n$ 'mod' $x == 0$

Since *filter* is a fold and *down* a build, we can apply the law to eliminate the intermediate list. If we define $fd\ pr = filter\ pr \circ down$, then $factors\ n = fd\ ('isFactorOf'\ n)\ (n\ 'div'\ 2)$ and by Law 1 we obtain $fd\ pr = gd\ (fnil, fcons)$. Inlining we get the following recursive definition for $fd\ pr$:

$fd\ pr\ 0 = [\,]$

$fd\ pr\ n = $ **if** $pr\ n$ **then** $n : fd\ pr\ (n-1)$ **else** $fd\ pr\ (n-1)$

It is possible to formulate an extended form of shortcut fusion which captures the case when the intermediate data structure is generated as part of another structure. This extension has been fundamental for the formulation of shortcut fusion laws for monadic programs [15,16], and for the derivation of (monadic) circular and higher-order programs [3]. It is based on an extended form of build:

$build_N :: (\forall b\ .\ (b, a \to b \to b) \to c \to N\ b) \to c \to N\ [a]$

$build_N\ g = g\ in_L$

where N represents a data structure in which the produced list is contained. Technically, N is a *functor*, i.e. a type constructor N of kind $\star \to \star$ equipped with a function $map_N :: (a \to b) \to (N\ a \to N\ b)$, which preserves identities and compositions: $map_N\ id = id$ and $map_N\ (f \circ g) = map_N\ f \circ map_N\ g$.

The above is a natural extension of the standard build function. In fact, *build* can be obtained from $build_N$ by considering the identity functor corresponding to the identity type constructor: **type** $N\ a = a$ and $map_N\ f = f$.

Based on this extended form of build an extended shortcut fusion law can be formulated (see [15] for a proof):

Law 2 (EXTENDED FOLD/BUILD) *For strictness-preserving* [1] N,

$$map_N\ (fold\ (nil, cons)) \circ build_N\ g = g\ (nil, cons)$$

To see an example consider the following composition, where *filterLen* is the function that, given a list of numbers, returns a pair formed by a list containing the positive numbers together with the length of the output list.

$sumFilLen = (sum \times id) \circ filterLen$

$sum \qquad :: \ Num\ a \Rightarrow [a] \to a$

$sum\ [\,] \qquad = \ 0$

$sum\ (a : as) = \ a + sum\ as$

$filterLen \qquad :: \ Num\ a \Rightarrow [a] \to ([a], Int)$

$filterLen\ [\,] \qquad = ([\,], 0)$

$filterLen\ (x : xs) = $ **if** $x > 0$ **then** $(x : ys, 1 + l)$ **else** (ys, l)

$\qquad$ **where** $(ys, l) = filterLen\ xs$

where $(f \times g)$ is defined as $(f \times g)\ (x, y) = (f\ x, g\ y)$; id is the identity function. To simplify the expression of *sumFilLen* we first observe that *filterLen* can be written as a $build_N$ with functor $N\ a = (a, Int)$ and $map_N\ f = f \times id$.

---

[1] By strictness-preserving we mean that map_N preserves strict functions, i.e. if f is strict, then so is $map_N\ f$.

$filterLen = build_N\ gfL$
   where
      $gfL\ (nil, cons)\ [\,]\qquad = (nil, 0)$
      $gfL\ (nil, cons)\ (x : xs) = \textbf{if}\ x > 0\ \textbf{then}\ (cons\ x\ ys, 1 + l)\ \textbf{else}\ (ys, l)$
         where $(ys, l) = gfL\ (nil, cons)\ xs$

It is easy to see that sum is a fold: $sum = fold\ (0, (+))$. Then, by applying Law 2 we can deduce: $sumFilLen = (fold\ (0, (+)) \times id) \circ build_N\ gfL = gfL\ (0, (+)))$, which corresponds to the following recursive definition:

$sumFilLen\ [\,]\qquad = (0, 0)$
$sumFilLen\ (x : xs) = \textbf{if}\ x > 0\ \textbf{then}\ (x + s, 1 + l)\ \textbf{else}\ (s, l)$
    where $(s, l) = sumFilLen\ xs$

3   Circular and Higher-Order Programs

In this section we review the laws that make it possible to derive circular as well as higher-order programs from function compositions that communicate through an intermediate pair (t, z), where t is a data structure and z some additional information. The derivation can be done both for pure and monadic programs (see [3]), and like for shortcut fusion, it requires both consumer and producer to be expressible in terms of certain program schemes. The consumer is required to be a structural recursive definition that can be written as a *pfold*, a program scheme which is similar to *fold* but that additionally takes a constant parameter for its computation. For lists, it corresponds to the following definition:

$pfold :: (z \to b, a \to b \to z \to b) \to ([a], z) \to b$
$pfold\ (hnil, hcons)\ ([\,], z)\quad = hnil\ z$
$pfold\ (hnil, hcons)\ (a : as, z) = hcons\ a\ (pfold\ (hnil, hcons)\ (as, z))\ z$

The producer is required to be expressible in terms of a kind of build function, called *buildp*, that returns a pair formed by a data structure and a value instead of simply a data structure. For lists:

$buildp\quad :: (\forall b\ .\ (b, a \to b \to b) \to c \to (b, z)) \to c \to ([a], z)$
$buildp\ g = g\ in_L$

Note that *buildp* corresponds to $build_N$ with functor $N\ a = (a, z)$ for some z.

3.1   Derivation of Circular Programs

The derivation of purely functional circular programs is stated by the following law (see [3] for further details and a proof). To improve the understanding of circular definitions we frame their circular arguments.

Law 3 (PFOLD/BUILDP)

$$pfold\ (hnil, hcons)\ (buildp\ g\ c) = v$$
$$\textbf{where}\ (v, \boxed{z}) = g\ (knil, kcons)\ c$$
$$knil = hnil\ \boxed{z}$$
$$kcons\ x\ r = hcons\ x\ r\ \boxed{z}$$

To see an example, let us consider $addLen = addL \circ filterLen$ where:

$$addL\ ([\,],l)\quad = [\,]$$
$$addL\ (x:xs,l) = (x+l) : addL\ (xs,l)$$

First, we express $addL$ and $filterLen$ in terms of pfold and buildp, respectively:

$$addL = pfold\ (hnil, hcons)\ \textbf{where}\ hnil\ l = [\,]$$
$$hcons\ x\ r\ l = (x+l):r$$

$$filterLen = buildp\ gfL$$

where gfL is the same function presented in Section 2. Then, by applying Law 3 we derive the following circular definition:

$$addLen\ xs = ys$$
$$\textbf{where}\ (ys, \boxed{l})\quad = gk\ xs$$
$$gk\ [\,]\quad\quad = ([\,],0)$$

$$gk\ (x:xs) = \textbf{if}\ x>0\ \textbf{then}\ ((x+\boxed{l}):ys, 1+n)\ \textbf{else}\ (ys,n)$$
$$\textbf{where}\ (ys,n) = gk\ xs$$

Law 3 can be generalized similarly to extended shortcut fusion. The generalization works on an extended form of $buildp$ and represents the case where the intermediate pair is produced within another structure given by a functor N.

$$buildp_N\quad :: (\forall\ b\ .\ (b, a \to b \to b) \to c \to N\ (b,z)) \to c \to N\ ([a],z)$$
$$buildp_N\ g = g\ in_L$$

Observe that $buildp_N = build_M$ for $M\ a = N\ (a,z)$.

For the formulation of the new law it is necessary to assume that functor N possesses an associated polymorphic function $\epsilon_N :: N\ a \to a$ that projects a value of type a from a structure of type $N\ a$. A free theorem [13] associated with the type of ϵ_N states that $f \circ \epsilon_N = \epsilon_N \circ map_N\ f$, for every f.

The desired generalization of Law 3 is as follows. Let $f\ \$\ x = f\ x$.

Law 4 (PFOLD/BUILDPN) *Let* (N, ϵ_N) *be a strictness-preserving.*

$$pfold\ (hnil, hcons) \circ \epsilon_N \circ buildp_N\ g\ \$\ c = v$$
$$\textbf{where}\ (v, \boxed{z}) = \epsilon_N\ (g\ (knil, kcons)\ c)$$
$$knil = hnil\ \boxed{z}$$
$$kcons\ x\ r = hcons\ x\ r\ \boxed{z}$$

3.2 Derivation of Higher-Order Programs

Starting from the same kind of compositions used to derive circular programs it is possible to derive, by alternative laws, higher-order programs [3]. Higher-order programs are sometimes preferred over circular ones as they are not restricted to a lazy evaluation setting and their running performance is often better than that of their circular equivalents.

The transformation into higher-order programs is based on the fact that every pfold can be expressed in terms of a higher-order fold. For example, given

$pfold\ (hnil, hcons) :: ([a], z) \to b$, with $hnil :: z \to b$ and $hcons :: a \to b \to z \to b$, we can write it as a fold of type $[a] \to z \to b$:

$$pfold\ (hnil, hcons)\ (xs, z) = fold\ (knil, kcons)\ xs\ z$$

where $knil = \lambda z \to hnil\ z :: z \to b$ and $kcons\ x\ r = \lambda z \to hcons\ x\ (r\ z)\ z ::$
$a \to (z \to b) \to (z \to b)$. With this relationship at hand we can state the following law, which is the instance to our context of a more general program transformation technique called lambda abstraction [17].

Law 5 (H-O PFOLD/BUILDP) *For left-strict hcons,*[2]

$$pfold\ (hnil, hcons)\ (buildp\ g\ c) = f\ z$$
$$\textbf{where}\ (f, z) = g\ (knil, kcons)\ c$$
$$knil = \lambda z \to hnil\ z$$
$$kcons\ x\ r = \lambda z \to hcons\ x\ (r\ z)\ z$$

Like in Law 3, $g\ (knil, kcons)$ returns a pair, but now composed by a function of type $z \to b$ and a value of type z. The final result then corresponds to the application of the function to that value.

To see an example of the use of this law, let us consider again the composition $addLen = addL \circ filterLen$. By applying Law 5 we get the following definition:

$$addLen\ xs = f\ l$$
$$\textbf{where}\ (f, l) = gk\ xs$$
$$gk\ [] \quad = (\lambda l \to [], 0)$$
$$gk\ (x : xs) = \textbf{if}\ x > 0\ \textbf{then}\ (\lambda l \to (x + l) : f'\ l, 1 + l')\ \textbf{else}\ (f', l')$$
$$\textbf{where}\ (f', l') = gk\ xs$$

The following is a generalization of the previous law.

Law 6 (H-O PFOLD/BUILDPN) *Let* (N, ϵ_N) *be a strictness-preserving functor.*

$$pfold\ (hnil, hcons) \circ \epsilon_N \circ buildp_N\ g\ \$\ c = f\ z$$
$$\textbf{where}\ (f, z) = \epsilon_N\ (g\ (knil, kcons)\ c)$$
$$knil = \lambda z \to hnil\ z$$
$$kcons\ x\ r = \lambda z \to hcons\ x\ (r\ z)\ z$$

4   Multiple Intermediate Structure Deforestation

In this section we analyse how can we deal with a sequence of compositions $f_n \circ \cdots \circ f_1$, for $n > 2$. We start with the analysis of the standard case in which a single data structure is generated in each composition. Our aim is to look at the conditions the functions f_i need to satisfy in order to be possible to derive a monolithic definition from such a composition. We then turn to the analysis of situations in which the intermediate data structures are passed between functions inside a pair. As we saw in Section 3, compositions of this kind give rise to circular and higher-order definitions.

---

[2] By left-strict we mean strict on the first argument, that is, $hcons\ (\bot, z) = \bot$.

4.1 Standard Case

Let us suppose that in every composition $f_{i+1} \circ f_i$ only an intermediate data structure is passed between the functions. To derive a monolithic definition from the whole sequence $f_n \circ \cdots \circ f_1$ the involved functions need to satisfy certain conditions. Clearly, f_1 needs to be a producer while f_n a consumer. Functions $f_2, \ldots, f_{n-1}$ are more interesting since they all need to be both consumers and producers in order to be possible to fuse them with their neighbour functions.

Suppose, for example, that we want to test whether a number is perfect. A number is said to be *perfect* when it is equal to the sum of its factors:

$perfect\ n = sumFactors\ n == n$

$sumFactors\ n = sum\ (factors\ n)$

Notice that two intermediate lists are generated by *sumFactors*: one by *factors* and the other in the composition of *sum* with *factors*. If we want to eliminate those data structures the essential expression to fuse is *sum* ∘ *filter pr* ∘ *down*. As shown in Section 2, *down* is a producer. On the other hand, *sum* is a consumer as it can be written as a fold. Concerning *filter pr*, it is a consumer, but it can also be a producer maintaining its formulation as a fold, appealing to the notion of an *algebra transformer*, traditionally used in the context of fusion laws known as *acid rain* [6]. Similar to the "template" of a build, a transformer makes it possible to abstract the occurrences of the constructors of the data structure produced as result from the body of a fold, or which is the same, from the operations of the algebra carried by a fold. In the case of *filter pr*, we can write:

$filter\ pr = fold\ (\tau\ in_L)$

where $\tau\ (nil, cons) = (nil, \lambda a\ r \rightarrow$ **if** $pr\ a$ **then** $cons\ a\ r$ **else** $r)$

The algebra transformer $\tau :: \forall\ b\ .\ (b, a \rightarrow b \rightarrow b) \rightarrow (b, a \rightarrow b \rightarrow b)$ simply abstracts the list constructors from the algebra $([], \lambda a\ r \rightarrow$ **if** $pr\ a$ **then** $a :$ r **else** $r)$ of the fold for *filter pr* by replacing its occurrences by the components of an arbitrary algebra $(nil, cons)$. As mentioned above, transformers are useful in the context of acid rain laws because they permit to specify producers given by folds. The following is an acid rain law with a transformer between list algebras.

Law 7 (FOLD-FOLD FUSION FOR LISTS)

$$\tau :: \forall\ b\ .\ (b, a \rightarrow b \rightarrow b) \rightarrow (b, a' \rightarrow b \rightarrow b)$$
$$\Rightarrow$$
$$fold\ (nil, cons) \circ fold\ (\tau\ in_L) = fold\ (\tau\ (nil, cons))$$

Acid rain laws can be expressed in terms of shortcut fusion [18]. For example, Law 7 can be seen as a particular case of Law 1. In fact, by defining $gfold\ k = fold\ (\tau\ k)$ it follows that $fold\ (\tau\ in_L) = build\ gfold$.

Returning to the composition *sum* ∘ *filter pr* ∘ *down*, there are various ways in which fusion can proceed in this case. One way is to proceed from left-to-right by first fusing *sum* with *filter pr*, and then fusing the result with *down*. For fusing *sum* ∘ *filter pr* we can apply Law 7, obtaining as result $fold\ (\tau\ (0, (+)))$. Fusing this fold with *down* by Law 1 we obtain $gd\ (\tau\ (0, (+)))$ as final result.

An equivalent alternative is to proceed from right-to-left by first fusing *filter pr* with *down* and then fusing the result with *sum*. Fusion of *filter pr* ∘ *down* is performed by applying Law 1, obtaining *gd* (τ in_L) as result; this coincides with the function *fd pr* shown in Section 2. If we now want to fuse *sum* with *gd* (τ in_L) then we first need to rewrite this function as a build. It is in such a situation that a new law, that we call *chain law*, comes into play. It states conditions under which the composition of a consumer with a producer, such that the consumer happens to be also a producer, can be fused resulting in a function that can be directly expressed as a producer. The key idea of this law is the appropriate combination of the fusion approaches represented by shortcut fusion and acid rain. We present the case of the chain law for an algebra transformer with same type as in Law 7.

Law 8 (CHAIN LAW FOR LISTS)

$$\tau :: \forall b . (b, a \to b \to b) \to (b, a' \to b \to b)$$
$$\Rightarrow$$
$$fold\ (\tau\ in_L) \circ build\ g = build\ (g \circ \tau)$$

Applying this law we have that *filter pr* ∘ *down* = *build* ($gd \circ \tau$), which can be directly fused with *sum*, obtaining *gd* (τ (0, (+))) as before. To see its recursive definition, let us define *sfd pr* = *gd* (τ (0, (+))). Inlining,

$sfd\ pr\ 0 = 0$

$sfd\ pr\ n = \textbf{if}\ pr\ n\ \textbf{then}\ n + sfd\ pr\ (n-1)\ \textbf{else}\ sfd\ pr\ (n-1)$

It is then natural to state a chain law associated with the extension of build.

Law 9 (EXTENDED CHAIN LAW) *For strictness-preserving N,*

$$\tau :: \forall b . (b, a \to b \to b) \to (b, a' \to b \to b)$$
$$\Rightarrow$$
$$map_N\ (fold\ (\tau\ in_L)) \circ build_N\ g = build_N\ (g \circ \tau)$$

The next law describes a more general situation where the transformer τ returns an algebra whose carrier is the result of applying a functor W to the carrier of the input algebra. Law 9 is then the special case when W is the identity functor. By NW we denote the composition of functors N and W, that is, $NW\ a = N\ (W\ a)$ and $map_{NW}\ f = map_N\ (map_W\ f)$.

Law 10 *Let W be a functor. For strictness-preserving N,*

$$\tau :: \forall b . (b, a \to b \to b) \to (W\ b, a' \to W\ b \to W\ b)$$
$$\Rightarrow$$
$$map_N\ (fold\ (\tau\ in_L)) \circ build_N\ g = build_{NW}\ (g \circ \tau)$$

4.2 Derivation of Programs with Multiple Circularities

We now analyse laws that make it possible the derivation of programs with multiple circularities. We consider that the sequence of compositions $f_n \circ \cdots \circ f_1$

is such that a pair (t_i, z_i) of a data structure t_i and a value z_i is generated in each composition. Like before, f_1 needs to be a producer, f_n a consumer, whereas $f_2, \ldots, f_{n-1}$ need to be simultaneously consumers and producers. Therefore, in this case the sequence of compositions is of the form $pfold \circ \cdots \circ pfold \circ buildp$.

Like in the standard case, we want to analyse the transformation in both directions: from left-to-right and right-to-left. We will see that in this case there are significant differences between the transformation in each direction, not in the result, but in the complexity of the laws that need to be applied.

Right-to-Left Transformation. Following a similar approach to the one used for the standard case, when the transformation proceeds from right to left it is necessary to state sufficient conditions that permit us to establish when the composition of a pfold with a buildp is again a buildp. Interestingly, the resulting definition would be not only a producer (a buildp) that can be fused with the next pfold in the sequence, but by Law 3 it would be also a circular program that internally computes a pair (v, z) formed by the result of the program (v) and the circular argument (z). Therefore, by successively fusing the compositions in the sequence from right to left we finally obtain a program with multiple circular arguments, one for each fused composition. During this process, we incrementally introduce a new circular argument at every fusion step without affecting the circular arguments previously introduced.

At the i-th step, the calculated circular program internally computes a nested product of the form $((\ldots (v_i, z_i), \ldots), z_1)$, where v_i is the value returned by that program and $z_1, \ldots, z_i$ are the circular arguments introduced so far. As a consequence of this, at each step it is necessary to employ an extended shortcut fusion law because the pair (t_i, z_i) to be consumed by the next pfold is generated within the structure formed by the nested product. Thus, we will be handling extensions with functors of the form $N\ a = ((\ldots (a, z_j), \ldots), z_1)$.

Therefore, to deal with this process appropriately we need to state a chain law in the sense of Law 9 but now associated with the composition of a pfold with an extended buildp. Given a transformer $\sigma :: \forall\, b\, .\, (b, a \to b \to b) \to (z \to W\ b, a' \to W\ b \to z \to W\ b)$, where W is a functor and, for each algebra k, $\sigma\ k = (\sigma_1\ k, \sigma_2\ k)$, it is possible to derive an algebra transformer: $\tau :: \forall\, b\, .\, (b, a \to b \to b) \to (W\ b, a' \to W\ b \to W\ b)$ such that $\tau\ k = (\tau_1\ k, \tau_2\ k)$ with $\tau_1\ k = \sigma_1\ k\ z$ and $\tau_2\ k\ x\ r = \sigma_2\ k\ x\ r\ z$, for a fixed z. Such a σ is used in the next law to represent a case when the consumer, given by a pfold, is also a producer. In fact, observe that the pfold in the law has type $([a'], z) \to ([a], y)$.

Law 11 (CHAIN RULE) *Let* (N, ϵ_N) *be a strictness-preserving functor, and* $M\ a = N\ (a, z)$. *Let* $W\ a = (a, y)$, *for some type* y. *Let* $\sigma\ k = (\sigma_1\ k, \sigma_2\ k)$.

$$\sigma :: \forall\, b\, .\, (b, a \to b \to b) \to (z \to W\ b, a' \to W\ b \to z \to W\ b)$$
$$\Rightarrow$$
$$pfold\ (\sigma\ in_L) \circ \epsilon_N \circ buildp_N\ g\ \$\ c = p$$
$$\textbf{where}\ (p, \boxed{z}) = \epsilon_N\ (buildp_M\ (g \circ \tau)\ c)$$
$$\tau\ k = (\tau_1\ k, \tau_2\ k)$$
$$\tau_1\ k = \sigma_1\ k\ \boxed{z}$$
$$\tau_2\ k\ x\ r = \sigma_2\ k\ x\ r\ \boxed{z}$$

Example 1. Consider the following program that given a set of points in a plane returns the maximum distance between the points located above the average height and the highest point below the average height. We assume that the height of all points is non-negative.

type *Point* $= (Float, Float)$
type *Height* $= Float$
type *Distance* $= Float$

$distance = maxDistance \circ takePoints \circ avrgHeight\ 0\ 0$

$avrgHeight :: Height \rightarrow Integer \rightarrow [Point] \rightarrow ([Point], Height)$
$avrgHeight\ h\ l\ [] = ([], h\ /\ fromInteger\ l)$
$avrgHeight\ h\ l\ ((x, y) : ps) = \textbf{let}\ (ps', avH) = avrgHeight\ (y + h)\ (1 + l)\ ps$
$\qquad\qquad\qquad\qquad\quad \textbf{in}\ ((x, y) : ps', avH)$

$takePoints :: ([Point], Height) \rightarrow ([Point], Point)$
$takePoints\ ([], avH) = ([], (0, 0))$
$takePoints\ ((x, y) : ps, avH) = \textbf{let}\ (ps', hp) = takePoints\ (ps, avH)$
$\qquad\qquad\qquad\qquad\qquad \textbf{in if}\ y > avH\ \textbf{then}\ ((x, y) : ps', hp)$
$\qquad\qquad\qquad\qquad\qquad\qquad \textbf{else}\ (ps', \textbf{if}\ y > snd\ hp\ \textbf{then}\ (x, y)\ \textbf{else}\ hp)$

$maxDistance :: ([Point], Point) \rightarrow Distance$
$maxDistance\ ([], hp) = 0$
$maxDistance\ ((x, y) : ps, hp@(hx, hy))$
$\quad = sqrt\ ((x - hx)^2 + (y - hy)^2)\ \text{`}max\text{`}\ maxDistance\ (ps, hp)$

To apply the rules, first we need to express these functions in terms of the corresponding program schemes.

$avrgHeight = buildp\ gavrgH$
$\quad \textbf{where}\ gavrgH\ (nil, cons)\ h\ l\ [] = (nil, h\ /\ fromInteger\ l)$
$\qquad\qquad\quad gavrgH\ (nil, cons)\ h\ l\ ((x, y) : ps)$
$\qquad\qquad\qquad = \textbf{let}\ (ps', avH) = gavrgH\ (nil, cons)\ (y + h)\ (1 + l)\ ps$
$\qquad\qquad\qquad\quad \textbf{in}\ (cons\ (x, y)\ ps', avH)$

$takePoints = pfold\ (tnil, tcons)$
$\quad \textbf{where}\ tnil\ avH \qquad\quad = ([], (0, 0))$
$\qquad\qquad\quad tcons\ (x, y)\ r\ avH = \textbf{let}\ (ps, hp) = r$
$\qquad\qquad\qquad\qquad\qquad\quad \textbf{in if}\ y > avH\ \textbf{then}\ ((x, y) : ps, hp)$
$\qquad\qquad\qquad\qquad\qquad\qquad \textbf{else}\ (ps, \textbf{if}\ y > snd\ hp\ \textbf{then}\ (x, y)\ \textbf{else}\ hp)$

$maxDistance = pfold\ (hnil, hcons)$
$\quad \textbf{where}\ hnil\ hp = 0$
$\qquad\qquad\quad hcons\ (x, y)\ r\ hp@(hx, hy) = sqrt\ ((x - hx)^2 + (y - hy)^2)\ \text{`}max\text{`}\ r$

Since $(tnil, tcons)$ can be expressed as $\sigma\ in_L$, where σ is a transformer:

$\sigma\ (nil, cons) = (\lambda avH \rightarrow (nil, (0, 0))$
$\qquad\qquad\qquad , \lambda(x, y)\ r\ avH \rightarrow$
$\qquad\qquad\qquad\qquad \textbf{let}\ (ps, hp) = r$

$$\textbf{in if } y > avH \textbf{ then } (cons\ (x, y)\ ps, hp)$$
$$\textbf{else } (ps, \textbf{if } y > snd\ hp \textbf{ then } (x, y) \textbf{ else } hp))$$

our program corresponds to the following composition:

$$distance = pfold\ (hnil, hcons) \circ pfold\ (\sigma\ in_L) \circ buildp\ gavrgH\ 0\ 0$$

The transformation from right to left essentially proceeds by first applying Law 11 and then Law 4. The program that is finally obtained is the following:

$distance\ inp = v$
   $\textbf{where } (v, \boxed{u}) = w$
      $(w, \boxed{z}) = gk\ 0\ 0\ inp$
      $gk\ h\ l\ [\,] = ((0, (0, 0)), h\ /\ fromInteger\ l)$
      $gk\ h\ l\ ((x, y) : ps) =$
         $\textbf{let } (ps', avH) = gk\ (y + h)\ (1 + l)\ ps$
         $\textbf{in } (\textbf{let } (qs, hp) = ps'$
            $\textbf{in if } y > \boxed{z}$
               $\textbf{then } (sqrt\ ((x - fst\,\boxed{u})^2 + (y - snd\,\boxed{u})^2)\ `max`\ qs, hp)$
               $\textbf{else } (qs, \textbf{if } y > snd\ hp \textbf{ then } (x, y) \textbf{ else } hp), avH)$

Left-to-right Transformation. When the transformation is in left to right order we worry about the opposite situation. Except for the last step, at each intermediate stage of the transformation process we are interested in that the definition that results from a fusion step is a consumer. If that is the case then it is guaranteed that we can successively apply fusion until cover all function compositions. It is then necessary to state sufficient conditions to establish when the composition of two pfolds is again a pfold.

The following acid rain law is inspired in fold-fold fusion (Law 7).

Law 12 (PFOLD-PFOLD FUSION)

$$\sigma :: \forall\ b\ .\ (b, a \to b \to b) \to (z \to b, a' \to b \to z \to b)$$
$$\Rightarrow$$
$$pfold\ (hnil, hcons)\ (pfold\ (\sigma\ in_L)\ c) = v$$
$$\textbf{where } (v, \boxed{z}) = pfold\ (\sigma\ (knil, kcons))\ c$$
$$knil = hnil\ \boxed{z}$$
$$kcons\ x\ r = hcons\ x\ r\ \boxed{z}$$

Like fold-fold fusion, this law can also be formulated in terms of shortcut fusion. By defining $gpfold\ k = pfold\ (\sigma\ k)$, it follows that $pfold\ (\sigma\ in_L) = buildp\ gpfold$. Then, by Law 3 we obtain the same result.

Observe that, unlike the right to left transformation, now we do not need to worry about any data structure (a nested pair) inside which fusion is performed. A nested pair is in fact created, but on the result side of the consumers that are successively calculated. It is interesting to see how the nested pair that appears in the final circular program is incrementally generated in each transformation. In the left-to-right transformation the nested pair is generated from inside to outside, i.e. the pair generated in each fusion step contains the previous existing pair, whereas in the right-to-left transformation the nested pair is generated from outside to inside.

Returning to the example of function *distance*, the transformation from left to right essentially proceeds by simply applying Law 12 and then Law 3. The program that is finally obtained is of course the same.

4.3   Derivation of Higher-Order Programs

During the transformation to a higher-order program we will deal again with a nested structure. Instead of a nested pair we will incrementally construct a structure of type $(z_1 \to (z_2 \to (\cdots \to (z_i \to a, z_i) \cdots), z_2), z_1)$ where the zs are the types of the context parameters that are passed in the successive compositions. So, a structure of this type is a pair (p_1, z_1) composed by a function p_1, which returns a pair (p_2, z_2) such that p_2 is a function that returns again a pair, and so on. Associated to each of these structures we can define a functor $N\ a = (z_1 \to (z_2 \to (\cdots \to (z_i \to a, z_i) \cdots), z_2), z_1)$ whose projection function $\epsilon_N :: N\ a \to a$ is given by iterated function application: $\epsilon_N(p_1, z_1) = p_i\ z_i$ where $(p_j, z_j) = p_{j-1}\ z_{j-1}, j = 2, i$.

Like for circular programs, we will see differences in the process of derivation of a a higher-order program when we transform a sequence of compositions $f_n \circ \cdots \circ f_1$ from right to left and left to right. Again one of the differences is the order in which the nested structure is generated.

Right-to-Left Transformation. For the transformation in this direction we need to consider again the situation in which the consumer (a pfold) composed with a producer (a buildp) is again a buildp, The situation is similar to the one faced with Law 11 with the only difference that now we are in the context of a higher-order program derivation. Given a transformer $\sigma :: \forall\ b\ .\ (b, a \to b \to b) \to (z \to W\ b, a' \to W\ b \to z \to W\ b)$, where W is a functor and, for each algebra k, $\sigma\ k = (\sigma_1\ k, \sigma_2\ k)$, it is possible to derive an algebra transformer: $\tau :: \forall\ b\ .\ (b, a \to b \to b) \to (z \to W\ b, a' \to (z \to W\ b) \to (z \to W\ b))$ such that $\tau\ k = (\tau_1\ k, \tau_2\ k)$ with $\tau_1\ k = \lambda z \to \sigma_1\ k\ z$ and $\tau_2\ k\ x\ r = \lambda z \to \sigma_2\ k\ x\ (r\ z)\ z$. Observe that the pfold in the next law has type $([a'], z) \to ([a], y)$.

Law 13 (H-O CHAIN RULE) *Let (N, ϵ_N) be a strictness-preserving functor and $M\ a = N\ (a, z)$. Let $W\ a = (a, y)$, for some type y. Let $\sigma\ k = (\sigma_1\ k, \sigma_2\ k)$.*

$$\sigma :: \forall\ b\ .\ (b, a \to b \to b) \to (z \to W\ b, a' \to W\ b \to z \to W\ b)$$
$$\Rightarrow$$
$$pfold\ (\sigma\ in_L) \circ \epsilon_N \circ buildp_N\ g\ \$\ c = f\ z$$
$$\textbf{where}\ (f, z) = \epsilon_N\ (buildp_M\ (g \circ \tau)\ c)$$
$$\tau\ k = (\tau_1\ k, \tau_2\ k)$$
$$\tau_1\ k = \lambda z \to \sigma_1\ k\ z$$
$$\tau_2\ k\ x\ r = \lambda z \to \sigma_2\ k\ x\ (r\ z)\ z$$

The higher-order program derivation in right to left order applied to *distance* essentially proceeds by first applying Law 13 and then Law 6. As result we obtain the following higher-order program:

$distance\ inp = f\ u$
   where $(f, u) = g\ z$
       $(g, z) = gk\ 0\ 0\ inp$
       $gk\ h\ l\ [\,] = (\lambda z \to (\lambda u \to 0, (0, 0)), h\ /\ fromInteger\ l)$
       $gk\ h\ l\ ((x, y) : ps) =$
       let $(ps', avH) = gk\ (y + h)\ (1 + l)\ ps$
       in $(\lambda z \to$
          let $(qs, hp) = ps'\ z$
          in if $y > z$
             then $(\lambda u \to sqrt\ ((x - fst\ u)^2 + (y - snd\ u)^2)\ `max`\ (qs\ u), hp)$
             else $(\lambda u \to qs\ u, \textbf{if}\ y > snd\ hp\ \textbf{then}\ (x, y)\ \textbf{else}\ hp), avH)$

Left-to-Right Transformation. For the transformation in this other direction we proceed similarly as we did for circular programs. The same considerations hold in this case. The calculation of the successive consumers from left to right is performed using the following acid rain law:

Law 14 (H-O PFOLD-PFOLD FUSION)

$$\sigma :: \forall\ b\ .\ (b, a \to b \to b) \to (z \to b, a' \to b \to z \to b)$$
$$\Rightarrow$$
$$pfold\ (hnil, hcons)\ (pfold\ (\sigma\ in_L)\ c) = f\ z$$
$$\textbf{where}\ (f, z) = pfold\ (\sigma\ (knil, kcons))\ c$$
$$knil = \lambda z \to hnil\ z$$
$$kcons\ x\ r = \lambda z \to hcons\ x\ (r\ z)\ z$$

This law can also be formulated in terms of shortcut fusion. By defining $gpfold\ k = pfold\ (\sigma\ k)$, we have that $pfold\ (\sigma\ in_L) = buildp\ gpfold$. Then, by Law 5 we obtain the same result.

Concerning the example of function $distance$, the higher-order program derivation from left to right essentially proceeds by applying Law 14 and then Law 5.

5 Conclusions

In this paper, we have presented an approach, based on shortcut fusion, to achieve deforestation in an arbitrary number of function compositions. Our work generalizes standard shortcut fusion [1], *circular* shortcut fusion [3] and *higher-order* shortcut fusion [3]. The derivation of circular programs is strongly associated with attribute grammar research [10,11], and we expect our work to clarify even further their similar nature. The derivation of higher-order programs is motivated by efficiency. Indeed, as the programs we consider here are of the same kind as the ones we have benchmarked in [19], we expect the derived higher-order programs to be significantly more efficient when compared to their multiple traversal and circular counterparts.

Our approach is calculational and establishes sufficient conditions for fusion to proceed. For now, we have not focused on implementation details, that we are considering to present in an extended version of this paper as well as further demonstrational examples that have not been included here due to space limitations.

References

1. Gill, A., Launchbury, J., Peyton Jones, S.: A short cut to deforestation. In: Functional Programming Languages and Computer Architecture. ACM (1993)
2. Bird, R.: Using circular programs to eliminate multiple traversals of data. Acta Informatica 21, 239–250 (1984)
3. Pardo, A., Fernandes, J.P., Saraiva, J.: Shortcut fusion rules for the derivation of circular and higher-order programs. Higher-Order and Symbolic Computation 24(1-2), 115–149 (2011)
4. Voigtländer, J.: Semantics and pragmatics of new shortcut fusion rules. In: Garrigue, J., Hermenegildo, M.V. (eds.) FLOPS 2008. LNCS, vol. 4989, pp. 163–179. Springer, Heidelberg (2008)
5. Swierstra, D., Chitil, O.: Linear, bounded, functional pretty-printing. Journal of Functional Programming 19(1), 1–16 (2009)
6. Onoue, Y., Hu, Z., Iwasaki, H., Takeichi, M.: A Calculational Fusion System HYLO. In: IFIP TC 2 Working Conference on Algorithmic Languages and Calculi, pp. 76–106. Chapman & Hall (1997)
7. Launchbury, J., Sheard, T.: Warm fusion: Deriving build-catas from recursive definitions. In: Funct. Prog. Lang. and Computer Architecture. ACM (1995)
8. Johnsson, T.: Attribute grammars as a functional programming paradigm. In: Kahn, G. (ed.) FPCA 1987. LNCS, vol. 274, pp. 154–173. Springer, Heidelberg (1987)
9. de Moor, O., Backhouse, K., Swierstra, S.D.: First-class attribute grammars. Informatica (Slovenia) 24(3) (2000)
10. Fernandes, J.P., Saraiva, J.: Tools and Libraries to Model and Manipulate Circular Programs. In: Workshop on Partial Eval. and Program Manipulation. ACM (2007)
11. Fernandes, J.P., Saraiva, J., Seidel, D., Voigtländer, J.: Strictification of circular programs. In: Workshop on Partial Eval. and Program Manipulation. ACM (2011)
12. Johann, P., Voigtländer, J.: Free theorems in the presence of seq. In: Symposium on Principles of Programming Languages, pp. 99–110. ACM (2004)
13. Wadler, P.: Theorems for free! In: Functional Programming Languages and Computer Architecture. ACM (1989)
14. Bird, R., de Moor, O.: Algebra of Programming. Prentice-Hall Inernational Series in Computer Science, vol. 100. Prentice-Hall (1997)
15. Manzino, C., Pardo, A.: Shortcut Fusion of Monadic Programs. Journal of Universal Computer Science 14(21), 3431–3446 (2008)
16. Ghani, N., Johann, P.: Short cut fusion for effects. In: TFP 2008. Trends in Functional Programming, vol. 9, pp. 113–128. Intellect (2009)
17. Pettorossi, A., Skowron, A.: The lambda abstraction strategy for program derivation. Fundamenta Informaticae 12(4), 541–561 (1989)
18. Takano, A., Meijer, E.: Shortcut deforestation in calculational form. In: Functional Programming Languages and Computer Architecture, pp. 306–313. ACM (1995)
19. Fernandes, J.P.: Desing, Implementation and Calculation of Circular Programs. PhD thesis, Dept. of Informatics, Univ. of Minho, Portugal (2009)

Zipper-Based Attribute Grammars
and Their Extensions*

Pedro Martins[1], João Paulo Fernandes[1,2], and João Saraiva[1]

[1] High-Assurance Software Laboratory (HASLAB/INESC TEC),
Universidade do Minho, Portugal
[2] Reliable and Secure Computation Group ((Rel)ease),
Universidade da Beira Interior, Portugal
{prmartins,jpaulo,jas}@di.uminho.pt

Abstract. Attribute grammars are a suitable formalism to express complex software language analysis and manipulation algorithms, which rely on multiple traversals of the underlying syntax tree. Recently, Attribute Grammars have been extended with mechanisms such as references and high-order and circular attributes. Such extensions provide a powerful modular mechanism and allow the specification of complex fix-point computations. This paper defines an elegant and simple, zipper-based embedding of attribute grammars and their extensions as first class citizens. In this setting, language specifications are defined as a set of independent, off-the-shelf components that can easily be composed into a powerful, executable language processor. Several real examples of language specification and processing programs have been implemented in this setting.

1 Introduction

Attribute Grammars (AGs) [1] are a well-known and convenient formalism not only for specifying the semantic analysis phase of a compiler but also to model complex multiple traversal algorithms. Indeed, AGs have been used not only to specify real programming languages, like for example Haskell [2], but also to specify powerful pretty printing algorithms [3], deforestation techniques [4] and powerful type systems [5], for example.

All these attribute grammars specify complex and large algorithms that rely on multiple traversals over large tree-like data structures. To express these algorithms in regular programming languages is difficult because they rely in complex recursive patterns, and, most importantly, because there are dependencies between values computed in one traversal and used in following ones. In such cases, an explicit data structure has to be used to glue different traversal functions. In an imperative setting those values are stored in the tree nodes (which work as a gluing data structure), while in a declarative setting such data structures have to

---

* This work is funded by ERDF - European Regional Development Fund through the COMPETE Programme (operational programme for competitiveness) and by National Funds through the FCT - Fundação para a Ciência e a Tecnologia (Portuguese Foundation for Science and Technology) within projects FCOMP-01-0124-FEDER-020532 and FCOMP-01-0124-FEDER-022701.

A. Rauber Du Bois and P. Trinder (Eds.): SBLP 2013, LNCS 8129, pp. 135–149, 2013.

be defined and constructed. In an AG setting, the programmer does not have to concern himself on scheduling traversals, nor on defining gluing data structures.

Recent research in attribute grammars is working in two main directions. Firstly, AG-based systems are supporting new extensions to the standard AG formalism that improve the AG expressiveness. Higher-order AGs (HOAGs) [6, 7] provide a modular extension to AGs. Reference AGs (RAGs) [8] allow the definition of references to remote parts of the tree, and, thus, extending the traditional tree-based algorithms to graphs. Finally, Circular AGs (CAGs) allow the definition of fix-point based algorithms. AG systems like Silver [9], JastAdd [10], and Kiama [11] all support such extensions. Secondly, attribute grammars are embedded in regular programming languages and AG fragments are first-class citizens: they can be analyzed, reused and compiled independently.

First class AGs provide: i) a full component-based approach to AGs where a language is specified/implemented as a set of reusable off-the-shelf components, and ii) semantic-based modularity, while traditional AG specifications use a (re-strict) syntax modular approach. Moreover, by using an embedding approach there is no need to construct a large AG (software) system to process, analyse and execute AG specifications: first class AGs reuse for free the mechanisms provided by the host language as much as possible, while increasing abstraction on the host language. Although this option may also entail some disadvantages, e.g. error messages relating to complex features of the host language instead of specificities of the embedded language, the fact is that an entire infrastructure, including libraries and language extensions, is readily available at a minimum cost. Also, the support and evolution of such infrastructure is not a concern.

This paper presents a novel technique combining these two AG advances.

First, we propose a concise embedding of AGs in Haskell. This embedding relies on the extremely simple mechanism of functional zippers. Zippers were originally conceived by Huet [12] to represent a tree together with a subtree that is the focus of attention, where that focus may move within the tree. By providing access to any element of a tree, zippers are very convenient in our setting: attributes may be defined by accessing other attributes in other nodes. Moreover, they do not rely on any advanced feature of Haskell. Thus, our embedding can be straightforwardly re-used in any other functional environment.

Second, we extend our embedding with the main AG extensions proposed to the AG formalism. In fact, we present the first embedding of HOAGs, RAGs and CAGs as first class attribute grammars. By this we are able to express powerful algorithms as the composition of AG reusable components. An approach that we have been using, e.g., in developing techniques for a language processor to implement bidirectional AG specifications and to construct a software portal.

2   Motivation

In this section we introduce the Desk language, that was proposed in [13], and that we will use as our running example throughout the paper. This language is small enough to be completely defined here while still holding central characteristics of real programming languages, such as mandatory but unique declaration of all name entities that are used. The Desk language allows the definition of simple arithmetic expressions whose single operator is addition and that uses globally scoped variables. A concrete sentence in this language defines the sum of variables x and y with the value 1, where x and y are set to 2 and 3, respectively:

```
PRINT x + y + 1 WHERE x = 2, y = 3
```

Our goal here is similar to the one of [13]: we want to define a mapping from Desk sentences to assembly code for a simple machine with one register only. For the sentence above, we want to transform it into the following assembly program:

```
{ LOAD 2 (the value of x); ADD 3 (the value of y); ADD 1; PRINT 0; HALT 0 }
```

Implementing this transformation introduces typical language processing challenges such as lexical and syntactical analysis, name analysis through symbol table management, verification of static conditions, right-to-left processing and interpretation and code generation. Since declaration of entities may come after their usage, a traditional approach to solve this problem relies on complex, multiple traversal algorithms. In his original paper [13], Paaki proposed to implement this mapping using an AG with the following set of attributes:

```
code  - synthesized target code
name  - synthesized name of a constant
value - synthesized value of a constant or a number
ok    - synthesized attribute that indicates correcteness
envs  - synthesized environment (symbol table)
envi  - inherited environment (symbol table)
```

Attributes envs and envi both have the form of a list with (name, value) pairs representing a symbol table. Attribute code is the actual meaning of the grammar, i.e., the final result of processing a sentence, and it has the form of a list of pairs (instruction, value). An important thing to notice is that an incorrect Desk phrase also yields a meaning. For example,

```
PRINT z WHERE x = 2, y = 3
```

produces the resulting code (i.e., has the following meaning):

```
{ HALT 0; PRINT 0; HALT 0 }
```

Next, we present the implementation of the Desk AG, as proposed in [13]:

```
(p1) Prog -> PRINT Exp Cons
     { Prog.code = if Cons.ok then Exp.code + (PRINT, 0) + (HALT, 0)
                              else (HALT,  0)
     , Exp.envi  = Cons.envs }
(p2) Exp1 -> Exp2 '+' Fact
     { Exp1.code = if Fact.ok then Exp2.code + (ADD, Fact.value)
                              else (HALT, 0)
     , Exp2.envi  = Exp1.envi
     , Fact.envi  = Exp1.envi }
(p3) Exp -> Fact
     { Exp.code  = if Fact.ok then (LOAD, Fact.value) else (HALT, 0)
     , Fact.envi  = Exp.envi }
```

```
(p4) Fact -> Name
     { Fact.ok    = isin (Name.name, Fact.envi)
     , Fact.value = getvalue (Name.name, Fact.envi) }
(p5) Fact -> Number
     { Fact.ok = true, Fact.value = Number.value }
(p6) Name -> Id
     { Name.name = Id.name }
(p7) Cons -> empty
     { Cons.ok = true, Cons.envs = () }
(p8) Cons -> WHERE DefList
     { Cons.ok = DefList.ok, Cons.envs = DefList.envs }
(p9) DefList₁ -> DefList₂ ',' Def
     { DefList₁.ok = DefList₂.ok and not isin (Def.name, DefList₂.envs)
     , DefList₁.envs = DefList₂.envs + (Def.name, Def.value) }
(p10) DefList -> Def
      { DefList.ok = true, DefList.envs = (Def.name, Def.value) }
(p11) Def -> Name '=' Number
      { Def.name = Name.name, Def.value = Name.value }
```

A definition (p n) production {semantic rules} is used to associate concrete semantics (using semantic rules to define attribute values) to the syntax (defined by context-free grammar productions) of a language. In a production, when the same non-terminal symbol occurs more than once, each occurrence is denoted by a subscript (starting from 1 and counting left to right).

In this particular case, it is assumed that the values of attributes name and value are externally provided, e.g., by a lexical analyzer. Also, we use constructions if then else, and and not assuming their standard interpretation; + is used for list consing, isin to check wether a value is contained within a symbol table and getvalue to extract a value from a symbol table, returning 0 if it does not exist[1]. Conventional constant functions are also used, such as the integer 0, the Boolean true and the empty list ().

3   Zipper-Based Attribute Grammars

In this section we show how we can implement Desk as an AG embedded in Haskell relying on the concept of functional zippers, that we start by revising.

3.1   Functional Zippers

In our work we have used the generic zipper library of [14]. It works for both homogeneous and heterogeneous datatypes, and data-types for which an instance of the Data and Typeable type classes [15] are available can be traversed.

In order to illustrate how we may use zippers, we consider the following Haskell data-type straightforwardly obtain from the syntax of the Desk language.

---

[1] The traditional definition of AGs only permits semantic rules of the form X.a = f(...), forcing the use of identity functions for constants. For clarity and simplicity, we allow their direct usage in attribute definitions.

```
data Root    = Root  Prog
data Prog    = PRINT Exp Cons
data Exp     = Add    Exp Fact   | Fact Fact
data Fact    = Name  Name        | Number String
data Name    = Id Constant
data Cons    = EmptyCons         | WHERE DefList
data DefList = Comma DefList Def | Def Def
data Def     = Equal Name Value
type Constant    = String
type Value       = Int
type SymbolTable = [(String,String)]
```

We may use this data-type to represent PRINT x + y + 1 WHERE x = 2, y = 3 as the following program:

```
exp     = Add (Add (Fact (Name (Id "x")))
                   (Name (Id "y")))
              (Number 1)
deflst  = WHERE (Comma (Def (Equal (Id "y") 5))
                       (Equal (Id "x") 3))
program = PRINT exp deflst
```

In order to navigate on program, we start by wrapping it up using the library-provided function toZipper :: Data a => a -> Zipper a:

```
program' = toZipper (Root program)
```

We end up with an aggregate data structure which is easy to traverse and update. For example, we may move the focus of attention on program' from the topmost node to the exp node as follows:[2]

```
exp' = (getHole . down . down) program'
```

The library function down goes down to the leftmost (immediate) child of a node whereas function getHole extracts the node under focus from a zipper.

3.2   Desk as an Embedded Attribute Grammar

On top of the zipper library of [14], we have implemented several simple combinators that facilitate the embedding of attribute grammars. In particular, we have defined: (.$) :: Zipper a -> Int -> Zipper a for accessing any child of a structure given by its index starting in 1; parent :: Zipper a -> Zipper a to move the focus to the parent of a concrete node, and, to check whether the current location is a sibling of a tree node, (.|) :: Zipper a -> Int -> Bool.

We may now define each attribute of the Desk attribute grammar. For synthesizing the name of a constant, as defined in the semantics of production (p6) and (part of) production (p11) we define an attribute name as follows[3].

---

[2] For totality, the results of functions down :: Zipper a -> Maybe (Zipper a) and getHole :: Zipper a -> Maybe b are within Maybe. As the analysis of their results is provided by our combinators, we simplify the example by abstracting this analysis.

[3] Function constructor exposes the type of the node under focus, and function lexeme simulates a standard lexer, and both can be automatically generated.

```
name :: Zipper Root -> String
name ag = case (constructor ag) of "Id"    -> lexeme ag
                                   "Equal" -> name (ag.$1)
```

where `Zipper Root` is the type of an instance of `Root` embedded inside the `Zipper`.

The purpose of the attributes `envs` and `envi` is, respectively, to compute and to appropriately pass around an environment mapping constant names to values in accordance with the bindings in `DefList`. For a node being a `Prog`, the inherited environment `envi` is given by the synthesized environment `envs` of its `Cons` child, as defined in (p1). For any other node, `envi` is accessed in its parent node:

```
envi :: Zipper Root -> SymbolTable
envi ag = case (constructor ag) of "PRINT"   -> envs (ag.$2)
                                   otherwise -> envi (parent ag)
```

Attribute `envi` is copied from the root node where it is computed to any other node. There is usually a primitive that allows the programmer to define this type of attributes without having to specify them throughout the grammar: in Silver [9], for example, this is called `autocopy`. Our solution relies on Haskell 's `case/otherwise` construction to implement a similar feature.

The synthesized environment `envs` goes down a sentence in search for the constants defined in it. When one such definition is found, a pair (c, v), where c is the constant `name` and v the `value` being set for it, is added to the environment:

```
envs :: Zipper Root -> SymbolTable
envs ag = case (constructor ag) of
            "EmptyCons" -> []
            "WHERE" -> envs (ag.$1)
            "Comma" -> (name (ag.$2), value (ag.$2)) : envs (ag.$1)
            "Def"   -> [(name (ag.$1), value (ag.$1))]
```

The value of a constant or a number is given by attribute `value` as follows:

```
value :: Zipper Root -> String
value ag = case (constructor ag) of
             "Name"   -> getValue (name (ag.$1)) (envi ag)
             "Number" -> lexeme ag
             "Equal"  -> lexeme ag
```

The value of a constant `Name` c occurring in the `Expression` part of a sentence must be searched for in the environment, which is precisely what `getValue` does. The value of `Number` v or the constant definition `Equal` c v is simply v.

The attribute `ok` checks if a variable is defined once and only once:

```
ok :: Zipper Root -> Bool
ok ag = case (constructor ag) of
          "Name"   -> isIn (name (ag.$1)) (envi ag)
          "Number" -> True
          "EmptyCons" -> True
          "WHERE"  -> ok (ag.$1)
          "Comma"  -> ok (ag.$1) && not isIn (name (ag.$2)) (envs (ag.$1))
          "Def"    -> True
```

The synthesized attribute `code` reuses the defined attributes to generate code.

```
code :: Zipper Root -> String
code ag = case (constructor ag) of
          "Root"  -> code (ag.$1)
          "PRINT" -> if ok (ag.$2)
                     then code (ag.$1) ++ "PRINT, 0" ++ "HALT, 0"
                     else "HALT, 0"
          "Add"   -> if (ok (ag.$2))
                     then code (ag.$1) ++ "ADD, " ++ value (ag.$2)
                     else "HALT, 0"
          "Fact"  -> if (ok (ag.$1))
                     then  "LOAD, " ++ value (ag.$1)
                     else "HALT, 0"
```

In this section, we have embedded the Desk analysis as an AG in Haskell. Our solution is simple and elegant, easy to implement, to analyze and to extend.

A difference between our embedding and the traditional definition of AGs is that in the former, an attribute is defined as a semantic function on tree nodes, while in the latter the programmer defines on one production exactly how many and how attributes are computed. Nevertheless, we argue that this difference does not impose increasing implementation costs as the main advantages of the attribute grammar setting still hold: attributes are modular, their implementation can be sectioned by sites in the tree and as we will see inter-attribute definitions work exactly the same way. What is more, our embedding might provide an easier setting for debugging as the entire definition of one attribute is localized in one semantic function. Furthermore, we believe that the individual attribute definitions in our embedding can straightforwardly be understood and derived from their traditional definition on an attribute grammar system, as can be observed comparing the attribute definitions in the previous section with the ones in this section.

A traditional advantage of the embedding of domain-specific languages in a host language is the use of target language features as native. In our case, this applies, e.g., to the Haskell functions && for Boolean conjunction, not for Boolean negation and ++ for list concatenation, whereas on specific AG systems the set of functions is usually limited and pre-defined. Also, regarding distribution of language features for dynamical load and separate compilation, it is posible to divide an AG in modules that, e.g., may contain contain data types (representing the grammar) and functions (representing the attributes).

4   Zipper-Based Attribute Grammar Extensions

After showing first class attribute grammars embedded in a zipper framework, we present the embedding of three well known AG extensions.

4.1   Referenced Attribute Grammars

Referenced Attribute Grammars [8] allow references to arbitrary nodes in the tree, and attributes attached to those nodes to be accessed via the referenced attributes. Because RAGs allow nodes to reference any node in the tree (not only their children), they allow the expression of graph-based algorithms.

In the original Desk AG, the inherited attribute `envi` is used to collect and pass context information to the expression part of a sentence. However, if this language evolves to allow, e.g., type definitions, then a complete re-write of the symbol table with the respective attributes and semantics may be needed. By using RAGs, the symbol table is promoted to contain references to locations in the tree. As a result, if the definition part evolves, then the attribute references still point to the evolved tree, and changes are much easier to carry.

In our embedding, references are represented by zippers whose focus points to relevant tree locations. This implies changes on the symbol table's data type, its construction and the lookup semantic function that uses it:

```
type SymbolTable = [(String, Zipper Root)]

envs :: Zipper Root -> SymbolTable
envs ag = case (constructor ag) of
            "EmptyCons" -> []
            "WHERE" -> envs (ag.$1)
            "Comma" -> envs (ag.$1) ++ [( name (ag.$2), ag.$2 )]
            "Def"    -> [( name (ag.$1), ag.$1 )]

isIn :: String -> SymbolTable -> Bool
isIn _ [] = False
isIn name ((a,b):xs) = if (name == a) then True else isIn name xs

getValue :: String -> SymbolTable -> Bool
getValue name ((a,b):xs) = if (name == a) then (value b)
                                          else (getValue name xs)
```

This definition is very similar to the AG in Section 3, with the main difference being the fact that, since the symbol table is composed by references, the semantic function `getValue` has to use the attribute `value` to extract the actual assigned values, where it only had to return information contained in the list. This is the general approach in RAGs.

4.2   Higher-Order Attribute Grammars

Higher-order attribute grammars [6] are an important extension of AGs because they allow both tree changes during attribute evaluation, and the definition of any (first-order) recursive functions as AG computations. Moreover, they also provide a component-based (modular) approach to AG specifications [7].

In our running example the functions `getValue` and `isIn` are semantically expressed, contrary to the AG, while on a HOAG setting those computations are promoted to higher-order attributes.

We start by creating a new data type for the symbol table:

```
data Root_ho = Root_ho SymbolTable
data SymbolTable = NilST | ConsST Tuple SymbolTable
type Tuple = (String, String)
```

The symbol table becomes a tree-based structure with clear constructors and names for tree nodes. Having defined these data types, we only need to express the lookup operations as attribute computations.

```
isIn :: String -> Zipper Root_ho -> Bool
isIn name ag = case (constructor_ho ag) of
          "Root_ho" -> isIn name (ag.$1)
          "NilST"   -> False
          "ConsST"  -> isIn name (ag.$1) || isIn name (ag.$2)
          "Tuple"   -> lexeme_ho z == name

getValue :: String -> Zipper Root_ho -> String
getValue name ag = case (constructor_ho ag) of
            "Root_ho" -> getValue (ag.$1)
            "ConsST" -> if (lexeme_ho (ag.$1) == name)
                        then (lexeme_ho (ag.$1))
                        else (getValue name (ag.$2))
```

Having modelled the two lookup functions, we now need to focus on the part of the specification where those functions are called. Instead of a function call, in a HOAG setting we need to instantiate the higher-order tree as a zipper, as shown next (we include the relevant productions only):

```
value :: Zipper Root -> String
value ag = case (constructor ag) of
          "Name" -> getValue (name ag.$1) (toZipper (Root_ho (envi ag)))

ok :: Zipper Root -> String
ok ag = case (constructor ag) of
        "Name"  -> isIn (name ag.$1) (toZipper (Root_ho (envi ag)))
        "Comma" -> (ok ag.$1) && not
                    isIn (name ag.$2) (toZipper (Root_ho (envs ag.$1)))
```

Like in standard HOAG specifications, as supported by LRC [16], a call to a semantic function (in a classical AG) is transformed into a higher-order tree/attribute. In our embedding the function toZipper is used to model this.

4.3 Circular Attribute Grammars

HOAGs allow expressing first-order computations but several algorithms, such as type inference, rely on fix-point computations. In order to express these algorithms in a AG setting, we need to consider Circular Attribute Grammars [17].

As an example, lets imagine the revised version of Desk as considered by [13], where assignments can be symbolical and their order is not relevant:

PRINT x + y + 1 WHERE x = y, z = 1, y = z

To process this Desk expression, we need a fixed-point evaluation strategy. The general idea is to start with a bottom value, $\perp$, and compute approximations of the final result until it is not changed anymore, that is, the least fixed point is reached: $x = \perp$; $x = f(x)$; $x = f(f(x))$; ....

To guarantee the termination of this computation, it must be possible to test the equality of the result (with ⊥ being its smallest value). With this, the sequence x = ⊥; x = f(x); x = f(f(x)); ... will return the final result, in the form f(f(...f(⊥)...)).

Of course, this solution might produce an infinite loop in cases such as:

PRINT x + y + 1 WHERE x = y, y = x

While this is undesired, this assignment is actually impossible to solve (besidesm it corresponds to an invalid Desk phrase).

Next, we present the Haskell function that implements this definition:

```
fixed-point :: Eq a => (a -> a) -> a -> a
fixed-point f s | s == next = s
                | otherwise = fixed-point f next
                where next = f s
```

This is a standard Haskell solution, that takes as argument f, an input s and applies the function indefinitely until it can not perform more changes to the input, i.e., until f(s) == s. It is easy to imagine in Desk a call such as fixed-point solver symbol-table, where solver solves as much assignments as possible in one traverse, and is applied until no more assignments can be resolved. Such improvement to Desk would successfully update the original implementation of the language to solve a new class of circular dependencies. Despite successful, this solution is not preferable since it forces standard semantic approaches and we loose part of the expressive power of AGs. Therefore, our approach is to define a new attribute, isSolved, that terminates the fixed-point computation. This is a more desirable way of controlling the fixed-point process since we are not constrained to function equality and we can do so in an AG fashion, by modularly creating definitions per tree node, as shown next.

```
isSolved :: Zipper Root_{ho} -> Bool
isSolved ag = case (constructor_{ho} ag) of
              "Root_{ho}" -> auxIsSolved (ag.$1)
              otherwise -> isSolved (parent ag)


auxIsSolved :: Zipper Root_{ho} -> Bool
auxIsSolved ag = case (constructor_{ho} ag) of
               "Root_{ho}"     -> auxIsSolved (ag.$1)
               "ConsST"      -> (auxIsSolved ag.$1) &&
                                (auxIsSolved ag.$2)
               "NilST"        -> True
               "TupleInt"     -> True
               "TupleString" -> False
```

The attribute isSolved exists only to ensure that this test is performed on the whole HOAG, and not only on a subpart of it. Therefore, it goes all the way to the top where it calls another attribute, auxIsSolved. The attribute auxIsSolved goes through the tree and checks if any of the position contains an assignment to another variable. If it does, the symbol table is not "complete", i.e., there are assignments still left to solve.

Secondly, to make the example more interesting, we shall implement this using a high-order AG. HOAG is being constantly calculated until a certain condition is met (remember, in the traditional fixed-point approach, this condition would be that two subsequent computations produce the same output). It is a good idea to use an HOAG because, as we have seen in Section 4.2, this type of grammars are much more easier to handle, to manage and to reason about.

Next, we present the attributes responsible for solving as much assignments as possible of the high-order symbol table in one traverse:

```
solve :: Zipper Root_ho -> Zipper Root_ho
solve ag = case (constructor_ho ag) of
            "Root_ho" -> solve (ag.$1)
            "NilST"   -> NilST
            "ConsST"  -> ConsST (check ag.$1) (solve ag.$2)

check :: Zipper Root_ho -> Bool
check ag = case (constructor_ho ag) of
            "TupleInt"    -> lexeme_ho ag
            "TupleString" -> substitute (solvedSymbols ag)
                                        (lexeme_ho ag)
```

The attribute `solve` goes recursively through the tree and calls the attribute `check` on every tree node. If this node contains an assignment to a number, `check` does not do anything. On the other hand, if the assignment is to a variable, `check` uses a supporting semantic function, `substitute`, that takes as argument the unresolved assignment and a list of all the resolved assignments that exist in the symbol table and sees if any of this information can be used. The attribute that creates the list of resolved assignments is presented next.

```
solvedSymbols :: Zipper Root_ho -> [(String, Int)]
solvedSymbols ag = case (constructor_ho ag) of
                    "Root_ho" -> auxSolvedSymbols (ag.$1)
                    otherwise -> solvedSymbols (parent ag)

auxSolvedSymbols :: Zipper Root_ho -> [(String, Int)]
auxSolvedSymbols ag = case (constructor_ho ag) of
                    "ConsST"      -> auxSolvedSymbols (ag.$1) ++
                                     auxSolvedSymbols (ag.$2)
                    "NilST"       -> []
                    "TupleInt"    -> [(lexeme z, lexeme z)]
                    "TupleString" -> []
```

With all the necessary attributes implemented, we only have to define the attribute that applies this fixed-point strategy on the HOAG. As stated earlier, the idea of this fixed-point computation is to indefinitely apply a computation (`solve`) until a stop condition is reached (`isSolved`).

```
fixed-point ag = case (constructor_ho ag) of
         "Root_ho" -> if (isSolved ag) then ag
                      else fixed-point (toZipper (Root_ho (solve ag.$1)))
         otherwise  -> fixed-point (parent ag)
```

This way, we solved the cyclic dependencies imposed by a new version of Desk without loosing the modularity and expressiveness of AGs in our embedding. What is left to do is to call this fixed-point attribute immediately after the symbol table is created, namely in the original attribute envi.

5   Related Work

In this paper, we have proposed a zippers-based embedding of attribute grammars in a functional language. The implementations we obtain are modular and do not rely on laziness. We believe that our approach is the first that deals with arbitrary tree structures while being applicable in both lazy and strict settings. Furthermore, we have been able to implement in our environment all the standard examples that have been proposed in the attribute grammar literature. This is the case of repmin [18], HTML table formatting [7], and smart parentesis, an illustrative example of [9], that are available from the first author's webpage and that we will include in an extended version of the paper.

Moreover, the navigation via a generic zipper that we envison here has applications in other domains: *i*) our setting is being used to create combinator languages for process management [19] which themselves are fundamental to a platform for open source software analysis and certification [20, 21]; and *ii*), the setting that we propose was applied on a prototype for bidirectional transformations applied to programming environments for scientific computing.

Below we survey only works most closely related to ours: works in the realm of functional languages and attribute grammar embeddings.

Zipper-based approaches. Uustalu and Vene have shown how to embed attribute computations using comonadic structures, where each tree node is paired with its attribute values [22]. This approach is notable for its use of a zipper as in our work. However, it appears that this zipper is not generic and must be instantiated for each tree structure. Laziness is used to avoid static scheduling. Moreover, their example is restricted to a grammar with a single non-terminal and extension to arbitrary grammars is speculative.

Badouel *et al.* define attribute evaluation as zipper transformers [23]. While their encoding is simpler than that of Uustalu and Vene, they also use laziness as a key aspect and the zipper representation is similarly not generic. This is also the case of [24], that also requires laziness and forces the programmer to be aware of a cyclic representation of zippers.

Yakushev *et al.* describe a fixed point method for defining operations on mutually recursive data types, with which they build a generic zipper [25]. Their approach is to translate data structures into a generic representation on which traversals and updates can be performed, then to translate back. Even though their zipper is generic, the implementation is more complex than ours and incurs the extra overhead of translation. It also uses more advanced features of Haskell such as type families and rank-2 types.

Non-zipper-based approaches. Circular programs have been used in the past to straightforwardly implement AGs in a lazy functional language [26, 27]. These works, in contrast to our own, rely on the target language to be lazy, and their goal is not to embed AGs: instead they show that there exists a direct correspondence between an attribute grammar and a circular program.

Regarding other notable embeddings of AGs in functional languages [28–30], they do not offer the modern AG extensions that we provided, with the exception of [30] that uses macros to allow the definition of higher-order attributes. Also, these embeddings are not based on zippers, rely on laziness and use extensible records [28] or heterogeneous collections [29, 30]. The use of heterogeneous lists in the second of these approaches replaces the use in the first approach of extensible records, which are no longer supported by the main Haskell compilers. In our framework, attributes do not need to be collected in a data structure at all: they are regular functions upon which correctness checks are statically performed by the compiler. The result is a simpler and more modular embedding. On the other hand, the use of these data structures ensures that an attribute is computed only once, being then updated to a data structure and later found there when necessary. In order to guarantee such a claim in our setting we need to rely on memoization strategies, often costly in terms of performance.

Our embedding does not require the programmer to explicitly combine different attributes nor does it require combination of the semantic rules for a particular node in the syntax tree, as is the case in the work of Viera *et al.* [29, 30]. In this sense, our implementation requires less effort from the programmer.

The Kiama library embeds attribute grammars in Scala [11]. This embedding is not purely functional, but uses generic 'parent' and similar operations to access the structure, instead of having more traditional inherited attribute definitions.

In general, when designing a Domain Specific Language (DSL), it is often the case that "syntax is not quite right" [31]. With this observation, the author claims that DSLs must be as close to the language being embedded as possible. Our DSL for AGs closely resembles custom AG languages, so we have the notational power without incurring the implementation cost of a custom language.

6   Conclusions and Future Work

In this paper we have presented the first embedding of modern AG extensions using a concise and elegant zipper-based implementation. We have presented how reference, higher-order and circular attribute grammars can be expressed as first class AGs in this setting. As a result, complex multiple traversal algorithms can be expressed in this setting in an off-the-shelf set of reusable components.

We have presented our embedding in the Haskell programming language, despite not relying on any advanced feature of Haskell (namely on lazy evaluation). Thus, similar concise embeddings can be defined in other declarative languages.

As we have shown both by the example presented and by the ones available online, our simple embedding provides the same expressiveness of modern, large and more complex attribute grammar based systems.

As part of our future research, we plan to: i) improve attribute definition by referencing non-terminals instead of (numeric) positions on the right-hand side of productions; and ii) wherever possible, benchmark our embedding against other AG embeddings and systems.

References

1. Knuth, D.: Semantics of Context-free Languages. Mathematical Systems Theory 2(2) (June 1968); Correction: Mathematical Systems Theory 5(1) (March 1971)
2. Dijkstra, A., Fokker, J., Swierstra, S.D.: The architecture of the utrecht haskell compiler. In: Weirich, S. (ed.) Haskell, pp. 93–104. ACM (2009)
3. Swierstra, D., Azero, P., Saraiva, J.: Designing and Implementing Combinator Languages. In: Swierstra, S.D., Oliveira, J.N. (eds.) AFP 1998. LNCS, vol. 1608, pp. 150–206. Springer, Heidelberg (1999)
4. Fernandes, J.P., Saraiva, J.: Tools and Libraries to Model and Manipulate Circular Programs. In: Proceedings of the ACM SIGPLAN 2007 Symposium on Partial Evaluation and Program Manipulation, PEPM 2007, pp. 102–111. ACM Press (2007)
5. Middelkoop, A., Dijkstra, A., Swierstra, S.D.: Iterative type inference with attribute grammars. In: Visser, E., Järvi, J. (eds.) GPCE, pp. 43–52. ACM (2010)
6. Vogt, H.H., Swierstra, S.D., Kuiper, M.F.: Higher order attribute grammars. SIGPLAN Not. 24(7), 131–145 (1989)
7. Saraiva, J., Swierstra, S.D.: Generating spreadsheet-like tools from strong attribute grammars. In: Pfenning, F., Macko, M. (eds.) GPCE 2003. LNCS, vol. 2830, pp. 307–323. Springer, Heidelberg (2003)
8. Magnusson, E., Hedin, G.: Circular reference attributed grammars - their evaluation and applications. Sci. Comput. Program. 68(1), 21–37 (2007)
9. Van Wyk, E., Bodin, D., Gao, J., Krishnan, L.: Silver: an extensible attribute grammar system. Electron. Notes Theor. Comput. Sci. 203(2), 103–116 (2008)
10. Ekman, T., Hedin, G.: The jastadd extensible java compiler. SIGPLAN Not. 42(10), 1–18 (2007)
11. Sloane, A.M., Kats, L.C.L., Visser, E.: A pure object-oriented embedding of attribute grammars. Electron. Notes Theor. Comput. Sci. 253(7), 205–219 (2010)
12. Huet, G.: The zipper. Journal of Functional Programming 7(5), 549–554 (1997)
13. Paakki, J.: Attribute grammar paradigms a high-level methodology in language implementation. ACM Comput. Surv. 27(2), 196–255 (1995)
14. Adams, M.D.: Scrap your zippers: a generic zipper for heterogeneous types. In: Proceedings of the 6th ACM SIGPLAN Workshop on Generic Programming, WGP 2010, pp. 13–24. ACM, New York (2010)
15. Lämmel, R., Jones, S.P.: Scrap your boilerplate: a practical design pattern for generic programming. In: Procs. of the 2003 ACM SIGPLAN Inter. WorkShop on Types in Language Design and Implementation, TLDI 2003, pp. 26–37. ACM (2003)
16. Kuiper, M., Saraiva, J.: Lrc - A Generator for Incremental Language-Oriented Tools. In: Koskimies, K. (ed.) CC 1998. LNCS, vol. 1383, pp. 298–301. Springer, Heidelberg (1998)

17. Magnusson, E., Hedin, G.: Circular reference attributed grammars - their evalua-
    tion and applications. Sci. Comput. Program. 68(1), 21–37 (2007)
18. Bird, R.: Using circular programs to eliminate multiple traversals of data. Acta
    Informatica 21, 239–250 (1984)
19. Martins, P., Fernandes, J.P., Saraiva, J.: A purely functional combinator language
    for software quality assessment. In: Symposium on Languages, Applications and
    Technologies, SLATE 2012. OASICS, vol. 21, pp. 51–69. Schloss Dagstuhl - Leibniz-
    Zentrum fuer Informatik (2012)
20. Martins, P., Fernandes, J.P., Saraiva, J.: A web portal for the certification of open
    source software. In: 6th International Workshop on Foundations and Techniques for
    Open Source Software Certification, OPENCERT 2012. LNCS (2012) (to appear)
21. Martins, P., Carvalho, N., Fernandes, J.P., Almeida, J.J., Saraiva, J.: A frame-
    work for modular and customizable software analysis. In: Murgante, B., Misra, S.,
    Carlini, M., Torre, C.M., Nguyen, H.-Q., Taniar, D., Apduhan, B.O., Gervasi, O.
    (eds.) ICCSA 2013, Part II. LNCS, vol. 7972, pp. 443–458. Springer, Heidelberg
    (2013)
22. Uustalu, T., Vene, V.: Comonadic functional attribute evaluation. In: Trends in
    Functional Programming, vol. (10), pp. 145–162. Intellect Books (2005)
23. Badouel, E., Fotsing, B., Tchougong, R.: Yet another implementation of attribute
    evaluation. Research Report RR-6315, INRIA (2007)
24. Badouel, E., Fotsing, B., Tchougong, R.: Attribute grammars as recursion schemes
    over cyclic representations of zippers. Electronic Notes Theory Computer Sci-
    ence 229(5), 39–56 (2011)
25. Yakushev, A.R., Holdermans, S., Löh, A., Jeuring, J.: Generic programming with
    fixed points for mutually recursive datatypes. In: Procs. of the 14th ACM SIG-
    PLAN International Conference on Functional Programming, pp. 233–244 (2009)
26. Johnsson, T.: Attribute grammars as a functional programming paradigm. In:
    Kahn, G. (ed.) Functional Programming Languages and Computer Architecture.
    LNCS, vol. 274, pp. 154–173. Springer, Heidelberg (1987)
27. Kuiper, M., Swierstra, D.: Using attribute grammars to derive efficient functional
    programs. In: Computing Science in the Netherlands (November 1987)
28. de Moor, O., Backhouse, K., Swierstra, S.D.: First-class attribute grammars. In-
    formatica (Slovenia) 24(3) (2000)
29. Viera, M., Swierstra, D., Swierstra, W.: Attribute Grammars Fly First-class: how
    to do Aspect Oriented Programming in Haskell. In: Procs. of the 14th ACM SIG-
    PLAN Int. Conf. on Functional Programming, ICFP 2009, pp. 245–256 (2009)
30. Viera, M.: First Class Syntax, Semantics, and Their Composition. PhD thesis,
    Utrecht University, The Netherlands (2013)
31. Siek, J.: General purpose languages should be metalanguages. In: Procs. of ACM
    SIGPLAN Workshop on Partial Evaluation and Program Manipulation, pp. 3–4
    (2010)

Author Index